PIT BOSS WOO GRILL & SMOKER COOKBOOK FOR BEGINNERS

The Ultimate Guide to Transform Your Backyard BBQs with 1700+ Days of Fail-proof Recipes, Pro Techniques, and Marinade Mastery

Maxwell Beaumont

© **Copyright 2024 by Maxwell Beaumont**
- All rights reserved.

The following book is provided below with the aim of delivering information that is as precise and dependable as possible. However, purchasing this book implies an acknowledgment that both the publisher and the author are not experts in the discussed topics, and any recommendations or suggestions contained herein are solely for entertainment purposes. It is advised that professionals be consulted as needed before acting on any endorsed actions.

This statement is considered fair and valid by both the American Bar Association and the Committee of Publishers Association, and it holds legal binding throughout the United States.

Moreover, any transmission, duplication, or reproduction of this work, including specific information, will be deemed an illegal act, regardless of whether it is done electronically or in print. This includes creating secondary or tertiary copies of the work or recorded copies, which are only allowed with the express written consent from the Publisher. All additional rights are reserved.

The information in the following pages is generally considered to be a truthful and accurate account of facts. As such, any negligence, use, or misuse of the information by the reader will result in actions falling solely under their responsibility. There are no scenarios in which the publisher or the original author can be held liable for any difficulties or damages that may occur after undertaking the information described herein.

Additionally, the information in the following pages is intended solely for informational purposes and should be considered as such. As fitting its nature, it is presented without assurance regarding its prolonged validity or interim quality. Mention of trademarks is done without written consent and should not be construed as an endorsement from the trademark holder.

TABLE OF CONTENTS

PIT BOSS WOOD PELLET GRILL & SMOKER COOKBOOK FOR BEGINNERS 1

Chapter 1: Discovering the Pit Boss Wood Pellet Grill & Smoker 15
- Exploring the Components of Your Pit Boss 15
- Initial Setup and Ensuring Safe Operation 16
- The Science of Heat: Managing Your Cooking Temperature 18

Chapter 2: Honing Your Pit Boss Skills 21
- Perfecting Marks and Mouthwatering Crusts 21
- The Art of Manipulating and Positioning 22
- Utilizing and Mastering the Grill's Heat Zones 23

Chapter 3: Maintenance and Care for Your Pit Boss 27
- A Detailed Cleaning Routine 27
- The Truth About Seasoning Your Grill 29
- Solutions for Common Pitfalls 30

Chapter 4: The Pit Boss Toolkit 33
- Essential Grilling Equipment 33
- Enhancements for Your Grilling Sessions 34
- Selecting the Best Tools for the Job 35

Chapter 5: Expanding Your Culinary Horizons 37
- Elevating Vegetables on the Grill 37
- Meat: Unlocking Succulence and Aroma 38
- Griddled Goods: Beyond Breakfast 39

Chapter 6: Seasonings and Marinades Mastery 41
- Grilling Spices and Herb Guide 41
- Crafting Your Marinades and Rubs 42
- Diverse Flavors for Global Dishes 43

Chapter 7: Smoke Crafting Techniques 47
- Fundamentals of Smoke Flavoring 47
- Advanced Smoking Strategies 48
- Pairing Woods with Foods 50

Chapter 8: Breakfast Delicacies 53
- Griddle Breakfast Classics 53

Recipe 1. SUNRISE SMASHED AVOCADO TOAST ... 53
Recipe 2. PIT BOSS PANCAKES ... 53
Recipe 3. COUNTRY STYLE HASH BROWNS ... 54
Recipe 4. GRIDDLE GRILLED CHEESE & TOMATO SOUP ... 54
Recipe 5. SAVORY MUSHROOM & HERB OMELETTE ... 54
Recipe 6. BLUEBERRY BANANA GRIDDLE CAKES ... 54
Recipe 7. SPICY CHORIZO BREAKFAST BURRITOS ... 54
Recipe 8. SMOKY MOUNTAIN HASH BROWNS ... 55
Recipe 9. GRIDDLE FRENCH TOAST ... 55
Recipe 10. SOUTHWESTERN OMELETTE ... 55
Recipe 11. BANANA PECAN PANCAKES ... 55

Innovative Morning Meals ... 56
Recipe 1. QUINOA POWER BOWLS ... 56
Recipe 2. SWEET POTATO AND BLACK BEAN BREAKFAST BURRITOS ... 56
Recipe 3. GREEN GODDESS SMOOTHIE BOWL ... 56
Recipe 4. AVOCADO EGG BOATS ... 56
Recipe 5. TURMERIC GINGER OATMEAL ... 57
Recipe 6. MUSHROOM SPINACH FRITTATA ... 57
Recipe 7. PEAR AND GORGONZOLA TOAST WITH HONEY DRIZZLE ... 57
Recipe 8. AVOCADO QUINOA BREAKFAST BOWL ... 57
Recipe 9. SWEET POTATO AND KALE HASH ... 58
Recipe 10. CHIA AND COCONUT MILK PORRIDGE ... 58
Recipe 11. TURMERIC GINGER TOFU SCRAMBLE ... 58

Light and Healthy Starts ... 58
Recipe 1. KALE AND BERRY SMOOTHIE ... 58
Recipe 2. COTTAGE CHEESE AND PINEAPPLE BOWL ... 59
Recipe 3. VEGAN TOFU SCRAMBLE ... 59
Recipe 4. CHIA SEED PUDDING ... 59
Recipe 5. AVOCADO AND EGG WHITE WRAP ... 59
Recipe 6. GREEK YOGURT WITH HONEY AND WALNUTS ... 59
Recipe 7. OATMEAL WITH ALMOND BUTTER AND BANANA ... 60
Recipe 8. BERRY SPIRALIZED CUCUMBER SALAD ... 60
Recipe 9. AVOCADO CITRUS BREAKFAST SALAD ... 60
Recipe 10. GREEN SMOOTHIE BOWL ... 60
Recipe 11. TOFU AND VEGETABLE BREAKFAST SCRAMBLE ... 60

Chapter 9: The Ultimate Burgers and Sandwiches ... 63

Crafting the Ultimate Patties ... 63
Recipe 1. CLASSIC BEEF BURGER PATTY ... 63

- Recipe 2. TURKEY AND SAGE BURGER PATTY 63
- Recipe 3. SPICY BLACK BEAN VEGGIE BURGER PATTY 64
- Recipe 4. SALMON AND DILL BURGER PATTY 64
- Recipe 5. CHICKPEA AND QUINOA VEGGIE BURGER PATTY 64
- Recipe 6. PORTOBELLO MUSHROOM BURGER PATTY 64
- Recipe 7. LENTIL AND WALNUT BURGER PATTY 64
- Recipe 8. SMOKED PAPRIKA CHICKPEA PATTIES 65
- Recipe 9. HERBED TURKEY AND QUINOA PATTIES 65
- Recipe 10. SPICY BLACK BEAN AND SWEET POTATO PATTIES 65
- Recipe 11. MEDITERRANEAN LENTIL PATTIES 65

Sandwich Creations and Innovations 66
- Recipe 1. GRILLED CHICKEN AND AVOCADO CLUB 66
- Recipe 2. ROASTED VEGETABLE AND HUMMUS PITA POCKET 66
- Recipe 3. APPLE, BRIE, AND WALNUT SANDWICH 66
- Recipe 4. SPICY TUNA AND CUCUMBER WRAP 67
- Recipe 5. MEDITERRANEAN VEGGIE SANDWICH 67
- Recipe 6. BUFFALO CHICKEN WRAP 67
- Recipe 7. PESTO CHICKPEA SALAD SANDWICH 67
- Recipe 8. ROASTED VEGETABLE AND HUMMUS GRILLED SANDWICH 67
- Recipe 9. CHIPOTLE CHICKEN AVOCADO WRAP 68
- Recipe 10. MEDITERRANEAN EGGPLANT PANINI 68
- Recipe 11. SMOKED SALMON AND CREAM CHEESE BAGEL 68

Vegetarian Delights Between the Buns 68
- Recipe 1. GRILLED PORTOBELLO MUSHROOM BURGER 68
- Recipe 2. SWEET POTATO AND BLACK BEAN BURGER 69
- Recipe 3. FALAFEL PITA SANDWICH 69
- Recipe 4. CAPRESE GRILLED CHEESE SANDWICH 69
- Recipe 5. AVOCADO AND SPINACH PANINI 69
- Recipe 6. EGGPLANT AND ROASTED PEPPER BURGER 70
- Recipe 7. ZUCCHINI AND GOAT CHEESE CIABATTA 70
- Recipe 8. CHICKPEA AND AVOCADO SMASH SANDWICH 70
- Recipe 9. BEETROOT AND GOAT CHEESE GRILLED CHEESE 70

Chapter 10: Reinventing Sides and Vegetables 73
Vegetable Dishes Reimagined 73
- Recipe 1. SMOKY CAULIFLOWER STEAKS 73
- Recipe 2. HERBED ZUCCHINI RIBBONS 73
- Recipe 3. BALSAMIC BRUSSELS SPROUTS 74
- Recipe 4. SPICED SWEET POTATO WEDGES 74

Recipe 5. GARLIC ROASTED GREEN BEANS 74
Recipe 6. MEDITERRANEAN STUFFED BELL PEPPERS 74
Recipe 7. CURRIED CAULIFLOWER RICE 74
Recipe 8. CHARRED BROCCOLINI WITH LEMON TAHINI DRIZZLE 75
Recipe 9. SPICED CAULIFLOWER STEAKS 75
Recipe 10. BALSAMIC GLAZED BRUSSELS SPROUTS WITH WALNUTS 75
Recipe 11. GRILLED ZUCCHINI RIBBONS WITH PINE NUT PESTO 75

Side Dishes to Complement Any Meal 76

Recipe 1. LEMON HERB QUINOA 76
Recipe 2. ROASTED GARLIC MASHED POTATOES 76
Recipe 3. CRISPY PARMESAN ASPARAGUS STICKS 76
Recipe 4. SWEET AND SPICY ROASTED CARROTS 76
Recipe 5. GRILLED CORN WITH CILANTRO LIME BUTTER 77
Recipe 6. BAKED ZUCCHINI FRIES 77
Recipe 7. CUCUMBER AND DILL SALAD 77
Recipe 8. CHARRED BRUSSELS SPROUTS WITH LEMON AIOLI 77
Recipe 9. ROASTED SWEET POTATO WEDGES WITH CINNAMON DIP 77
Recipe 10. GRILLED CORN WITH COTIJA CHEESE AND LIME 78
Recipe 11. BALSAMIC ROASTED CARROT SALAD 78

Creative Salads and Slaws 78

Recipe 1. CRUNCHY APPLE AND FENNEL SLAW 78
Recipe 2. KALE AND QUINOA SALAD WITH AVOCADO DRESSING 78
Recipe 3. BEETROOT AND GOAT CHEESE SALAD 79
Recipe 4. SPICY SOUTHWESTERN SLAW 79
Recipe 5. MEDITERRANEAN CHICKPEA SALAD 79
Recipe 6. ASIAN SESAME BROCCOLI SALAD 79
Recipe 7. PEAR AND WALNUT ARUGULA SALAD 80
Recipe 8. POMEGRANATE PEARL COUSCOUS SALAD 80
Recipe 9. CRUNCHY ASIAN RAMEN NOODLE SLAW 80
Recipe 10. WATERMELON FETA MINT SALAD 80
Recipe 11. GRILLED ZUCCHINI RIBBON SALAD 81

Chapter 11: Celebrating Beef 83

Mastering Steaks and Ribs 83

Recipe 1. RUSTIC HERB CRUSTED RIB EYE 83
Recipe 2. SMOKEY BOURBON BBQ RIBS 83
Recipe 3. CHARRED CHIMICHURRI STEAK SKEWERS 84
Recipe 4. PEPPER CRUSTED T-BONE WITH GARLIC HERB BUTTER 84
Recipe 5. SWEET AND SPICY ASIAN BEEF SHORT RIBS 84

- Recipe 6. GARLIC LOVER'S GRILLED FLANK STEAK 84
- Recipe 7. BALSAMIC GLAZED BEEF RIBS 84
- Recipe 8. HERB-CRUSTED RIB-EYE STEAK 85
- Recipe 9. SMOKEY BBQ BEEF RIBS 85
- Recipe 10. GARLIC BUTTER FILET MIGNON 85
- Recipe 11. BALSAMIC GLAZED FLANK STEAK 85

Beef Skewers and More 86

- Recipe 1. MEDITERRANEAN BEEF KEBABS 86
- Recipe 2. ASIAN-INSPIRED BEEF SATAY 86
- Recipe 3. TEX-MEX BEEF SKEWERS 86
- Recipe 4. BALSAMIC GLAZED STEAK ROLLS 86
- Recipe 5. HERB MARINATED BEEF KABOBS 87
- Recipe 6. SPICY CAJUN BEEF STICKS 87
- Recipe 7. GREEK-STYLE BEEF SKEWERS 87
- Recipe 8. ASIAN-STYLE BEEF SKEWERS 87
- Recipe 9. ARGENTINIAN CHIMICHURRI BEEF SKEWERS 88

Innovative Beef Dishes 89

- Recipe 1. BEEF AND QUINOA STUFFED BELL PEPPERS 89
- Recipe 2. SLOW-COOKED BEEF RAGU OVER POLENTA 89
- Recipe 3. BEEF BRISKET PHO 89
- Recipe 4. BEEF STUFFED ACORN SQUASH 89
- Recipe 5. BEEF AND SWEET POTATO CURRY 90
- Recipe 6. KOREAN BEEF BOWL WITH KIMCHI 90
- Recipe 7. ARGENTINIAN BEEF EMPANADAS 90
- Recipe 8. BEEF AND MUSHROOM BOURGUIGNON 90
- Recipe 9. SPICY BEEF LETTUCE WRAPS 91
- Recipe 10. BEEF STROGANOFF WITH SPIRALIZED ZUCCHINI 91

Chapter 12: Exploring Pork and Lamb 93

Flavorful Pork Preparations 93

- Recipe 1. HONEY GLAZED PORK TENDERLOIN 93
- Recipe 2. SPICY PORK BELLY TACOS 93
- Recipe 3. HERB CRUSTED PORK CHOPS 94
- Recipe 4. PORK LOIN WITH APPLE CIDER GLAZE 94
- Recipe 5. SMOKED PORK SHOULDER WITH BBQ RUB 94
- Recipe 6. PORK AND PINEAPPLE KEBABS 94
- Recipe 7. SLOW COOKER PORK RAGOUT 95
- Recipe 8. HERB-ENCRUSTED PORK TENDERLOIN 95
- Recipe 9. SPICY MAPLE GLAZED PORK CHOPS 95

Recipe 10. PORK BELLY WITH CRISPY SKIN 95
Recipe 11. SMOKED PORK RIBS WITH APPLE BBQ SAUCE 96

Lamb: Techniques and Tastes 96

Recipe 1. ROSEMARY AND GARLIC LAMB CHOPS 96
Recipe 2. MINTED LAMB BURGERS 96
Recipe 3. SLOW-ROASTED LAMB SHOULDER WITH ROOT VEGETABLES 96
Recipe 4. GRILLED LAMB SKEWERS WITH YOGURT SAUCE 97
Recipe 5. LAMB TAGINE WITH APRICOTS 97
Recipe 6. LAMB AND FETA STUFFED PEPPERS 97
Recipe 7. ROASTED LAMB RACK WITH MINT PESTO 97
Recipe 8. ROSEMARY AND GARLIC ROAST LAMB 97
Recipe 9. LAMB SHANKS BRAISED IN RED WINE 98
Recipe 10. GRILLED LAMB KEBABS WITH MINT YOGURT SAUCE 98
Recipe 11. MOROCCAN SPICED LAMB MEATBALLS 98

Fusion Dishes Featuring Pork and Lamb 99

Recipe 1. SICILIAN PORK AND LAMB INVOLTINI 99
Recipe 2. KOREAN BBQ PORK AND LAMB WRAPS 99
Recipe 3. MEDITERRANEAN STUFFED PORK AND LAMB CHOPS 99
Recipe 4. ARGENTINIAN PORK AND LAMB CHIMICHURRI SKEWERS 99
Recipe 5. ITALIAN HERB CRUSTED PORK AND LAMB RACK 100
Recipe 6. LAMB AND PORK BELLY VINDALOO 100
Recipe 8. PORK GYOZA WITH LAMB BROTH 100
Recipe 9. LAMB AND PORK BELLY BAO BUNS 101
Recipe 10. SPICED LAMB AND PORK RAGOUT WITH POLENTA 101
Recipe 11. CURRIED LAMB AND PORK STUFFED PEPPERS 101

Chapter 13: Poultry Perfection 103

Beyond the Basics with Chicken 103

Recipe 1. CHICKEN CONFIT WITH GARLIC AND THYME 103
Recipe 2. SMOKED PAPRIKA AND HONEY GLAZED CHICKEN 103
Recipe 3. LEMON AND HERB ROASTED CHICKEN DRUMSTICKS 104
Recipe 4. CHICKEN TIKKA SKEWERS 104
Recipe 5. ASIAN-STYLE CHICKEN LETTUCE WRAPS 104
Recipe 6. BALSAMIC-GLAZED CHICKEN WITH ROASTED VEGETABLES 104
Recipe 7. SZECHUAN PEPPER CHICKEN STIR-FRY 105
Recipe 8. LEMON AND HERB ROASTED CHICKEN 105
Recipe 9. SPICY CHICKEN TIKKA KEBABS 105
Recipe 10. CHICKEN AND ASPARAGUS LEMON STIR-FRY 106
Recipe 11. SMOKED PAPRIKA CHICKEN THIGHS 106

Turkey, Duck, and More Poultry Dishes 106

- Recipe 1. TURKEY BREAST WITH MAPLE-MUSTARD GLAZE 106
- Recipe 2. DUCK BREAST WITH CHERRY SAUCE 106
- Recipe 3. QUAIL STUFFED WITH WILD RICE AND MUSHROOMS 107
- Recipe 4. ROASTED PHEASANT WITH APPLES AND CIDER 107
- Recipe 5. GRILLED CORNISH HEN WITH LEMON AND HERBS 107
- Recipe 6. TURDUCKEN ROLLS WITH CRANBERRY GLAZE 107
- Recipe 7. SPICED GOOSE WITH RED WINE POACHED PEARS 108
- Recipe 8. ORANGE AND THYME ROASTED TURKEY BREAST 108
- Recipe 9. CRISPY DUCK BREAST WITH BALSAMIC GLAZE 108
- Recipe 10. HERBED CORNISH HEN WITH LEMON BUTTER 108
- Recipe 11. SMOKED PAPRIKA CHICKEN QUARTERS 109

Healthful and Hearty Poultry Recipes 109

- Recipe 1. TURKEY AND QUINOA STUFFED BELL PEPPERS 109
- Recipe 2. CHICKEN AND VEGETABLE STIR-FRY 109
- Recipe 3. SPICY TURKEY LETTUCE WRAPS 109
- Recipe 4. GRILLED CHICKEN WITH AVOCADO SALSA 110
- Recipe 5. BAKED LEMON HERB CHICKEN 110
- Recipe 6. TURKEY ZUCCHINI MEATBALLS 110
- Recipe 7. CHICKEN AND SWEET POTATO STEW 110
- Recipe 8. TURKEY AND QUINOA STUFFED PEPPERS 111
- Recipe 9. GRILLED CHICKEN AND VEGETABLE KEBABS 111
- Recipe 10. DUCK BREAST SALAD WITH BERRY VINAIGRETTE 111
- Recipe 11. SPICY THAI CHICKEN LETTUCE WRAPS 111

Chapter 14: Seafood Adventures 113

Grilling Fish to Perfection 113

- Recipe 1. CEDAR-PLANKED SALMON WITH LEMON-HERB BUTTER 113
- Recipe 2. GRILLED TUNA STEAKS WITH AVOCADO SALSA 113
- Recipe 3. HERB-CRUSTED GRILLED TROUT 114
- Recipe 4. GRILLED MAHI-MAHI WITH MANGO LIME SAUCE 114
- Recipe 5. GRILLED SWORDFISH WITH OLIVE TAPENADE 114
- Recipe 6. SPICY GRILLED SHRIMP WITH GARLIC LIME BUTTER 114
- Recipe 7. BLACKENED CATFISH WITH CUCUMBER DILL YOGURT SAUCE 115
- Recipe 8. LEMON-HERB GRILLED SALMON 115
- Recipe 9. SPICY GRILLED SHRIMP WITH GARLIC LIME SAUCE 115
- Recipe 10. GRILLED MAHI-MAHI WITH MANGO SALAD 115

Shellfish and Beyond 116

- Recipe 1. GRILLED SCALLOPS WITH HERB BUTTER 116

- Recipe 2. LEMON-GRILLED SHRIMP SKEWERS 116
- Recipe 3. CHAR-GRILLED OYSTERS WITH PARMESAN 116
- Recipe 4. GRILLED CLAMS WITH CHORIZO 116
- Recipe 5. SPICY GRILLED LOBSTER TAILS WITH GARLIC BUTTER 117
- Recipe 6. GRILLED MUSSELS WITH HERB CRUMBS 117
- Recipe 7. CEDAR-PLANKED SCALLOPS WITH SMOKY CHILI SAUCE 117
- Recipe 8. SMOKED SCALLOPS WITH HERB BUTTER 117
- Recipe 9. CHAR-GRILLED OYSTER MUSHROOMS 118
- Recipe 10. LEMON-HERB GRILLED SHRIMP 118
- Recipe 11. SPICY GRILLED CRAB LEGS 118

Seafood Mixes and Matches 118

- Recipe 1. SEAFOOD PAELLA ON THE GRILL 118
- Recipe 2. GRILLED SEAFOOD AND VEGETABLE SKEWERS 119
- Recipe 3. SPICY GRILLED FISH TACOS 119
- Recipe 4. GRILLED SALMON AND SHRIMP SCAMPI 119
- Recipe 5. MIXED SEAFOOD GRILL WITH GARLIC LEMON BUTTER 119
- Recipe 6. GRILLED MEDITERRANEAN SEAFOOD PIZZA 120
- Recipe 7. CIOPPINO-STYLE GRILLED SEAFOOD STEW 120
- Recipe 8. GRILLED SEAFOOD PAELLA 120
- Recipe 9. CEDAR-PLANKED SALMON AND SCALLOP DUO 121
- Recipe 10. SMOKEY SHRIMP AND CHORIZO SKILLET 121
- Recipe 11. GRILLED CLAMS AND MUSSELS WITH GARLIC BUTTER 121

Chapter 15: Snacking and Sharing 123

Quick Bites and Finger Foods 123

- Recipe 1. GRILLED PROSCIUTTO-WRAPPED ASPARAGUS 123
- Recipe 2. MINI GRILLED CHEESE SANDWICHES WITH TOMATO SOUP SHOTS 123
- Recipe 3. GRILLED SHRIMP AND PINEAPPLE SKEWERS 124
- Recipe 4. SMOKY GRILLED GUACAMOLE 124
- Recipe 5. BACON-WRAPPED STUFFED JALAPEÑOS 124
- Recipe 6. GRILLED PEACHES WITH BALSAMIC GLAZE 124
- Recipe 7. SPICY GRILLED CORN WITH COTIJA CHEESE 125
- Recipe 8. GRILLED PARMESAN GARLIC SHRIMP SKEWERS 125
- Recipe 9. BBQ CHICKEN SLIDERS 125
- Recipe 10. SPICY GRILLED CORN JALAPEÑO POPS 125

Shared Plates for Social Grilling 126

- Recipe 1. SMOKY PAPRIKA SHRIMP SKEWERS 126
- Recipe 2. GRILLED CORN WITH CILANTRO-LIME BUTTER 126
- Recipe 3. BALSAMIC GLAZED BRUSSELS SPROUTS 126

    Recipe 4. ASIAN-STYLE GRILLED EGGPLANT 126

    Recipe 5. CHARRED BELL PEPPER DIP 127

    Recipe 6. ZESTY LIME AND CILANTRO CHICKEN WINGS 127

    Recipe 7. SWEET AND SPICY GRILLED PINEAPPLE 127

    Recipe 8. GRILLED PROSCIUTTO-WRAPPED PEACHES 127

    Recipe 9. GRILLED VEGETABLE PLATTER WITH ROMESCO SAUCE 128

    Recipe 10. GRILLED HALLOUMI AND VEGETABLE TACOS 128

  Healthy Snacks and Dips 128

    Recipe 1. AVOCADO HUMMUS 128

    Recipe 2. SPICY KALE CHIPS 128

    Recipe 3. CARROT AND GINGER SOUP 129

    Recipe 4. CUCUMBER YOGURT DIP 129

    Recipe 5. ROASTED CHICKPEAS 129

    Recipe 6. QUINOA SALAD WITH LEMON VINAIGRETTE 129

    Recipe 7. PEANUT BUTTER BANANA BITES 130

    Recipe 8. ZESTY LIME AND BLACK BEAN DIP 130

    Recipe 9. CRUNCHY KALE CHIPS WITH SEA SALT 130

    Recipe 10. SWEET POTATO HUMMUS 130

    Recipe 11. GRILLED PEACH AND MOZZARELLA SKEWERS 131

Chapter 16: Grilling and Smoking FAQs 133

  Overcoming Common Challenges 133

  Pit Boss Tips and Tricks 134

  Recipe Adjustments and Substitutions 136

Chapter 17: From the Griddle to the Table 139

  Presentation and Plating Techniques 139

  Pairings: Drinks and Side Dishes 141

  Themed Meal Planning 142

Chapter 18: The Journey Ahead 145

  Continuing Your Grilling Education 145

  Joining the Pit Boss Community 147

  Elevating Your Grilling Game 148

  Conclusion 150

  Index 152

Chapter 1: Discovering the Pit Boss Wood Pellet Grill & Smoker

Embarking on a culinary adventure with the Pit Boss Wood Pellet Grill & Smoker isn't just about mastering a new cooking device; it's about unlocking a universe of flavors, techniques, and experiences that transform your backyard BBQs into gourmet feasts. This chapter is your gateway into that world, where the aroma of smoked meats and the sizzle of grilling vegetables beckon you to explore beyond the conventional.

The Pit Boss is more than a grill; it's a versatile companion that promises to elevate your culinary skills through smoking, grilling, baking, and even roasting. Imagine the possibilities—tender briskets that fall apart at the touch of a fork, succulent chicken with perfectly crisped skin, and vegetables infused with a smoky depth that only wood pellets can impart. This is not just cooking; it's an art form where fire meets flavor in a dance orchestrated by you, the grill master.

As we dive into the specifics, remember, the journey with your Pit Boss is as much about the process as it is about the outcome. From understanding the nuances of temperature control to mastering the smoke's timing, each step is a learning opportunity that builds your confidence and skills. This chapter aims to set a strong foundation, ensuring you're well-equipped to tackle any culinary challenge the Pit Boss throws your way.

So, whether you're a novice eager to embark on your grilling journey or a seasoned pitmaster looking to refine your skills, let's begin this adventure together. As you turn these pages, envision the backyard gatherings, the impressed guests, and the personal satisfaction of knowing you're creating something truly special with every meal you grill. Welcome to the world of Pit Boss Wood Pellet Grill & Smoker—where every flame tells a story, and every meal is a memory in the making.

Exploring the Components of Your Pit Boss

Diving into the world of Pit Boss Wood Pellet Grill & Smoker is akin to opening a treasure chest of culinary possibilities. This marvel of modern grilling technology combines the traditional essence of wood-fired flavors with the precision and ease of contemporary cooking. As you stand before this impressive piece of equipment, it's essential to familiarize yourself with its components. Understanding each part's role is the first step in mastering the art of pellet grilling, enabling you to transform ordinary meals into memorable feasts.

At the heart of your Pit Boss is the firepit, where the magic begins. Pellets, made from compressed hardwood, are fed into this small, but mighty chamber, igniting to provide the heat and smoke that will infuse your food with those sought-after, complex flavors. The beauty of the firepit lies in its simplicity and efficiency, capable of reaching high temperatures while ensuring a consistent cooking environment.

Perched above the firepit, the heat deflector plays a crucial role in distributing heat evenly across the grill. This unassuming piece of metal shields your food from direct flames, preventing harsh char and allowing for a gentler cooking process. The deflector also aids in creating a convection-like environment, perfect for baking and roasting, making your Pit Boss remarkably versatile.

The grease management system, often overlooked yet vital, ensures your grilling experience is as clean as it is enjoyable. By channeling excess fats and juices away from your food, it not only maintains the purity of your flavors but also minimizes flare-ups, keeping your Pit Boss safe and easy to maintain.

Central to the Pit Boss experience is the digital control board, your command center for precision grilling. This interface allows you to set your cooking temperature with the touch of a button, offering unparalleled control over the cooking process. Whether you're aiming for a low and slow smoke or a high-heat sear, the control board makes it effortless, allowing you to focus on the flavors and aromas that make grilling such a pleasure.

Beneath the gleaming surface of the grill grates lies the pellet hopper, a reservoir for your hardwood pellets. Its capacity dictates how long you can cook without refueling, making it an essential component for those long smoking sessions. The hopper's design ensures a steady flow of pellets to the firepit, maintaining consistent temperature and smoke levels for optimal cooking conditions.

Now, let's not forget about the smoke stack. This chimney-like feature is more than just an exit for smoke; it's a critical component in regulating airflow and smoke density within your Pit Boss. By adjusting the smoke stack, you can control the amount of smoke that circulates around your food, allowing you to fine-tune the intensity of the wood-fired flavor.

As you become more acquainted with your Pit Boss, you'll discover the significance of the grill's mobility features. Sturdy wheels and casters enable you to easily move your grill to the perfect spot in your backyard or patio, transforming any space into a gourmet outdoor kitchen. These mobility features underscore the Pit Boss's design philosophy: high-quality grilling should be accessible and enjoyable, regardless of your outdoor space's size or layout.

The meat probe, a tool of precision, is your insider to the internal temperature of your culinary creations. By providing real-time temperature readings directly to the control board, the meat probe ensures that your dishes are cooked to perfection, eliminating guesswork and enhancing your confidence as a pitmaster.

Lastly, the warming rack, often underutilized by novices, is a hidden gem within the Pit Boss. This elevated platform offers additional cooking space, ideal for keeping food warm, toasting buns, or slow-cooking delicate items away from the main heat source. It exemplifies the thoughtful design of the Pit Boss, aimed at maximizing your grilling efficiency and expanding your culinary repertoire.

Each component of your Pit Boss Wood Pellet Grill & Smoker has been meticulously designed to work in harmony, creating a seamless and enjoyable grilling experience. From the robust firepit to the intuitive digital control board, every element plays a crucial role in your culinary journey. As you explore these components, remember that your Pit Boss is more than a grill; it's a partner in your quest for grilling perfection. With this comprehensive understanding, you're well-equipped to embark on a journey of flavor, technique, and joy, bringing the best of wood-fired cooking to your backyard.

INITIAL SETUP AND ENSURING SAFE OPERATION

Stepping into the world of Pit Boss Wood Pellet Grill & Smoker brings with it the thrill of anticipation, a promise of countless flavorful adventures that await. However, before you embark on this exciting journey, a crucial first step must be taken: the initial setup and ensuring the safe operation of your new culinary companion. This is not just about following instructions; it's about laying the foundation for countless successful and enjoyable grilling experiences.

Unboxing and Assembly

Your Pit Boss arrives as a testament to the potential of countless grilled masterpieces yet to be created. As you unbox your grill, treat this moment with the reverence it deserves. Each component, from the smallest screw to the main body of the grill, plays a pivotal role in your grilling success. Assembly is straightforward, but don't rush through it. Follow the manufacturer's instructions carefully, ensuring each piece is securely fitted. This meticulous attention to detail during assembly will pay dividends in the reliability and longevity of your grill.

Location, Location, Location

Choosing the perfect spot for your Pit Boss isn't just about convenience; it's about safety and performance. Select a well-ventilated area, far removed from walls and any flammable materials. This ensures not only the safe operation of your grill but also enhances your grilling experience by providing a comfortable and spacious environment for you to work your culinary magic.

Powering Up

With your grill assembled and perfectly positioned, it's time to fuel it up. Fill the pellet hopper with high-quality hardwood pellets, your choice of flavor complementing the dishes you anticipate crafting. Then, power on your grill, following the specific ignition instructions provided. This initial firing is crucial, not just for the practical purpose of heating up your grill, but as a ceremonial beginning to your grilling journey.

The Burn-Off

Before the first cook, a "burn-off" is essential. This process involves heating your grill to a high temperature for a set period, usually around 30 minutes to an hour, to burn away any residues from the manufacturing process. It's a purification ritual, preparing your grill to produce clean, unadulterated flavors that will elevate your dishes.

Temperature Control Mastery

Understanding and mastering the temperature controls of your Pit Boss is akin to a musician learning the nuances of their instrument. The digital control board offers precision, but it's up to you to learn how your grill responds. Start with simple recipes that allow you to experiment with different temperature settings, observing how each affects the cooking process and the final outcome of your dishes.

Safety First

Safety should always be at the forefront of your grilling adventures. Regularly check for any pellet build-up in the firepit and ensure the grease management system is clean and functional. A clean grill is a safe grill, preventing flare-ups and ensuring consistent performance. Always keep a fire extinguisher nearby, a silent guardian ready to protect your culinary dreams.

Maintaining a Pellet Paradise

The pellets are the lifeblood of your Pit Boss, providing the heat and smoke that will infuse your food with flavor. Store your pellets in a dry, cool place, ensuring they remain in prime condition. Moist or degraded pellets can impede your grill's performance, diminishing the quality of your cooking.

The Art of the Grill Shutdown

Concluding your grilling session properly is as important as the initial setup. Allow the grill to cool down naturally, and then clean it thoroughly. This not only prolongs the life of your grill but also ensures that it's ready and waiting for your next culinary adventure. Regular maintenance, following the guidelines provided by Pit Boss, will keep your grill in peak condition, always ready to perform.

Embracing the Pit Boss Community

You're not just buying a grill; you're joining a community of like-minded individuals passionate about the art of grilling. Share your experiences, seek advice, and engage with the wealth of knowledge available. The Pit Boss community is a vibrant forum for exchange, full of tips, recipes, and stories of grilling triumphs and challenges overcome.

Setting up your Pit Boss Wood Pellet Grill & Smoker is the first step in a journey that promises to transform your culinary landscape. This initial process, approached with care and respect, sets the stage for the countless meals you will craft. It's about more than just preparing your grill for use; it's about embracing a lifestyle that celebrates the joy of cooking, the beauty of sharing meals with loved ones, and the endless pursuit of perfecting your craft. Welcome to the Pit Boss family, where every meal is an opportunity to create something extraordinary.

The Science of Heat: Managing Your Cooking Temperature

In the grand tapestry of culinary arts, the mastery of heat is akin to the brushstrokes of a painter—both subtle and bold, capable of transforming the mundane into the magnificent. Within the realm of the Pit Boss Wood Pellet Grill & Smoker, understanding and harnessing the science of heat is not just a technique; it's an art form that elevates grilling from mere cooking to a gastronomic spectacle. This chapter delves into the heart of pellet grilling—managing your cooking temperature—to ensure that every meal is a masterpiece worthy of the canvas that is your Pit Boss.

A Symphony of Fire and Smoke

At its core, the Pit Boss operates on a simple principle: the combustion of wood pellets to generate heat and smoke. Yet, within this simplicity lies a complex interplay of factors that influence the temperature and cooking environment. The quality of the pellets, the airflow within the grill, and the precision of the digital control board work in harmony to create a consistent cooking temperature. Understanding this symphony of elements allows you to control the heat with the finesse of a maestro, ensuring that your dishes are cooked to perfection.

The Pellet Conductor

The type and quality of pellets you choose serve as the conductor of this symphony, dictating the flavor profile and heat output. Hardwoods like hickory, mesquite, and oak deliver robust flavors and a high heat output, perfect for searing steaks or grilling burgers. Fruitwoods, such as apple and cherry, offer a subtler flavor and a milder heat, ideal for smoking fish or poultry. The uniformity of the pellets ensures a steady burn, providing a consistent temperature for even cooking.

Airflow: The Breath of the Grill

Airflow within the Pit Boss plays a crucial role in temperature management. The intake and exhaust work together to regulate the oxygen supply, fueling the fire and controlling the heat. Too little airflow can smother the fire, leading to a drop in temperature, while too much can cause the temperature to spike. By adjusting the smoke stack and ensuring the grill is well-ventilated, you maintain a balanced airflow that supports even cooking and optimal smoke flavor infusion.

The Digital Maestro

The digital control board of your Pit Boss is the maestro of this operation, allowing you to set and maintain your desired cooking temperature with the push of a button. This precision control takes the guesswork out of grilling, enabling you to focus on the flavors and textures that make your dishes stand out. Whether you're aiming for the gentle heat required for slow-smoking a brisket or the intense fire needed for searing a steak, the control board ensures your grill performs exactly as needed.

Mastering the Zones
Understanding the heat zones within your Pit Boss can transform your grilling experience. Unlike traditional grills, where heat is often concentrated in the center, the Pit Boss's design ensures an even distribution of heat and smoke. However, subtle variations still exist, providing you with the opportunity to utilize different zones for different cooking needs. The areas closer to the firepit tend to be warmer, perfect for searing, while the outer edges offer a slightly cooler environment, ideal for slower cooking or warming. By mastering these zones, you can cook multiple dishes simultaneously, each at their optimal temperature.

The Dance of the Thermometers
While the digital control board provides a general guide to the grill's temperature, the use of meat probes and external thermometers allows for precision cooking. Inserting a meat probe into the thickest part of your dish gives you an accurate reading of its internal temperature, ensuring that it's cooked safely and to your desired level of doneness. An external thermometer can offer a secondary perspective on the grill's temperature, providing additional assurance that your cooking environment remains stable.

The Ritual of Preheating
Just as an artist prepares their canvas, preheating your Pit Boss is a ritual that sets the stage for culinary success. Allowing the grill to reach the desired temperature before adding your food stabilizes the cooking environment, ensuring that your dishes cook evenly and develop the perfect crust or bark. This step is crucial, especially when grilling at high temperatures, as it prevents sticking and ensures that the beautiful grill marks that are the signature of expert grilling are achieved.

Adjusting to the Elements
Grilling is an outdoor activity, and as such, it's at the mercy of Mother Nature. Ambient temperature, humidity, and wind can all affect your grill's performance. On cold or windy days, your Pit Boss may take longer to preheat and may require a higher setting to maintain the desired cooking temperature. Conversely, on hot days, it may heat up faster and run hotter than expected. Being attuned to these environmental factors allows you to adjust your grilling technique accordingly, ensuring that no matter the weather, your results remain consistently delicious.

The Endless Quest for Perfection
Mastering the science of heat on your Pit Boss is an ongoing journey, one that offers endless opportunities for experimentation, learning, and, most importantly, enjoyment. Each grilling session is a chance to refine your skills, to learn more about how different foods react to different temperatures and cooking methods. Embrace the challenges and the triumphs, for it is through them that you will grow as a pitmaster, continually elevating your culinary creations.

In mastering the science of heat, you not only become adept at controlling your Pit Boss; you unlock the door to a world of flavor, texture, and aroma that will delight your senses and impress your guests. This knowledge, combined with your passion for grilling, sets you on the path to becoming not just a grill master, but a culinary artist, painting with smoke and fire on the canvas of your Pit Boss.

Chapter 2: Honing Your Pit Boss Skills

Welcome to the next stage of your culinary journey with the Pit Boss Wood Pellet Grill & Smoker. As you step into Chapter 2, you're not just moving forward; you're elevating your game. This chapter is about refining those initial skills you've acquired and stretching the boundaries of what you thought possible in your backyard. It's here that you transition from a novice, grasping the basics of pellet grilling, to a burgeoning pitmaster who commands the grill with confidence and creativity.

Honing your skills is more than learning a set of techniques; it's about developing a deep understanding of the subtleties of grilling and smoking. You'll explore the artistry behind perfect grill marks, the science of achieving a mouthwatering crust, and the meticulous strategy of heat zone manipulation. This chapter aims to sharpen your instincts, enabling you to make split-second decisions that turn good dishes into great ones.

Imagine the satisfaction of serving up a perfectly seared steak, its exterior a testament to your mastery over the intense heat of the grill. Envision the delight in your guests' eyes as they bite into a piece of smoked chicken, the skin crisp and flavorful, the meat inside juicy and infused with a delicate smokiness. These are the moments we're working towards—moments of culinary brilliance that become not just meals, but memories.

As you delve into this chapter, remember: every tip, every technique, and every recipe are a step on the path to greatness. Your Pit Boss is the tool, but you, the aspiring pitmaster, are the craftsman. Let's begin this journey of refinement together, turning your backyard into the stage for your grilling masterpieces.

Perfecting Marks and Mouthwatering Crusts

In the symphony of flavors that is grilling, the mastery of perfect grill marks and the achievement of a mouthwatering crust stand out as critical movements, each contributing to the final culinary masterpiece. As you hone your Pit Boss skills, understanding the subtleties behind these techniques is essential. This subchapter is dedicated to transforming you into a maestro of the grill, capable of eliciting the richest flavors and textures from your ingredients.

Grill Marks: The Signature of Mastery

Grill marks are not just about aesthetics; they are a testament to your ability to control heat and timing. They add texture and flavor while presenting your culinary creations in their most appetizing form. Achieving the perfect grill marks with your Pit Boss begins with the grill itself. Ensure your grill grates are clean and well-oiled, preventing sticking and promoting even cooking. Preheat your Pit Boss to a high temperature—this is crucial for searing the surface of the meat quickly, creating those coveted marks without overcooking the interior.

The secret lies in the placement and movement. Lay your meat down at a 45-degree angle to the grates. After a few minutes, rotate it 90 degrees on the same side. This method creates the classic crosshatch pattern, a hallmark of grilling expertise. Patience is key; the meat will release from the grill when it's ready to be flipped. Resist the urge to move it too soon.

Cultivating a Crust to Crave

The crust on a piece of grilled meat is the pinnacle of flavor—a rich, caramelized exterior that encapsulates the tender, juicy interior. Achieving this involves more than just high heat; it's an artful balance of moisture, seasoning, and timing. The process begins well before the meat hits the grill, with the application of a dry rub or simple seasoning. Salt plays a crucial role, drawing moisture to the surface where it can evaporate, leaving behind concentrated flavors ready to caramelize under heat.

Moisture is the enemy of crust formation. Pat your meat dry before seasoning, and if you're aiming for the ultimate crust, consider letting it sit uncovered in the refrigerator for a few hours. This dry-brining method enhances flavor and texture, ensuring a crust that's richly caramelized and packed with taste.

High heat is essential, but so is knowing when to move your meat to a cooler part of the grill. After searing, allow it to finish cooking at a lower temperature. This technique ensures a crust that's not burnt but beautifully browned, encasing meat that's cooked to perfection.

Beyond Meat: Vegetables and Crusts

The principles of grill marks and crusts aren't limited to meat. Vegetables also benefit from these techniques, transforming into charred, flavor-packed delights. The key difference lies in the preparation and cooking times. Vegetables require a watchful eye and often a lighter touch, with a focus on ensuring they retain their natural moisture and sweetness while gaining that charred exterior.

A Symphony on the Grill

Mastering the art of perfect grill marks and mouthwatering crusts on your Pit Boss is akin to conducting a symphony. Each element, from the preparation of the grill to the final touch of seasoning, contributes to a culinary composition that delights the senses. Remember, the goal is not just to cook but to create an experience, turning each meal into an occasion and every bite into a memory. As you practice these techniques, you'll find yourself not just cooking, but crafting dishes that speak to the heart of grilling: flavor, texture, and the joy of sharing good food with good company.

The Art of Manipulating and Positioning

Crafting the perfect meal on your Pit Boss Grill isn't just about the ingredients you choose or the recipes you follow; it's also about the art of manipulating and positioning. Mastery over these techniques allows you to unlock the full potential of your grill, turning simple backyard barbecues into gourmet experiences. This sub-chapter delves into the nuances of these practices, empowering you to elevate your grilling game to new heights.

Understanding Your Grill's Zones

The first step in mastering the art of manipulating and positioning is understanding your Pit Boss Grill's heat zones. Unlike a traditional grill, your Pit Boss allows for incredible precision with its temperature control, offering a range of heat zones from the intense direct heat necessary for searing to the gentler indirect heat perfect for slow cooking. By learning how to utilize these zones effectively, you can manipulate your cooking environment to suit any dish, from a perfectly seared steak to a delicately smoked salmon.

Positioning for Perfection

The positioning of your food on the grill is critical. Each section of the grill offers a unique cooking property. The center often provides the most consistent heat, ideal for cooking meats evenly.

Meanwhile, the edges offer a slightly cooler temperature, perfect for vegetables or more delicate items that require gentler cooking. Understanding these subtleties allows you to position your food in a way that each piece comes out perfectly cooked, tailored to the specific needs of the dish.

The Dance of Flipping and Rotating

Flipping and rotating your food isn't just about ensuring even cooking; it's a dance that, when performed correctly, can significantly enhance the flavor and texture of your meal. By paying close attention to the cooking process and knowing precisely when to flip or rotate your food, you can achieve an even caramelization and crust, imbuing your dishes with a depth of flavor that is truly unparalleled. This technique requires patience and attention to detail, but the results are well worth the effort.

Utilizing Accessories for Ultimate Control

Your Pit Boss Grill is incredibly versatile, but by incorporating accessories, you can take your grilling to the next level. From grill baskets for vegetables to rotisserie attachments for that perfect roast, each accessory offers a new way to manipulate and position your food, providing even more control over the cooking process. By exploring these options, you can expand your culinary repertoire, experimenting with new dishes and techniques that were previously beyond reach.

Mastering the Use of Foil and Smoke

Foil is not just a tool for wrapping leftovers; in the hands of a skilled griller, it becomes an instrument of culinary precision. By wrapping certain foods in foil, you can manipulate the cooking environment, retaining moisture, and infusing your dishes with delicate flavors. Similarly, mastering the use of smoke through wood chips or pellets allows you to add a new dimension of taste to your meals, transforming simple ingredients into complex, flavor-packed dishes.

The Importance of Resting

Manipulation and positioning don't end once the food is off the grill. Understanding the importance of resting your meat allows the juices to redistribute, ensuring that every bite is as flavorful and tender as possible. This final step is crucial in the art of grilling, a testament to the patience and care that goes into creating the perfect meal.

A Symphony of Skills

Mastering the art of manipulating and positioning on your Pit Boss Grill is like conducting a symphony, where each movement and decision plays a crucial role in the final outcome. It's about more than just cooking; it's about creating an experience, one that delights the senses and brings people together. As you refine these skills, remember that each meal is an opportunity to explore, experiment, and excel. With your Pit Boss by your side, the possibilities are endless, and the journey is just as rewarding as the destination.

UTILIZING AND MASTERING THE GRILL'S HEAT ZONES

The Pit Boss Wood Pellet Grill & Smoker isn't just a tool for outdoor cooking; it's a canvas where the art of temperature control paints the masterpiece. Mastering your grill's heat zones means understanding the subtle dance of fire and flavor, where each decision impacts the symphony of taste and texture that emerges from your kitchen. This sub-chapter delves into the intricacies of utilizing and mastering these zones, turning every grilling session into an opportunity for culinary excellence.

The Essence of Heat Zones

Heat zones on your Pit Boss are not just areas of varying temperature; they are the heartbeats of your culinary creations. The direct zone offers high heat, perfect for searing and creating those iconic grill marks that signify a chef's touch. The indirect zone, cooler and more forgiving, is ideal for slow-cooking and smoking, where flavors deepen and meats tenderize into succulent masterpieces. Understanding these zones is the first step in harnessing the full potential of your grill.

Creating and Managing Zones

Achieving mastery over your grill's heat zones begins with the setup. On a Pit Boss, the pellet-driven system offers unparalleled control over temperature distribution. By adjusting the flow of pellets and managing the grill's settings, you can create distinct zones even within the uniform environment of a pellet grill. Experiment with different pellet types and quantities to see how they influence heat intensity and flavor profile.

The Art of Direct Grilling

Direct grilling is about intimacy with the flame. It's where steaks sear, burgers char, and vegetables gain a smoky exterior while retaining a crunchy interior. This method isn't just about applying heat; it's about engaging with your food, understanding when to flip, rotate, or move it to a less intense area. Mastering direct grilling on your Pit Boss involves not only managing the grill's temperature but also interpreting the subtle cues from your food, ensuring each piece reaches its peak of perfection.

The Mastery of Indirect Grilling

Indirect grilling is the realm of patience and precision. It's where the magic of slow cooking unfolds, transforming cuts of meat into tender, fall-off-the-bone delicacies. Utilizing this zone requires an understanding of time and temperature, recognizing that low and slow is the path to unlocking flavors and textures that high heat cannot achieve. It's about setting your Pit Boss to a lower temperature and allowing the convection-like flow of smoke and heat to gently cook your food to perfection.

Transitioning Between Zones

The true mark of a pitmaster is knowing when and how to move food between these zones. Starting a thick steak on the direct heat for a perfect sear, then moving it to the indirect zone to finish cooking, ensures a crusty exterior with a juicy interior. This technique, often referred to as reverse searing, epitomizes the strategic utilization of heat zones. It requires not just knowledge of your grill's capabilities but also an instinct for timing and adjustment developed through experience.

Tips and Techniques

- **Preheat your grill**: Ensure your Pit Boss reaches the desired temperature before adding food. This step is crucial for effective zone cooking.
- **Use a meat thermometer**: To avoid guesswork, especially when using the indirect zone, a meat thermometer ensures your food is cooked safely and to perfection.
- **Rest your meat**: After cooking, allow your meat to rest. This step redistributes juices and ensures maximum flavor, particularly when utilizing both direct and indirect zones.

The Path to Mastery

Utilizing and mastering the heat zones of your Pit Boss Wood Pellet Grill & Smoker is an ongoing journey. It combines the science of temperature control with the art of cooking, where each session on the grill is a lesson in flavor, texture, and technique. As you experiment with different foods, settings, and methods, remember that each meal is an opportunity to refine your skills, deepen your understanding, and, most importantly, enjoy the process. The path to becoming a pitmaster is not just about the meals you create but about the experiences you cultivate and the memories you make along the way.

Chapter 3: Maintenance and Care for Your Pit Boss

Embarking on your grilling journey with a Pit Boss Wood Pellet Grill & Smoker is a commitment—not just to the craft of cooking but to the stewardship of your culinary tool. Chapter 3 delves into the essential practices of maintenance and care, transforming the routine upkeep of your grill into an act of respect for the art of grilling itself. This isn't about mundane chores; it's about preserving and enhancing your grill's performance, ensuring that each flame you light is as potent as the first. Your Pit Boss, with its robust capabilities and innovative features, is more than a mere appliance; it's a partner in your culinary adventures. Like any good partnership, this one thrives on attention and care. From the simple, like regular cleaning to prevent build-up and ensure efficient operation, to the nuanced, like understanding the importance of pellet management and storage to maintain flavor integrity, this chapter covers it all.

Maintenance and care go beyond prolonging the life of your grill; they're about honoring the meals you've shared and those yet to come. It's about ensuring that each time you fire up your Pit Boss, it's ready to perform, capable of bringing your culinary visions to life. So, as we delve into the practicalities of keeping your grill in top condition, remember: this is an integral part of your journey as a pitmaster, a ritual that underscores your dedication to the craft and to the experiences created around the glow of the grill.

A Detailed Cleaning Routine

Creating a detailed cleaning routine for your Pit Boss Wood Pellet Grill & Smoker is not just about upkeep; it's about ensuring every grilling session can be as flawless as the first. A clean grill is a testament to a pitmaster's dedication, impacting everything from the longevity of the grill to the taste of the food. Here, we'll break down the steps to a comprehensive cleaning routine, ensuring your Pit Boss remains a reliable companion in your culinary adventures.

Before You Begin: Safety First
- Ensure the grill is completely cooled down before starting any cleaning procedure.
- Disconnect any electrical connections to prevent accidents.
- Wear gloves to protect your hands from grease and possible sharp edges.

Step 1: The Exterior
- Start with the grill's exterior. Wipe down the outer surfaces with a mild detergent and warm water solution. For stainless steel components, use a cleaner designed for stainless steel to avoid streaks and maintain its luster.
- Inspect the grill for any signs of wear, rust, or damage. Address these issues promptly to prevent them from worsening.

Step 2: The Grill Grates
- Remove the grates and soak them in soapy water for about 15 to 20 minutes to loosen any stuck-on food particles.
- Use a grill brush or a scouring pad to scrub the grates clean. For cast iron grates, avoid using soap too often, as it can strip the seasoning. Instead, opt for hot water and a stiff brush.
- Rinse thoroughly and dry before replacing.

Step 3: The Firepit and Heat Deflector
- Vacuum out the firepit to remove ash and unburned pellets. This is crucial for maintaining proper airflow and ensuring efficient pellet combustion.
- The heat deflector plate should be wiped down to remove any grease or food residue. This helps in preventing flare-ups and maintaining even heat distribution.

Step 4: The Grease Management System
- Clean out the grease bucket and replace any disposable liners. Ensure the grease chute leading to the bucket is clear of any obstructions to prevent grease build-up and potential fire hazards.
- Inspect and clean the grease tray, ensuring it's free from excessive grease and debris.

Step 5: The Pellet Hopper
- Empty the pellet hopper to check for any moisture, pellet dust, or debris. Moisture can cause the pellets to swell and potentially jam the auger system.
- Vacuum the inside of the hopper and inspect the auger for any signs of blockage.

Step 6: The Interior Walls and Lid
- Wipe down the interior walls and the underside of the grill lid with a damp cloth. Over time, smoke and grease can accumulate, affecting the flavor of your food.
- Avoid using harsh chemicals inside the grill to prevent any unwanted flavors transferring to your food.

Step 7: Inspecting and Cleaning the Burners
- For models with gas assist or side burners, ensure the burners are clear of debris and the ports are not obstructed.
- Use a pipe cleaner or a small wire to clear any blockages in the burner ports.

Step 8: Checking and Maintaining Connections
- Inspect all electrical connections, including the igniter, for any signs of wear or damage. Replace any faulty components as necessary.
- Check the condition of hoses and regulators on models equipped with gas assist features. Look for any signs of cracking, wear, or leaks.

Step 9: Final Inspection and Function Test
- Once the grill is clean and reassembled, conduct a function test. Turn on the grill and observe it running for a few minutes to ensure everything is working correctly.
- Listen for any unusual sounds that might indicate a problem, and make sure the grill is heating up as expected.

Routine After Each Use
- After each grilling session, brush the grates clean while they're still warm to remove food particles and prevent buildup.
- Wipe down the exterior to keep it looking new.

Seasonal Deep Clean
- Schedule a deep clean at least twice a year or more frequently based on usage. This ensures your grill remains in peak condition and ready for any impromptu BBQ sessions.

Conclusion
Adopting a detailed cleaning routine for your Pit Boss Grill is an integral part of your journey as a pitmaster. Not only does it prolong the life of your grill, but it also ensures that the flavors of your grilled creations remain true, free from the interference of old residues. Remember, a clean grill is the cornerstone of great grilling, setting the stage for countless memorable meals to come. Your

dedication to this ritual reflects your passion for the craft, ensuring your Pit Boss is always ready to perform at its best.

THE TRUTH ABOUT SEASONING YOUR GRILL

Seasoning your Pit Boss Wood Pellet Grill & Smoker is a rite of passage, a ceremonial initiation that transcends mere preparation—it's the beginning of a relationship between pitmaster and grill. Yet, many are shrouded in myths about what seasoning really entails and why it's essential. This sub-chapter demystifies the process, providing you with the knowledge and techniques to properly season your grill, ensuring it performs at its peak for years to come.

Understanding Seasoning
At its core, seasoning a grill is the process of coating the interior surfaces with a layer of oil and heating it to a point where the oil breaks down and polymerizes, creating a protective barrier. This barrier not only prevents rust but also creates a non-stick surface that improves with each cook. It's a process akin to seasoning a cast-iron skillet, enhancing both the grill's longevity and performance.

Choosing the Right Oil
The first step in seasoning your Pit Boss is selecting the right oil. High-smoke point oils are preferred due to their ability to withstand high temperatures without breaking down. Canola, vegetable, and flaxseed oils are excellent choices, each contributing to a durable and effective seasoning layer.

The Initial Seasoning
The initial seasoning of your Pit Boss is a momentous occasion, setting the stage for all future culinary exploits. To begin, ensure your grill is clean and dry. Apply a thin, even coat of your chosen oil to all interior surfaces, including the grates, using a cloth or spray bottle. Avoid using too much oil, as this can lead to a sticky residue rather than a smooth, protective layer.
With the oil applied, ignite your Pit Boss, setting it to a high temperature, usually around 350°F to 400°F. Let the grill run for at least an hour, during which the oil will smoke and eventually polymerize, bonding to the metal. This process emits a significant amount of smoke, so ensure your grill is in a well-ventilated area.

Post-Seasoning Care
After the initial seasoning, allow your grill to cool completely. You may notice a glossy sheen on the treated surfaces, a sign of a successful seasoning. From this point forward, the care you take after each cooking session will reinforce and build upon this foundational layer.

Maintaining the Seasoning
The beauty of a well-seasoned grill is that it becomes better with use. However, this doesn't mean it's maintenance-free. After each use, it's important to clean the grates gently to remove food particles without stripping the seasoned surface. A brush with soft bristles or a wooden scraper can effectively clean the grates without damaging the seasoning.
In the event of rust formation or if the seasoning layer is compromised, a re-seasoning may be necessary. The process mirrors the initial seasoning, ensuring your grill remains a reliable, high-performance cooking instrument.

Seasoning Misconceptions

One common misconception is that seasoning is a one-time process. In reality, the seasoning of your grill evolves with use, developing a patina that enhances its non-stick properties and flavor contribution to your dishes. Additionally, while seasoning does provide a form of rust protection, regular maintenance and care are still vital to prevent moisture-induced corrosion.

Conclusion

The act of seasoning your Pit Boss Wood Pellet Grill & Smoker is a testament to your commitment to the art of grilling. It's a procedure that not only prepares your grill for its culinary duties but also begins the process of creating a cooking surface that imparts incomparable flavor and texture to your dishes. By understanding and embracing the truth about seasoning, you ensure that your grill is not just a tool, but a cherished companion in your journey toward grilling mastery. Remember, a well-seasoned grill reflects the care, patience, and passion of the pitmaster who tends it.

SOLUTIONS FOR COMMON PITFALLS

In the journey of mastering the Pit Boss Wood Pellet Grill & Smoker, even the most seasoned pitmasters can encounter hurdles. This sub-chapter is dedicated to navigating those common pitfalls with grace and expertise, ensuring your grilling experience remains enjoyable and your results, exceptional.

Pitfall 1: Fluctuating Temperatures

One of the challenges you might face is maintaining a consistent temperature. Such fluctuations can disrupt the cooking process, affecting the texture and doneness of your meals.
Solutions:
- **Check the Pellets:** Ensure you're using high-quality pellets that are free from moisture, as poor-quality or damp pellets can cause temperature instability.
- **Clean Regularly:** Build-up in the firepit can hinder airflow and pellet combustion, leading to temperature issues. Regular cleaning ensures unimpeded operation.

Pitfall 2: Inefficient Smoke Production

For those who cherish the rich, smoky flavor in their barbecued dishes, insufficient smoke can be disappointing.
Solutions:
- **Pellet Choice Matters:** Different woods produce varying amounts of smoke and flavor profiles. Experiment with different types of pellets to find your preferred smoke intensity and taste.
- **Manage Airflow:** Adjusting the grill's vents can help control smoke density. More oxygen means a hotter fire but less visible smoke, so find the right balance for your cooking needs.

Pitfall 3: Grease Fires

A grease fire can be alarming and dangerous, turning a pleasant grilling session into a safety hazard.
Solutions:
- **Regular Cleaning:** Prevent grease buildup by cleaning the grease tray and firepit regularly. This is the most effective way to prevent grease fires.

- **Temperature Control:** Cooking at the right temperature for your food can reduce fat drippings and flare-ups. High heat is not always the answer.

Pitfall 4: Pellet Auger Jamming

An auger jam can bring your cooking to a standstill, often caused by pellet quality or maintenance issues.

Solutions:
- **Quality Pellets:** Again, the importance of high-quality, properly stored pellets cannot be overstated. Avoid using pellets that are broken or have absorbed moisture.
- **Regular Inspections:** Periodically inspect and clean the auger to prevent any buildup that could lead to a jam.

Pitfall 5: Rust and Wear

Exposure to the elements can cause your grill to rust or wear prematurely, affecting its functionality and lifespan.

Solutions:
- **Protective Covering:** When not in use, protect your Pit Boss with a grill cover to shield it from moisture and extreme weather conditions.
- **Touch-ups:** Use rust-resistant paint to touch up any chips or scratches on the grill's exterior, preventing rust from taking hold.

Pitfall 6: Ignition Failure

An unresponsive grill on a day planned for barbecuing can be frustrating.

Solutions:
- **Check Connections:** Ensure that all electrical connections are secure and that the grill is properly plugged in.
- **Clean the Igniter:** A dirty igniter can prevent the grill from lighting. Carefully cleaning the igniter area can resolve this issue.

Pitfall 7: Uneven Cooking

Uneven cooking can result from various factors, including grill setup, placement of food, or internal components needing adjustment.

Solutions:
- **Zone Cooking:** Utilize the grill's different heat zones for cooking various items simultaneously, adjusting their placement for even cooking.
- **Rotate Regularly:** Rotate and flip your food regularly to ensure even cooking, especially when cooking large quantities or pieces.

Conclusion

Every pitfall presents an opportunity to deepen your understanding and mastery of the Pit Boss Wood Pellet Grill & Smoker. By addressing these common issues proactively, you not only enhance your grilling experience but also extend the life of your grill, ensuring it remains a faithful companion in your culinary explorations. Remember, part of the joy of grilling lies in overcoming challenges, turning them into opportunities for learning and growth. With these solutions in hand, you're well-equipped to face any hurdle with confidence, keeping your focus on the art of creating delicious, smoked, and grilled masterpieces that bring joy to the table.

Chapter 4: The Pit Boss Toolkit

Embarking on a grilling adventure with your Pit Boss Wood Pellet Grill & Smoker is akin to setting out on a grand culinary expedition. Just as a skilled craftsman relies on a set of precision tools to bring visions to life, a pitmaster's success hinges on the arsenal at their disposal. Chapter 4, "The Pit Boss Toolkit," is designed to be your guide through the essential tools and accessories that elevate your grilling experience from ordinary to extraordinary.

Within these pages, you'll discover not only the fundamental gadgets that every grill master should possess but also delve into the specialized equipment that can transform your backyard barbecues into a gastronomic spectacle. From the basic, like a durable set of tongs and a reliable meat thermometer, to the more advanced, such as a cast iron griddle for those perfect sear marks and a digital meat probe for precision cooking, each tool plays a pivotal role in the symphony of flavors you create.

This chapter is more than a mere inventory; it's a roadmap to mastering your Pit Boss, equipping you with the knowledge to select, use, and care for these tools effectively. As you journey through the pages, remember, the right tool in the right hands can turn a simple meal into a memorable feast. Welcome to your Pit Boss Toolkit, the cornerstone of culinary excellence in the world of pellet grilling.

Essential Grilling Equipment

High-Quality Grill Tools
A robust set of grill tools is the foundation of effective grilling. These should include a long-handled spatula, tongs, and a basting brush, crafted from high-quality, durable materials capable of withstanding the high temperatures and rigors of grilling. Stainless steel is preferred for its strength and ease of cleaning, ensuring your tools remain hygienic and reliable over time.

Meat Thermometer
The importance of a precise meat thermometer cannot be overstated. Achieving the perfect doneness requires more than intuition; it demands accuracy. A digital meat thermometer provides instant readings, allowing you to ensure your meats are cooked safely and to your desired level of doneness, every single time.

Grill Gloves
Safety is paramount in the art of grilling, making a pair of high-temperature resistant grill gloves an essential tool. They protect your hands from burns while enabling you to handle hot utensils, move grill grates, or even manage the food directly with confidence and ease.

Grill Brushes
Keeping your grill clean is not just about maintenance; it's about flavor preservation and safety. A durable grill brush with a long handle allows for effective cleaning of the grates post-grilling, removing food particles and grease that can affect taste and increase the risk of flare-ups.

Grill Covers
Protection of your Pit Boss from the elements extends its lifespan and maintains its performance. A quality grill cover, tailored to fit your model, shields your grill from rain, dust, and sun, preventing rust and wear from compromising your grill's integrity.

Wood Pellets and Storage
The choice of wood pellets significantly influences the flavor profile of your grilled dishes. Investing in a variety of high-quality pellets enables you to experiment with different smoke flavors, enhancing your culinary creations. Equally important is a proper storage solution for your pellets, ensuring they remain dry and free from contamination, ready for your next grilling session. As we delve deeper into the nuances of each essential tool, remember that each piece of equipment serves as an extension of your skills, enhancing your ability to express culinary creativity and precision on the grill. The right tools not only simplify the grilling process but elevate the entire experience, allowing you to focus on the art of flavor and the joy of sharing your creations with others. Equipped with these essentials, you stand ready to master the Pit Boss Wood Pellet Grill & Smoker, transforming simple ingredients into extraordinary meals that linger in memory long after the last bite.

ENHANCEMENTS FOR YOUR GRILLING SESSIONS

Beyond the basic toolkit lies a world of enhancements designed to elevate your grilling sessions from ordinary to extraordinary. These are not merely accessories but invaluable allies in your quest to unlock the full potential of your Pit Boss Wood Pellet Grill & Smoker. This sub-chapter delves into the essential enhancements that will transform your grilling into an art form, ensuring each session is as rewarding as it is flavorful.

Cast Iron Cookware
The first enhancement in any pitmaster's arsenal should be quality cast iron cookware. A cast iron skillet or griddle introduces a new dimension to your grilling, allowing for unparalleled heat retention and distribution. Perfect for searing steaks, cooking vegetables, or even baking, cast iron cookware is as versatile as it is durable. Its ability to withstand high temperatures makes it ideal for use on your Pit Boss, enhancing the smoky flavor that pellet grilling is renowned for.

Smoking Boxes and Tubes
To infuse your dishes with a deeper, more nuanced smoke flavor, consider incorporating a smoking box or tube into your setup. Filled with wood chips or pellets, these devices produce a concentrated smoke that permeates your food, enhancing its flavor complexity without overpowering. This is especially beneficial for shorter cooks where traditional smoking methods may fall short.

Rotisserie Kit
A rotisserie kit offers a hands-off approach to cooking that ensures even cooking and basting. Ideal for roasting whole chickens, pork loins, or even ribs, the rotisserie slowly turns your food over the heat, enveloping it in a constant heat that locks in moisture and flavor. This enhancement not only simplifies cooking larger cuts of meat but also elevates the texture and taste to professional levels.

Grill Baskets and Mats
For those delicate items or smaller vegetables that might fall through the grates, grill baskets and mats are indispensable. These enhancements provide a smooth surface for cooking, ensuring nothing is lost to the flames. They're particularly useful for grilling fish, vegetables, or even smaller items like shrimp and scallops, allowing for an even cook without the fear of sticking or falling.

Digital Meat Probes
While a basic meat thermometer is essential, upgrading to a digital meat probe offers the ultimate in precision and convenience. With real-time temperature monitoring and alerts, you can ensure

your meat is cooked to perfection without constant supervision. This is invaluable for longer smokes, allowing you to maintain the perfect temperature throughout the cook for consistent, mouthwatering results.

Bluetooth Thermometers
Taking temperature monitoring a step further, Bluetooth thermometers connect to your smartphone, providing updates and alerts directly to your device. This technology not only frees you from constant grill-side monitoring but also offers the flexibility to entertain guests or prepare other dishes, secure in the knowledge that your grilling is progressing perfectly.

Custom Grill Grates
Custom grill grates, tailored to your specific Pit Boss model, can significantly enhance your grill's performance and ease of use. With options ranging from non-stick surfaces to specific designs for improved airflow, these grates can improve heat distribution, reduce sticking, and even imprint your food with signature grill marks, adding both beauty and flavor to your dishes.

The journey of a pitmaster is one of continuous exploration and improvement. Each session at your Pit Boss is an opportunity to experiment and refine your techniques, and these enhancements are tools to aid in that pursuit. Whether it's through the use of specialized cookware, innovative technology, or customized equipment, the goal remains the same: to elevate the grilling experience, ensuring each meal is a testament to the craft of grilling. With these enhancements, your Pit Boss becomes more than just a grill—it becomes an extension of your culinary creativity, capable of producing dishes that delight, inspire, and bring people together.

SELECTING THE BEST TOOLS FOR THE JOB

In the world of pellet grilling, the difference between the ordinary and the extraordinary lies in the details—the precise selection of tools that elevate a simple meal into a culinary masterpiece. This sub-chapter is dedicated to guiding you through the process of selecting the best tools for your Pit Boss Wood Pellet Grill & Smoker, ensuring that each choice you make adds to the richness of your grilling experience.

Understanding Your Needs
Before diving into the vast sea of grilling tools and accessories, start with a clear understanding of your needs. Consider the types of dishes you frequently cook, the size of your gatherings, and your personal grilling style. Whether you're a fan of slow-smoked briskets, seared steaks, or delicately grilled vegetables, each preference dictates a unique set of tools designed to enhance those specific experiences.

Quality Over Quantity
In the pursuit of the perfect grilling setup, it's easy to be tempted by the latest gadgets and gizmos. However, the cornerstone of a truly effective toolkit lies not in its size, but in the quality of each piece. opt for tools made from durable materials like stainless steel, which can withstand the high temperatures and rigors of grilling while maintaining their integrity over time. A well-made set of tongs, a sturdy spatula, and a reliable meat thermometer are indispensable allies in your quest for grilling perfection.

Versatility and Functionality
When selecting tools, consider their versatility and functionality. A tool that serves multiple purposes not only offers better value but also reduces clutter around your grill. For example, a spatula with a serrated edge can double as a knife for quick cuts, while a set of tongs with a built-in thermometer combines two essential functions in one, streamlining your grilling process and allowing you to adapt with ease to whatever the grill throws your way.

Personal Comfort and Ergonomics
The best tools are the ones that feel right in your hand. Ergonomics play a crucial role in the selection process, ensuring that prolonged use doesn't lead to discomfort or strain. Look for tools with handles that offer a comfortable grip and are designed to keep your hands away from the heat, ensuring safety as well as comfort during those long grilling sessions.

Maintenance and Care
Consider the maintenance required to keep your tools in top condition. Tools that are easy to clean and care for will not only last longer but will also ensure that your grilling remains hygienic and safe. Those with dishwasher-safe components offer added convenience, allowing you to focus more on the joy of grilling and less on the cleanup that follows.

Adapting to Technological Advances
In the ever-evolving world of grilling, new technologies offer opportunities to enhance your grilling experience further. Digital meat probes and Bluetooth-enabled thermometers provide precision and convenience, allowing you to monitor your cook from a distance. Embrace these advancements, selecting tools that integrate seamlessly with your Pit Boss, and expand your capabilities as a pitmaster.

A Tailored Approach
Ultimately, selecting the best tools for the job is a highly personal decision. What works for one pitmaster may not suit another, emphasizing the importance of a tailored approach. Assess your individual needs, preferences, and aspirations as a grill master, and build your toolkit accordingly. Remember, each tool you choose is a reflection of your journey in the art of grilling, a step closer to mastering the Pit Boss Wood Pellet Grill & Smoker.

The path to grilling excellence is paved with the choices we make; from the recipes we select to the tools we wield. By carefully selecting the best tools for your Pit Boss, you empower yourself to explore new culinary horizons, tackle any grilling challenge, and share unforgettable meals with friends and family. This sub-chapter is not just a guide to choosing tools; it's an invitation to enhance your grilling journey, equipping you with the knowledge and confidence to achieve greatness on the grill.

Chapter 5: Expanding Your Culinary Horizons

Embarking on a culinary adventure with your Pit Boss Wood Pellet Grill & Smoker is akin to charting a course into unexplored territories, where the thrill of discovery awaits at every turn. Chapter 5, "Expanding Your Culinary Horizons," is dedicated to those intrepid pitmasters eager to push beyond the familiar landscapes of burgers and briskets, into a realm were creativity and curiosity reign supreme. Here, we explore the boundless possibilities that pellet grilling offers, inviting you to experiment with ingredients, techniques, and cuisines that may have once seemed beyond reach.

This journey is not just about mastering new dishes; it's a quest to deepen your understanding of flavor, texture, and the subtle interplay between fire, smoke, and food. Whether it's elevating vegetables to the centerpiece of your meal, exploring the delicate art of grilled desserts, or incorporating global flavors that span continents, this chapter is your guide to broadening your culinary repertoire.

As you turn these pages, remember that each recipe, each technique, and each new ingredient is a step toward redefining what it means to grill. With your Pit Boss as your companion, there are no limits to the culinary heights you can achieve. So, light the fire, open your mind, and prepare to expand your culinary horizons in ways you never imagined possible.

Elevating Vegetables on the Grill

In a culinary world often dominated by proteins, vegetables on the grill can transform from mere sides to the stars of the show. This sub-chapter, "Elevating Vegetables on the Grill," invites you to reimagine the role of vegetables in your grilling repertoire, showcasing techniques and flavors that bring out the best in garden-fresh produce.

The Foundation: Choosing Your Vegetables

Selecting the right vegetables is the first step toward grilling success. Look for freshness and seasonality as your guides; vibrant, in-season vegetables not only bring superior flavor and texture but also connect your cooking with the rhythms of the natural world. Hardy vegetables like zucchini, bell peppers, and eggplant excel on the grill, their flesh transforming into tender, charred delicacies.

Preparation: The Key to Perfection

Prepping your vegetables for the grill involves more than just slicing and dicing. Marinating your vegetables can infuse them with depth and complexity, while a simple brush of olive oil and a sprinkle of salt can enhance their natural flavors. Consider size and shape for even cooking; larger, flatter pieces maximize surface area for those desirable grill marks.

Mastering the Heat

Understanding how different vegetables interact with heat allows you to achieve perfect results every time. Dense vegetables like potatoes and carrots benefit from a slower, indirect heat, allowing them to cook through without charring excessively. In contrast, quick-cooking vegetables like asparagus and green beans thrive over direct heat, which crisps their exteriors while keeping the interiors crunchy and bright.

The Role of Smoke
Introducing wood pellets specifically chosen for their flavor profiles can elevate grilled vegetables into a new realm of taste. Mesquite imparts a bold smokiness, while applewood offers a subtler, sweeter note. Experimenting with different woods provides an opportunity to pair vegetable dishes with complementary smoke flavors, adding an extra layer of complexity to your culinary creations.

Techniques for Excellence
Beyond the basic grill-and-serve approach, consider techniques that showcase the versatility of vegetables. Grilling in foil packets steams the vegetables in their own juices, preserving moisture and flavor. Using a grill basket can prevent smaller, delicate pieces from falling through the grates, ensuring every bit of your carefully chosen produce is savored and enjoyed.

Finishing Touches
The final flourish comes with the application of dressings, herbs, and spices after grilling. A drizzle of balsamic glaze, a sprinkle of fresh herbs, or a dusting of exotic spices can transform grilled vegetables from simple to sublime. These finishing touches not only add flavor but also create visually stunning dishes that delight the senses.

Pairings and Presentations
Elevating vegetables on the grill isn't just about the cooking—it's also about how these dishes integrate into your overall meal. Consider the balance of flavors and textures, pairing smoky, charred vegetables with creamy sauces or fresh, zesty salads. Presentation matters; arrange your grilled vegetables with care and creativity, making every plate a testament to the beauty and bounty of the garden.

Conclusion
Grilling vegetables offers a world of culinary possibilities, inviting you to explore the vast spectrum of flavors, textures, and techniques available. This sub-chapter is not merely a guide but an inspiration, encouraging you to see vegetables in a new light and to elevate them from side dishes to centerpieces. With your Pit Boss Grill as your canvas and the garden's bounty as your palette, the art of grilling vegetables becomes a celebration of nature's richness, enhancing your culinary horizons and bringing joy and satisfaction to every meal.

MEAT: UNLOCKING SUCCULENCE AND AROMA

The allure of perfectly grilled meat, with its irresistible aroma and succulence, is the cornerstone of any pitmaster's repertoire. This sub-chapter, "Meat: Unlocking Succulence and Aroma," is devoted to the art and science behind mastering meat on your Pit Boss Wood Pellet Grill & Smoker. Here, we explore the techniques, tips, and insights necessary to transform good meat into an extraordinary culinary experience, celebrating the rich flavors and textures that only pellet grilling can achieve.

Choosing the Right Cut
Selecting the right cut of meat is the first step in the journey toward grilling excellence. Each cut possesses unique characteristics that influence its flavor, tenderness, and cooking requirements. From the robust, marbled texture of a ribeye steak to the lean, delicate nature of a pork tenderloin, understanding these nuances allows you to tailor your grilling technique to highlight the best attributes of each cut.

Marination and Seasoning

Marination and seasoning are not just about adding flavor; they're about enhancing the natural taste of the meat. Whether you prefer a simple salt and pepper rub or a complex marinade infused with herbs and spices, the key is balance. Allow the meat to marinate for several hours, or even overnight, to ensure that the flavors penetrate deeply, tenderizing the meat and setting the stage for a sensory explosion upon grilling.

Mastering Temperature Control

The essence of pellet grilling lies in its precise temperature control, offering the ability to cook meat to perfection. Understanding the ideal temperature for each type of meat—and how to maintain it on your Pit Boss—is crucial. Whether searing a steak over high heat to lock in juices or slowly smoking a brisket to achieve melt-in-your-mouth tenderness, temperature control is your greatest ally in achieving the desired doneness and texture.

The Magic of Smoke

Smoke is the soul of pellet grilling, imparting a depth of flavor that transcends ordinary cooking methods. Experiment with different wood pellets—each type offers a unique flavor profile, from the sweet notes of applewood to the bold intensity of hickory. The right choice of wood can complement the natural flavors of the meat, enhancing its aroma and taste without overwhelming it.

Resting: The Unsung Hero

Often overlooked, resting is a critical step in ensuring meat retains its succulence. After grilling, allow the meat to rest, covered loosely with foil, for several minutes. This pause lets the juices redistribute throughout the meat, ensuring that every bite is moist and flavorful. The patience required to rest meat properly is a testament to the art of grilling, where time itself becomes an ingredient.

The Finer Details: Slicing and Serving

The final steps of slicing and serving can significantly impact the eating experience. Slice meat against the grain to maximize tenderness, and consider the presentation on the plate. The visual appeal of grilled meat, highlighted with the perfect garnish or side, can elevate the dining experience, turning a meal into a memorable event.

Unlocking the succulence and aroma of meat on a Pit Boss Grill is a journey of discovery, experimentation, and passion. It's about more than just cooking; it's about creating moments that linger long after the last bite. As you explore the limitless possibilities that pellet grilling offers, remember that each choice—from the cut of meat to the type of wood pellets—plays a crucial role in crafting the ultimate grilling experience. Embrace the adventure, and let the rich flavors and aromas of perfectly grilled meat inspire your culinary journey to new horizons.

GRIDDLED GOODS: BEYOND BREAKFAST

The griddle, with its smooth, flat surface, is a versatile tool in the world of grilling, often relegated to breakfast duties of pancakes and bacon. Yet, this culinary canvas offers a vast expanse for creativity, inviting you to explore the delights of griddled goods beyond the morning fare. This sub-chapter, "Griddled Goods: Beyond Breakfast," ventures into the uncharted territories of lunch, dinner, and everything in between, showcasing the griddle's prowess in transforming simple ingredients into gourmet experiences.

The Art of the Griddle
The key to mastering griddled cooking lies in understanding its uniform heat distribution, a stark contrast to the direct flame of grilling. This consistent surface temperature is ideal for foods requiring a delicate touch or a crisp exterior without the threat of charring. Here, you'll learn to wield this tool with the precision of an artist, turning everyday meals into griddled masterpieces.

Lunchtime Reinvented
Imagine the humble grilled cheese elevated on the griddle, with golden, buttery bread encasing a molten core of artisanal cheeses, or quesadillas stuffed with gourmet fillings, their edges crisped to perfection. The griddle transforms lunch from a midday necessity into a culinary event, offering endless possibilities from flatbreads adorned with seasonal toppings to gourmet burgers with that perfect crust.

Dinner: A Griddled Affair
As the sun sets, the griddle becomes the stage for dinner's main act. Delicate fillets of fish, seasoned and cooked to tender perfection, or slices of eggplant and zucchini, marinated and griddled until they melt in your mouth, redefine what's possible in outdoor cooking. This section explores techniques for cooking meats to perfection, achieving that coveted Maillard reaction that elicits depth and complexity of flavor.

Vegetables and Sides
Vegetables find a new lease on life on the griddle. Asparagus spears, brussels sprouts halved and kissed by the heat, or sweet slices of bell pepper become vibrant, charred, and deliciously tender. Here, you'll uncover secrets to griddled sides that complement any dish, infusing your meals with the essence of flame and smoke, yet with the griddle's unique touch.

Sweet Endings
The journey doesn't end with the main course. The griddle's even heat is perfect for crafting desserts that surprise and delight. From griddled fruits, like peaches and pineapple caramelized with a touch of brown sugar, to sweet crepes filled with indulgent creams and fresh berries, these recipes will inspire you to look at the griddle in a whole new light.

Mastering Techniques
Beyond recipes, this sub-chapter delves into the techniques that elevate your griddled cooking—managing heat, mastering flip and timing, and the nuances of cooking with and without oil. These skills are your toolkit for innovation, allowing you to adapt, experiment, and create with the seasons and your inspirations.

"Griddled Goods: Beyond Breakfast" is an ode to the potential that lies in every square inch of your griddle. It's a call to explore, to experiment, and to elevate. As you turn each page, you'll discover not just recipes, but a new way of thinking about cooking—a celebration of the joy and artistry found in the simple act of preparing food. Let your griddle be a canvas for culinary exploration, and let the journey transform not just your meals, but your approach to grilling.

Chapter 6: Seasonings and Marinades Mastery

Venturing into the realm of seasonings and marinades is akin to embarking on a grand culinary expedition, where each spice, herb, and concoction unlocks new dimensions of flavor and aroma. Chapter 6, "Seasonings and Marinades Mastery," is your guide to the alchemy of flavors that will transform your grilling into a symphony of taste sensations. This chapter is not just about mixing herbs and spices; it's an exploration of how to layer flavors, creating dishes that resonate with depth, complexity, and harmony.

As you navigate through this chapter, you'll learn the art of balancing the bold with the subtle, the art of marrying spices with the inherent flavors of your ingredients. From the rustic charm of classic barbecue rubs to the exotic allure of international marinades, you'll discover how to elevate meats, vegetables, and even fruits from their humble origins to the stars of the dining table.

Moreover, "Seasonings and Marinades Mastery" delves into the science behind why certain combinations work, offering you the knowledge to experiment with confidence. You'll understand how acidity, sweetness, fat, and heat interact, transforming the texture and enhancing the flavors of your grilled masterpieces.

Prepare to journey through a world where every pinch of spice and every splash of marinade holds the potential to inspire, delight, and surprise. Welcome to the chapter that will change the way you grill, one seasoning and marinade at a time, turning each meal into an unforgettable culinary adventure.

Grilling Spices and Herb Guide

Embarking on the aromatic journey of grilling, spices and herbs are the compass and map that guide us through the vast landscape of flavor. This sub-chapter, "Grilling Spices and Herb Guide," is your toolkit for navigating this terrain, unlocking the secrets to infusing your grilled dishes with layers of complexity and character. Here, we delve into the heart of seasoning mastery, exploring how the right combination of spices and herbs can transform the simple act of grilling into an art form.

The Essentials of Spice

Understanding the essentials of spice begins with recognizing the role heat plays in releasing their full potential. Spices such as paprika, cumin, and coriander bring warmth and depth, acting as the foundation upon which flavors are built. These ground powders are best added before grilling, allowing the heat to unlock their aromatic oils and imbue the meat with rich undertones.

The Delicate Touch of Herbs

Herbs, with their delicate fragrances, offer a counterbalance to the robustness of spices. Fresh herbs like rosemary, thyme, and basil impart a brightness that elevates the natural flavors of the food. These green notes are especially complementary to lighter fare such as vegetables and fish, where they can shine without overpowering the dish's inherent qualities.

Creating Harmony

The art of seasoning is in creating harmony — a balance where no single note overwhelms the others. This section provides guidance on pairing spices and herbs with different types of meat and vegetables, crafting blends that enhance without dominating. From the peppery bite of black pepper paired with the sweetness of basil for chicken, to the earthy duo of cumin and cilantro for grilled vegetables, each pairing is a discovery in flavor synergy.

Marinades and Rubs: The Flavor Infusers

Marinades and rubs are the vehicles that carry spices and herbs deep into the heart of the food. This part of the sub-chapter explores how to craft these flavor infusers, using acid, oil, and seasoning to tenderize and enrich. You'll learn the ratios and techniques for creating marinades that moisten and tenderize, and rubs that form a flavorful crust, locking in juices and aroma.

Experimentation and Personalization

At its core, the mastery of spices and herbs is an invitation to experiment. Encouraging personalization, this section inspires you to create your own signature blends, adapting the guidelines to suit your palate and daring to combine unexpected flavors. Here, you'll find tips on starting with base blends and gradually incorporating more exotic spices, expanding your flavor repertoire and personalizing your grilling style.

Preservation and Storage

Maintaining the potency of your spices and herbs is critical to their effectiveness. Learn the best practices for storing both dried spices and fresh herbs, ensuring they retain their vibrancy and aroma for your next grilling session. From the cool, dark locations for spices to the refrigeration techniques for prolonging the life of fresh herbs, this guidance is key to preserving the essence of your seasonings.

"Grilling Spices and Herb Guide" is more than a directory of flavors; it's a journey into the heart of culinary creativity, where the grill serves as the canvas and spices and herbs the palette. Embrace the exploration, let your intuition guide you, and remember that the ultimate goal is not just to cook, but to create experiences that linger in the memory long after the meal has ended. Through the mastery of seasoning, you unlock not just the taste, but the soul of grilling, crafting dishes that speak to the senses and celebrate the joy of cooking with fire.

Crafting Your Marinades and Rubs

Crafting the perfect marinade or rub is akin to composing a melody, where each ingredient contributes a note to the harmonious blend of flavors that will dance upon the palate. This sub-chapter, "Crafting Your Marinades and Rubs," is a deep dive into the artistry behind these essential grilling companions, guiding you through the creation of concoctions that not only enhance flavor but also tenderize and transform the texture of your grilled dishes.

The Essence of Marinades

Marinades are magical mixtures that imbue meats and vegetables with moisture and flavor. At their core, they consist of three key components: acids, oils, and seasonings. The acid, whether it's lemon juice, vinegar, or yogurt, tenderizes the meat by breaking down tough proteins. Oils help dissolve fat-soluble flavor compounds in spices and herbs, ensuring they penetrate deeply. Seasonings, the soul of your marinade, impart unique flavors that can transport your taste buds across the globe.

Creating the Perfect Marinade

To craft your marinade, start by considering the flavor profile you wish to achieve. Are you seeking the zesty tang of citrus for a summer barbecue, or the deep, rich spices of a Moroccan feast? Once you've chosen your theme, balance your acids and oils in a 1:3 ratio, ensuring there's enough acidity to tenderize without overpowering the oil's ability to carry flavors. Add your spices and herbs, whisking vigorously to combine. Always taste your marinade before adding the meat or vegetables, adjusting seasonings as necessary.

The Rub: A Dry Alternative

Rubs, in contrast, are dry mixes of spices and herbs applied directly to the surface of the meat. They create a crust that seals in flavors and juices, adding texture and depth. Rubs are particularly suited for shorter cooking times, where their direct contact with heat intensifies the flavors, creating a caramelized, crispy exterior.

Crafting Your Rub

The creation of a rub begins with selecting your base spices. Salt and sugar are common starting points, drawing moisture to the surface to mingle with the spices for a more flavorful crust. From there, the world of spices is your oyster. Paprika for smokiness, black pepper for heat, garlic powder for savoriness—the combinations are endless. For a cohesive rub, grind your spices to a similar consistency, ensuring even application and flavor distribution.

Marinade and Rub Techniques

- **Marinating Time:** The duration should match the type and cut of meat. Delicate items like fish require shorter marinating times, typically 30 minutes to an hour, while tougher cuts of beef can benefit from several hours to overnight.
- **Applying Rubs:** Ensure the meat is dry before application. A light brush of oil can help the rub adhere better. Apply generously, massaging the mix into every crevice for maximum flavor impact.
- **Cooking Considerations:** When cooking with a rub, be mindful of ingredients like sugar that can burn at high temperatures. Adjust your grilling technique to prevent charring, moving the meat to cooler parts of the grill if necessary.

Innovation and Experimentation

The beauty of marinades and rubs lies in their infinite variability. Encouraging experimentation, this section explores how combining different cultures' flavors can result in innovative and surprising taste experiences. It also touches on the importance of documenting your creations, noting what works and what can be improved for future grilling sessions.

Preservation Tips

For those who find their signature blend, making larger batches for future use can save time. Learn how to properly store your rubs and marinades, ensuring they retain their potency and are ready at a moment's notice. From airtight containers for rubs to freezing options for marinades, these tips are crucial for any grill master.

"Crafting Your Marinades and Rubs" is not just a guide; it's an invitation to explore the alchemy of flavors that elevate grilling from cooking to an expression of creativity. As you blend, taste, and adjust, remember that each marinade and rub is a reflection of personal taste and the joy of discovery. Whether you're a seasoned pitmaster or a curious novice, the journey of crafting these concoctions is one of the most rewarding aspects of grilling, offering endless opportunities to infuse love and flavor into every dish you create.

DIVERSE FLAVORS FOR GLOBAL DISHES

Embarking on a journey through the world of grilling, the pursuit of flavor knows no boundaries. The sub-chapter "Diverse Flavors for Global Dishes" is a celebration of the rich tapestry of global cuisine, inviting you to explore the depths of flavor that can be achieved on your Pit Boss Wood Pellet Grill & Smoker. Here, we traverse continents and cultures, uncovering the secrets to infusing your grilled dishes with the authentic essence of international culinary traditions.

The Spice Routes: A Global Expedition

The journey begins on the ancient spice routes, where the exchange of spices and herbs between civilizations laid the foundation for some of the world's most beloved cuisines. From the smoky paprika of Spain to the vibrant turmeric of India, each spice carries with it a story of trade, discovery, and culinary innovation. This section guides you through selecting and combining these spices to create marinades and rubs that are true to the flavors of their origin.

Mediterranean Marvels

The sun-drenched shores of the Mediterranean offer a palette of flavors characterized by the freshness of herbs, the richness of olive oil, and the tang of citrus. Learn to craft marinades that embody the simplicity and elegance of Mediterranean cooking, perfect for enhancing the natural flavors of fish, poultry, and vegetables.

The Heat of Latin America

Latin American cuisine is a vibrant fusion of indigenous, European, and African influences, renowned for its bold use of chilies, lime, and cilantro. This section delves into the art of creating rubs and marinades that capture the fiery spirit of Latin America, bringing the zest and zing of its markets and kitchens to your grill.

Asian Aromatics

From the soy-sauce-infused marinades of Japan to the complex spice blends of Southeast Asia, this part of the chapter explores the delicate balance of flavors that defines Asian cuisine. Discover the techniques for marrying umami with sweetness, heat with acidity, crafting marinades, and rubs that elevate grilled dishes with the nuanced flavors of Asia.

Middle Eastern Mystique

Middle Eastern cuisine, with its aromatic spices and emphasis on grilling, offers a wealth of inspiration for the pitmaster. This section introduces you to the spices and herbs that are staples of the region, such as sumac, za'atar, and saffron. Learn how to blend these into marinades and rubs that impart a deep, complex flavor profile reminiscent of Middle Eastern feasts.

African Adventures

Africa's diverse cuisines provide a rich source of culinary exploration, with flavors ranging from the earthy richness of berbere in Ethiopia to the fragrant spices of Ras ell hanout in Morocco. Here, you'll find guidance on creating rubs and marinades that pay homage to Africa's wide-ranging palette of flavors, perfect for transforming simple grilled meats and vegetables into exotic dishes.

Balancing Act: The Art of Seasoning

Mastering global flavors requires an understanding of the delicate balance between the four basic taste elements: sweet, salty, sour, and bitter. This section offers tips on achieving this balance within your marinades and rubs, ensuring that every bite is a harmonious reflection of its cultural origins.

Experimentation and Fusion

The final part of this sub-chapter encourages bold experimentation and the fusion of flavors from different cultures. It's a reminder that while traditions provide the foundation, great culinary innovation often occurs at the crossroads of cultures. Here, you'll learn to trust your palate and creativity, blending global flavors in ways that are uniquely your own.

"Diverse Flavors for Global Dishes" is not just a guide to seasoning and marinating; it's an invitation to embark on a global grilling adventure. It's about bringing the world to your backyard, one dish at a time, using your Pit Boss Grill as the vehicle for culinary exploration. As you delve into the flavors of different cultures, remember that each dish you create is a bridge between worlds, a celebration of the universal language of food.

Chapter 7: Smoke Crafting Techniques

In the realm of grilling, smoke is the alchemist's fire, transforming the simple act of cooking into a craft capable of eliciting depth, complexity, and nuance from the humblest ingredients. Chapter 7, "Smoke Crafting Techniques," is dedicated to this sublime culinary element, guiding you through the mastery of smoke to elevate your Pit Boss grilling to artistry. This chapter is not merely about smoking meat; it's an exploration into the very essence of flavor, where the choice of wood, the control of temperature, and the patience of the pitmaster converge to create dishes that resonate with the soul of the fire.

Within these pages, you'll discover the science behind smoke and how its compounds weave their magic into your meals. From the delicate wisps that kiss seafood to the robust plumes that envelop briskets, learning to control smoke is to command one of the most potent forces in cooking. You'll navigate through the selection of woods, each with its unique flavor profile, and learn techniques for managing smoke density, timing, and temperature to achieve the perfect balance of flavor.

Whether you're a novice seeking to understand the basics or an experienced pitmaster ready to refine your smoke crafting skills, this chapter promises to deepen your appreciation for the transformative power of smoke. Welcome to a journey into the heart of grilling, where the mastery of smoke crafting techniques opens new horizons for culinary creativity.

Fundamentals of Smoke Flavoring

Delving into the world of smoke flavoring is akin to exploring the essence of fire itself—a primal element that, when harnessed correctly, transforms the act of grilling into an art form. The subchapter "Fundamentals of Smoke Flavoring" is your gateway to understanding how smoke, meticulously controlled and applied, becomes the invisible ingredient that imparts depth, character, and soul to your dishes.

The Nature of Smoke

At the heart of smoke flavoring lies the combustion of wood. This process releases a complex bouquet of volatile compounds, each contributing to the distinctive aroma and taste smoke imparts to food. Understanding the types of wood and their corresponding flavors is crucial; from the sweet, mild notes of applewood to the strong, earthy essence of mesquite, each type of wood brings a unique profile to the table.

Selecting Your Wood

The choice of wood is your first, most critical decision in smoke flavoring. Hardwoods, dense and slow-burning, are preferred for their clean smoke and rich flavors. Fruitwoods like cherry and peach offer subtle sweetness, ideal for poultry and pork, while hickory and oak provide a robust backdrop perfect for beef and game. The selection of wood should complement the natural flavors of your food, enhancing rather than overpowering.

The Technique of Smoking

Smoke flavoring is as much about technique as it is about ingredient choice. The introduction to smoking techniques covers:
- **Direct vs. Indirect Smoking:** Positioning food directly over the smoke source for intense flavor or off to the side for a gentler infusion.

- **Managing Smoke Flow:** Ensuring adequate ventilation to prevent the smoke from becoming stale and bitter.
- **Temperature Control:** Maintaining a consistent temperature to ensure smoke is produced steadily, allowing for a controlled flavoring process.

Smoke Layering

Layering smoke involves applying smoke at different stages of cooking, building complexity in flavor. Begin with a stronger wood for the initial smoke, then transition to milder woods. This technique creates a nuanced flavor profile, where the initial robustness is softened by subtle, sweet notes, offering a sophisticated, layered tasting experience.

Moisture and Smoke

Moisture plays a pivotal role in smoke adherence. A dry surface can repel smoke, while a moist one welcomes it, allowing the compounds to cling and penetrate the food. Discussing methods to maintain moisture—through basting, marinating, or even placing a water pan beneath the food—this section underscores the importance of moisture in achieving a rich, smoky flavor.

Timing and Patience

The application of smoke is not a race but a marathon. The length of smoking time impacts the depth of flavor; too short, and the smoke barely whispers its presence; too long, and it overwhelms. This section guides you through timing your smoking process, teaching patience and attention as you wait for the smoke to weave its magic.

Personalization and Experimentation

Encouraging personalization, this part invites you to experiment with different woods, techniques, and timings to discover your signature smoke flavor. It's a process of trial and error, learning from each grilling session to refine your approach and develop a style that is uniquely yours.

The fundamentals of smoke flavoring provide the foundation upon which your grilling artistry is built. As you explore the nuances of smoking, remember that each choice—from the type of wood to the timing of its application—is a brushstroke in the larger picture of your culinary creation. Smoke, in its ethereal beauty, is more than just a technique; it's a journey into the heart of grilling, promising dishes imbued with the primal essence of fire and flavor.

ADVANCED SMOKING STRATEGIES

Embarking beyond the basics into the realm of advanced smoking strategies requires not just skill and knowledge but an intuitive understanding of fire, smoke, and flavor. This sub-chapter, "Advanced Smoking Strategies," is designed for those ready to deepen their mastery over smoke, exploring techniques that challenge and elevate the traditional smoking process. Here, you will learn to manipulate smoke in ways that transform good dishes into unforgettable culinary masterpieces.

The Art of Cold Smoking

Cold smoking separates the process of flavoring from cooking, imbuing foods with the delicate essence of smoke without applying heat. This technique is perfect for cheeses, nuts, and certain types of fish, such as salmon. Cold smoking requires precise temperature control, typically below 90°F, ensuring that the food remains uncooked while taking on a smoky aroma and flavor. This section delves into the setup for cold smoking, including the use of a smoke generator and the importance of ventilation.

Layering Flavors with Multiple Woods
Just as a chef layers flavors in a dish, a pitmaster can layer smoke from different woods to create complex flavor profiles. Starting with a base of mild wood and gradually introducing stronger, more aromatic woods can add depth and intrigue to your smoked dishes. This strategy involves not just the selection of woods but also timing their introduction to balance and complement the food's natural flavors.

The Smoke-then-Sear Technique
Traditionally, meats are seared before being transferred to a smoker. The smoke-then-sear technique reverses this process, smoking the meat at a low temperature to infuse it with flavor, then finishing it with a high-heat sear. This method locks in the smoky taste while ensuring a crispy, caramelized exterior. Tips on managing this transition, including resting the meat between smoking and searing, are explored to achieve perfect results.

Utilizing Smoke in Sous Vide Cooking
Combining smoking with sous vide cooking offers the best of both worlds: the deep, penetrating flavors of smoke and the precise, even cooking of sous vide. This section guides you through the process of smoking food lightly before sealing and cooking it sous vide, resulting in dishes that are moist, tender, and richly flavored. The technique is particularly effective for meats and fish, where the gentle cooking method preserves texture and moisture.

Refining Smoke Intensity
Controlling smoke intensity is crucial for dishes that benefit from a hint of smoke without overwhelming the palate. Techniques such as using smoking pellets in moderation, adjusting the airflow to manage smoke density, and selecting the right moment to introduce and remove food from the smoker are discussed. This nuanced approach allows for a subtler incorporation of smoke, enhancing rather than dominating the dish.

Creating Smoked Ingredients
Advanced smoking strategies extend beyond direct application to foods, venturing into the creation of smoked ingredients that can be used in a variety of dishes. From smoked salts and sugars to oils and butters, these ingredients introduce smoky notes to dishes without the need for a smoker. The process for smoking these pantry staples is outlined, along with ideas for their use in enhancing everyday cooking.

Innovation and Experimentation
At its heart, the mastery of advanced smoking techniques is an invitation to innovate and experiment. This final section encourages you to push the boundaries of traditional smoking, combining techniques and flavors in new and exciting ways. Whether it's incorporating smoked ingredients into desserts for an unexpected twist or exploring cold smoking for vegetarian dishes, the possibilities are as limitless as your creativity.

"Advanced Smoking Strategies" is more than a guide; it's a journey into the heart of what makes smoking such a revered and transformative cooking method. By embracing these advanced techniques, you open a new chapter in your culinary adventures, one where smoke becomes not just a flavor but a medium for expression. As you explore, remember that each technique refined and each flavor unlocked brings you closer to the essence of pitmaster artistry, where fire and smoke dance in the service of flavor.

PAIRING WOODS WITH FOODS

In the nuanced world of smoke crafting, the marriage between wood and food is one of the most critical elements, shaping the soul of the dish. "Pairing Woods with Foods" is a deep dive into this delicate balance, offering insights into how different woods can complement, enhance, or transform a variety of ingredients. Here, we explore the art of selecting the perfect wood to pair with your culinary creations, ensuring that each dish is a masterpiece of flavor.

The Symphony of Smoke

Smoke, the ethereal ingredient, carries with it the essence of the wood it originates from. This essence, when paired correctly, can accentuate the natural flavors of food, adding layers of depth that elevate the dish. Understanding the characteristics of different woods and how they harmonize with various foods is akin to conducting a symphony, where each note contributes to a greater culinary harmony.

Hardwoods: The Foundation of Flavor

Hardwoods, with their dense structure, are the cornerstone of smoking. Each type offers a unique flavor profile:

- **Hickory:** Robust and hearty, hickory imparts a strong, bacon-like flavor. Ideal for pork and beef, it's a classic choice that stands up to rich, fatty meats.
- **Oak:** Versatile and mild, oak provides a subtle smokiness that enhances without overpowering, making it suitable for a wide range of dishes, from beef to seafood.
- **Mesquite:** Intense and earthy, mesquite's bold smoke is best used sparingly. It's perfect for short cooks, lending its signature punch to red meats and poultry.

Fruitwoods: A Lighter Touch

Fruitwoods, with their sweeter, milder smoke, offer a gentle way to introduce smoky flavors:

- **Apple:** Delicate and slightly sweet, apple wood pairs beautifully with poultry, pork, and even fish, adding a light, fruity smoke that complements rather than dominates.
- **Cherry:** Offering a hint of sweetness with a deeper color, cherry wood is versatile, enhancing everything from chicken to vegetables with its pleasant aroma.
- **Peach:** Similar to apple but with a softer sweetness, peach wood is excellent for delicate meats, including poultry and seafood, infusing them with a subtle, fruity smoke.

Exotic Woods: Unique Flavor Profiles

Exploring exotic woods can uncover unique flavors:

- **Alder:** Traditionally used for smoking salmon, alder imparts a clean, mild flavor that's also excellent with other seafood and poultry.
- **Pecan:** Rich and buttery, pecan wood offers a sweetness that's akin to hickory but milder, perfect for poultry and pork.

Matching Woods to Foods

The key to successful wood-food pairings lies in balance:

- **For Robust Meats (Beef, Lamb):** Choose woods with stronger flavors, such as hickory or mesquite, that can stand up to the meat's richness.
- **For Delicate Dishes (Poultry, Seafood):** opt for lighter woods like apple or cherry, which lend a subtle smokiness without overwhelming the dish.
- **For Vegetables and Cheeses:** Experiment with a variety of woods, leaning towards milder options like alder or fruitwoods to enhance their natural flavors.

The Role of Blending Woods

For those seeking to craft a signature smoke flavor, blending woods offers endless possibilities. Combining the robustness of hickory with the sweetness of cherry, for instance, can create a balanced, complex smoke ideal for versatile applications. This section provides guidelines for starting your journey into wood blending, including tips on ratios and pairing principles.

"Pairing Woods with Foods" is more than just a guide; it's an invitation to explore the rich, aromatic world of smoke crafting. With each pairing, you're not just cooking; you're weaving flavor, tradition, and innovation into every bite. As you experiment with different woods and their affinities for various foods, remember that each choice is a step toward defining your unique voice in the vast chorus of grilling. Embrace the journey, let intuition be your guide, and discover the transformative power of smoke in elevating the ordinary to the extraordinary.

Chapter 8: Breakfast Delicacies

In the symphony of flavors that is the culinary world, breakfast holds a special place—a morning ritual that awakens the senses and sets the tone for the day ahead. Chapter 8, "Breakfast Delicacies," turns the spotlight onto the first meal of the day, transforming it with the magic of the grill. This chapter is a celebration of morning meals, an invitation to explore the richness of breakfast cuisine through the lens of smoke and fire.

Here, you'll discover how the Pit Boss Wood Pellet Grill & Smoker brings a new dimension to breakfast classics. From smoky bacon and eggs to grilled French toast, each recipe is reimagined with the unique flavors that only a grill can impart. But we don't stop at the traditional; this chapter ventures into the realm of the extraordinary, introducing dishes that challenge the conventions of breakfast.

Prepare to be inspired by recipes that blend the savory with the sweet, the hearty with the delicate. Learn techniques for infusing classic breakfast ingredients with the nuanced flavors of wood smoke, transforming simple dishes into gourmet experiences. Whether it's a leisurely weekend brunch or a quick weekday bite, "Breakfast Delicacies" is your guide to elevating the first meal of the day from ordinary to exceptional.

Welcome to a chapter where breakfast becomes not just a meal, but a culinary adventure, inviting you to start your day with creativity, flavor, and the warmth of the grill.

Griddle Breakfast Classics

Recipe 1. Sunrise Smashed Avocado Toast

PREPARATION TIME: 10 min - **COOKING TIME:** 5 min **MODE OF COOKING:** Griddling - **SERVINGS:** 2
INGREDIENTS: 4 slices of whole grain bread; 2 ripe avocados; 1 Tbsp. lemon juice; 1/4 tsp salt; 1/4 tsp black pepper; 1/2 cup cherry tomatoes, halved; 2 Tbsp. feta cheese, crumbled; 2 tsp pumpkin seeds; 1 Tbsp. olive oil
DIRECTIONS: Halve avocados and remove pits. Scoop flesh into a bowl, adding lemon juice, salt, and pepper, then mash roughly. Heat griddle over medium heat and brush with olive oil. Grill bread until golden. Spread mashed avocado on toasted bread, top with cherry tomatoes, feta, and pumpkin seeds.
N.V.: Calories: 370, Fat: 20g, Carbs: 42g, Protein: 9g, Sugar: 6g

Recipe 2. Pit Boss Pancakes

PREPARATION TIME: 10 min - **COOKING TIME:** 15 min **MODE OF COOKING:** Griddling - **SERVINGS:** 4
INGREDIENTS: 1 1/2 cups all-purpose flour; 2 Tbsp. sugar; 1/2 tsp salt; 2 tsp baking powder; 1 egg, beaten; 1 1/4 cups milk; 3 Tbsp. unsalted butter, melted; 1 tsp vanilla extract
DIRECTIONS: In a large bowl, whisk together flour, sugar, salt, and baking powder. In another bowl, mix egg, milk, melted butter, and vanilla extract. Combine wet and dry ingredients until

smooth. Preheat griddle to medium-high (375°F/190°C). Pour 1/4 cup batter for each pancake. Cook until bubbles form, then flip. Serve hot.
N.V.: Calories: 250, Fat: 8g, Carbs: 38g, Protein: 7g, Sugar: 9g

RECIPE 3. COUNTRY STYLE HASH BROWNS

PREPARATION TIME: 15 min - **COOKING TIME:** 20 min **MODE OF COOKING:** Griddling - **SERVINGS:** 4
INGREDIENTS: 3 large potatoes, peeled and shredded; 1/4 cup onion, finely chopped; 1/4 tsp salt; 1/4 tsp black pepper; 4 Tbsp. unsalted butter
DIRECTIONS: Rinse shredded potatoes in cold water, squeeze dry. Mix potatoes with onion, salt, and pepper. Melt butter on griddle over medium heat. Spread potato mixture, press down lightly. Cook until golden brown, about 10 min each side. Serve immediately.
N.V.: Calories: 210, Fat: 12g, Carbs: 24g, Protein: 3g, Sugar: 2g

RECIPE 4. GRIDDLE GRILLED CHEESE & TOMATO SOUP

PREPARATION TIME: 5 min - **COOKING TIME:** 10 min **MODE OF COOKING:** Griddling - **SERVINGS:** 2
INGREDIENTS: 4 slices sourdough bread; 4 slices cheddar cheese; 2 Tbsp. butter, softened; 2 cups tomato soup, prepared
DIRECTIONS: Spread butter on one side of each bread slice. Place two slices, butter-side down, on a preheated griddle over medium heat. Top each with two cheese slices and remaining bread, butter-side up. Cook until golden brown, flipping once. Heat soup and serve alongside sandwiches.
N.V.: Calories: 550, Fat: 32g, Carbs: 46g, Protein: 22g, Sugar: 12g

RECIPE 5. SAVORY MUSHROOM & HERB OMELETTE

PREPARATION TIME: 10 min - **COOKING TIME:** 8 min **MODE OF COOKING:** Griddling - **SERVINGS:** 2
INGREDIENTS: 4 eggs; 1/4 cup milk; 1/2 cup mushrooms, sliced; 2 Tbsp. chives, chopped; 2 Tbsp. parsley, chopped; Salt and pepper to taste; 1 Tbsp. olive oil; 1/4 cup grated cheese
DIRECTIONS: Whisk eggs, milk, salt, and pepper. Heat oil on griddle over medium heat. Cook mushrooms until soft. Pour in egg mixture, sprinkle with herbs. As eggs set, lift edges, letting uncooked eggs flow underneath. Sprinkle cheese on one half, fold over. Serve when cheese melts.
N.V.: Calories: 300, Fat: 22g, Carbs: 4g, Protein: 20g, Sugar: 3g

RECIPE 6. BLUEBERRY BANANA GRIDDLE CAKES

PREPARATION TIME: 15 min - **COOKING TIME:** 15 min **MODE OF COOKING:** Griddling - **SERVINGS:** 4
INGREDIENTS: 1 1/2 cups whole wheat flour; 2 tsp baking powder; 1/2 tsp salt; 1 Tbsp. honey; 1 egg; 1 cup milk; 1 banana, mashed; 1/2 cup blueberries; 2 Tbsp. unsalted butter, for griddling
DIRECTIONS: Mix flour, baking powder, and salt. In another bowl, blend honey, egg, and milk, then add to dry ingredients. Stir in mashed banana and blueberries. Preheat griddle to medium (375°F/190°C), melt butter. Pour batter, cook until bubbles form, then flip. Serve warm.
N.V.: Calories: 280, Fat: 8g, Carbs: 46g, Protein: 8g, Sugar: 14g

RECIPE 7. SPICY CHORIZO BREAKFAST BURRITOS

PREPARATION TIME: 20 min - **COOKING TIME:** 10 min **MODE OF COOKING:** Griddling - **SERVINGS:** 4

INGREDIENTS: 8 oz. chorizo sausage, crumbled; 4 large eggs, beaten; 1/4 cup onion, diced; 1/4 cup bell pepper, diced; 4 flour tortillas; 1/2 cup cheddar cheese, shredded; 1 avocado, sliced; 1/4 cup salsa; Salt and pepper to taste
DIRECTIONS: Cook chorizo, onion, and bell pepper on a griddle over medium heat until chorizo is fully cooked. Add eggs, scramble until set. Warm tortillas on griddle. Divide egg mixture among tortillas, top with cheese, avocado, and salsa. Roll up burritos. Serve immediately.
N.V.: Calories: 450, Fat: 26g, Carbs: 35g, Protein: 22g, Sugar: 4g

RECIPE 8. SMOKY MOUNTAIN HASH BROWNS

PREPARATION TIME: 10 min - **COOKING TIME:** 15 min
MODE OF COOKING: Griddle - **SERVINGS:** 4
INGREDIENTS: 3 large russet potatoes, grated; 1/4 cup onion, finely chopped; 1/4 cup bell pepper, diced; 1/4 cup sharp cheddar, shredded; 1 tsp smoked paprika; Salt and pepper to taste; 2 Tbsp. olive oil
DIRECTIONS: Combine grated potatoes, onion, bell pepper, cheddar, smoked paprika, salt, and pepper in a bowl; Heat olive oil on a griddle over medium heat; Spread potato mixture evenly, cooking until golden brown on each side, about 7-8 min per side; Serve hot.
N.V.: Calories: 220, Fat: 7g, Carbs: 35g, Protein: 5g, Sugar: 2g

RECIPE 9. GRIDDLE FRENCH TOAST

PREPARATION TIME: 10 min - **COOKING TIME:** 10 min
MODE OF COOKING: Griddle - **SERVINGS:** 4
INGREDIENTS: 8 slices thick-cut bread; 4 eggs; 1 cup milk; 2 tsp cinnamon; 1 tsp vanilla extract; Butter for griddle; Maple syrup for serving
DIRECTIONS: Whisk together eggs, milk, cinnamon, and vanilla; Soak bread slices in mixture for 30 seconds on each side; Heat butter on a griddle over medium heat; Cook bread until golden brown, about 2-3 min per side; Serve with maple syrup.
N.V.: Calories: 310, Fat: 9g, Carbs: 45g, Protein: 12g, Sugar: 8g

RECIPE 10. SOUTHWESTERN OMELETTE

PREPARATION TIME: 5 min - **COOKING TIME:** 8 min
MODE OF COOKING: Griddle - **SERVINGS:** 2
INGREDIENTS: 4 eggs; 1/4 cup milk; 1/2 cup cheddar cheese, shredded; 1/4 cup black beans, drained; 1/4 cup corn; 1/4 cup diced tomatoes; 1/4 cup green onions, chopped; Salt and pepper to taste; 1 Tbsp. olive oil
DIRECTIONS: Beat eggs and milk; Stir in cheese, beans, corn, tomatoes, and green onions; Season with salt and pepper; Heat oil on a griddle over medium heat; Pour in egg mixture, cooking until edges start to set, about 4 min; Fold omelette in half, cook until set.
N.V.: Calories: 350, Fat: 22g, Carbs: 12g, Protein: 24g, Sugar: 4g

RECIPE 11. BANANA PECAN PANCAKES

PREPARATION TIME: 10 min - **COOKING TIME:** 15 min
MODE OF COOKING: Griddle - **SERVINGS:** 4
INGREDIENTS: 2 cups all-purpose flour; 2 Tbsp. sugar; 2 tsp baking powder; 1 tsp baking soda; 1/2 tsp salt; 2 cups buttermilk; 2 eggs; 4 Tbsp. melted butter; 1 ripe banana, mashed; 1/2 cup pecans, chopped; Butter for griddle; Maple syrup for serving

DIRECTIONS: Mix flour, sugar, baking powder, baking soda, and salt; In another bowl, whisk buttermilk, eggs, and melted butter; Combine wet and dry ingredients; Fold in banana and pecans; Cook batter on a buttered griddle over medium heat until bubbles form and edges are dry.
N.V.: Calories: 520, Fat: 26g, Carbs: 62g, Protein: 13g, Sugar: 15g

INNOVATIVE MORNING MEALS

RECIPE 1. QUINOA POWER BOWLS

PREPARATION TIME: 15 min - **COOKING TIME:** 20 min **MODE OF COOKING:** Boiling & Sautéing - **SERVINGS:** 4
INGREDIENTS: 1 cup quinoa; 2 cups water; 1/2 tsp salt; 1 Tbsp. olive oil; 1 cup kale, chopped; 1/2 cup cherry tomatoes, halved; 4 eggs; 1 avocado, sliced; 2 tsp chia seeds; Salt and pepper to taste
DIRECTIONS: Rinse quinoa under cold water. In a saucepan, bring water and quinoa to a boil, reduce heat, cover, and simmer for 15 min until water is absorbed. In a skillet, heat olive oil over medium heat, sauté kale until wilted. Poach eggs in simmering water for 4 min. Assemble bowls with quinoa, kale, tomatoes, a poached egg, avocado slices, and sprinkle with chia seeds. Season with salt and pepper.
N.V.: Calories: 320, Fat: 15g, Carbs: 36g, Protein: 12g, Sugar: 3g

RECIPE 2. SWEET POTATO AND BLACK BEAN BREAKFAST BURRITOS

PREPARATION TIME: 20 min - **COOKING TIME:** 15 min **MODE OF COOKING:** Sautéing & Wrapping - **SERVINGS:** 4
INGREDIENTS: 2 medium sweet potatoes, cubed; 1 Tbsp. olive oil; 1/2 tsp cumin; 1 cup black beans, drained; 4 whole wheat tortillas; 1/2 cup cheddar cheese, shredded; 1 avocado, sliced; 1/4 cup salsa; Salt and pepper to taste
DIRECTIONS: Heat olive oil in a skillet over medium heat. Add sweet potatoes, season with cumin, salt, and pepper. Cook until tender. Stir in black beans and heat through. Divide mixture among tortillas, top with cheese, avocado, and salsa. Roll up tightly.
N.V.: Calories: 450, Fat: 20g, Carbs: 58g, Protein: 14g, Sugar: 8g

RECIPE 3. GREEN GODDESS SMOOTHIE BOWL

PREPARATION TIME: 10 min - **COOKING TIME:** 0 min **MODE OF COOKING:** Blending - **SERVINGS:** 2
INGREDIENTS: 1 avocado; 1 banana; 1/2 cup spinach; 1/2 cup kale; 1 cup almond milk; 2 Tbsp. honey; 1/4 cup granola; 1 Tbsp. chia seeds; 1/4 cup mixed berries
DIRECTIONS: In a blender, combine avocado, banana, spinach, kale, almond milk, and honey. Blend until smooth. Pour into bowls and top with granola, chia seeds, and mixed berries.
N.V.: Calories: 310, Fat: 14g, Carbs: 44g, Protein: 6g, Sugar: 22g

RECIPE 4. AVOCADO EGG BOATS

PREPARATION TIME: 5 min - **COOKING TIME:** 15 min **MODE OF COOKING:** Baking - **SERVINGS:** 4
INGREDIENTS: 2 avocados, halved and pitted; 4 eggs; Salt and pepper to taste; 2 Tbsp. chives, chopped; 1/4 cup shredded cheese

DIRECTIONS: Preheat oven to 425°F (220°C). Scoop out a bit of avocado flesh to enlarge the pit hole. Crack an egg into each avocado half. Season with salt and pepper. Sprinkle with chives and cheese. Bake for 15 min until egg whites are set.
N.V.: Calories: 220, Fat: 18g, Carbs: 9g, Protein: 8g, Sugar: 1g

RECIPE 5. TURMERIC GINGER OATMEAL

PREPARATION TIME: 5 min - **COOKING TIME:** 10 min **MODE OF COOKING:** Boiling - **SERVINGS:** 2
INGREDIENTS: 1 cup rolled oats; 2 cups almond milk; 1/2 tsp turmeric; 1/4 tsp ground ginger; 1 Tbsp. honey; 1 apple, diced; 1/4 cup walnuts, chopped
DIRECTIONS: In a saucepan, bring almond milk to a boil. Add oats, turmeric, and ginger. Reduce heat and simmer for 5 min, stirring occasionally. Stir in honey. Serve topped with diced apple and walnuts.
N.V.: Calories: 310, Fat: 12g, Carbs: 44g, Protein: 8g, Sugar: 16g

RECIPE 6. MUSHROOM SPINACH FRITTATA

PREPARATION TIME: 10 min - **COOKING TIME:** 20 min **MODE OF COOKING:** Baking - **SERVINGS:** 4
INGREDIENTS: 8 eggs; 1/2 cup milk; 1 cup mushrooms, sliced; 1 cup spinach, chopped; 1/2 cup feta cheese, crumbled; Salt and pepper to taste; 1 Tbsp. olive oil
DIRECTIONS: Preheat oven to 375°F (190°C). In a bowl, whisk eggs and milk. Season with salt and pepper. In an ovenproof skillet, heat olive oil over medium heat. Sauté mushrooms and spinach until softened. Pour egg mixture over vegetables. Sprinkle with feta. Bake for 20 min until set.
N.V.: Calories: 250, Fat: 18g, Carbs: 6g, Protein: 18g, Sugar: 3g

RECIPE 7. PEAR AND GORGONZOLA TOAST WITH HONEY DRIZZLE

PREPARATION TIME: 5 min - **COOKING TIME:** 10 min **MODE OF COOKING:** Griddling - **SERVINGS:** 4
INGREDIENTS: 4 slices of whole grain bread; 1 pear, thinly sliced; 4 oz Gorgonzola cheese, crumbled; 2 Tbsp. honey; 1/4 cup walnuts, chopped
DIRECTIONS: Preheat griddle to medium heat. Toast bread slices until golden brown. Top each slice with pear slices and Gorgonzola. Drizzle with honey and sprinkle with walnuts. Serve immediately.
N.V.: Calories: 320, Fat: 14g, Carbs: 42g, Protein: 9g, Sugar: 20g

RECIPE 8. AVOCADO QUINOA BREAKFAST BOWL

PREPARATION TIME: 15 min - **COOKING TIME:** 20 min
MODE OF COOKING: Boiling - **SERVINGS:** 4
INGREDIENTS: 1 cup quinoa, rinsed; 2 cups water; 2 ripe avocados, halved and sliced; 4 eggs; 1 cup cherry tomatoes, halved; 1/4 cup red onion, finely chopped; 2 Tbsp. cilantro, chopped; Juice of 1 lime; Salt and pepper to taste; 1 Tbsp. olive oil
DIRECTIONS: Cook quinoa in boiling water until fluffy, about 15 min; Drain and let cool. In a skillet, heat olive oil over medium heat, fry eggs to desired doneness. Assemble bowls with quinoa, top with avocado slices, fried eggs, cherry tomatoes, red onion, and cilantro. Drizzle with lime juice, season with salt and pepper.
N.V.: Calories: 350, Fat: 18g, Carbs: 38g, Protein: 12g, Sugar: 2g

RECIPE 9. SWEET POTATO AND KALE HASH

PREPARATION TIME: 10 min - **COOKING TIME:** 20 min
MODE OF COOKING: Sautéing - **SERVINGS:** 4
INGREDIENTS: 2 medium sweet potatoes, cubed; 1 Tbsp. olive oil; 1/2 red onion, diced; 2 cups kale, chopped; 4 cloves garlic, minced; 1 tsp smoked paprika; Salt and pepper to taste; 4 eggs; 1/4 cup feta cheese, crumbled
DIRECTIONS: Heat olive oil in a large skillet over medium heat. Add sweet potatoes, cook until tender, about 10 min. Add onion, garlic, cook until softened. Stir in kale, smoked paprika, salt, and pepper, cook until kale is wilted. Create four wells, crack an egg into each, cover, cook until eggs are set. Sprinkle with feta cheese before serving.
N.V.: Calories: 280, Fat: 12g, Carbs: 34g, Protein: 12g, Sugar: 6g

RECIPE 10. CHIA AND COCONUT MILK PORRIDGE

PREPARATION TIME: 5 min - **COOKING TIME:** 0 min (Refrigerate overnight)
MODE OF COOKING: Refrigeration - **SERVINGS:** 4
INGREDIENTS: 1 cup chia seeds; 4 cups coconut milk; 2 Tbsp. maple syrup; 1 tsp vanilla extract; 1/2 tsp cinnamon; Pinch of salt; Fresh berries and sliced almonds for topping
DIRECTIONS: In a bowl, mix chia seeds, coconut milk, maple syrup, vanilla extract, cinnamon, and salt until well combined. Cover and refrigerate overnight. Before serving, stir well, add more coconut milk if too thick. Top with fresh berries and sliced almonds.
N.V.: Calories: 350, Fat: 25g, Carbs: 25g, Protein: 8g, Sugar: 10g

RECIPE 11. TURMERIC GINGER TOFU SCRAMBLE

PREPARATION TIME: 10 min - **COOKING TIME:** 15 min
MODE OF COOKING: Sautéing - **SERVINGS:** 4
INGREDIENTS: 14 oz firm tofu, drained and crumbled; 1 Tbsp. olive oil; 1/2 tsp turmeric; 1/4 tsp ginger, grated; 1 bell pepper, diced; 1/2 cup spinach, chopped; 1/4 cup green onions, chopped; Salt and pepper to taste; 1 avocado, sliced; Hot sauce, optional
DIRECTIONS: Heat olive oil in a skillet over medium heat. Add turmeric and ginger, cook for 1 min. Add crumbled tofu, bell pepper, cook for 5 min. Stir in spinach and green onions, cook until wilted. Season with salt and pepper. Serve with avocado slices and hot sauce if desired.
N.V.: Calories: 220, Fat: 14g, Carbs: 12g, Protein: 15g, Sugar: 2g

LIGHT AND HEALTHY STARTS

RECIPE 1. KALE AND BERRY SMOOTHIE

PREPARATION TIME: 5 min - **COOKING TIME:** 0 min **MODE OF COOKING:** Blending - **SERVINGS:** 2
INGREDIENTS: 2 cups fresh kale, stems removed; 1 cup mixed berries, frozen; 1 banana; 1 Tbsp. flaxseed, ground; 1 cup almond milk; 1 tsp honey
DIRECTIONS: Place kale, mixed berries, banana, flaxseed, and almond milk in a blender. Blend on high until smooth. Sweeten with honey to taste. Serve immediately.
N.V.: Calories: 150, Fat: 2g, Carbs: 31g, Protein: 5g, Sugar: 17g

RECIPE 2. COTTAGE CHEESE AND PINEAPPLE BOWL

PREPARATION TIME: 5 min - **COOKING TIME:** 0 min **MODE OF COOKING:** Assembly - **SERVINGS:** 1
INGREDIENTS: 1/2 cup cottage cheese; 1/2 cup pineapple, chopped; 1 Tbsp. chia seeds; 1 tsp honey
DIRECTIONS: In a bowl, combine cottage cheese and pineapple. Sprinkle chia seeds over the top and drizzle with honey. Serve chilled.
N.V.: Calories: 180, Fat: 3g, Carbs: 24g, Protein: 14g, Sugar: 18g

RECIPE 3. VEGAN TOFU SCRAMBLE

PREPARATION TIME: 10 min - **COOKING TIME:** 10 min **MODE OF COOKING:** Sautéing - **SERVINGS:** 2
INGREDIENTS: 1 Tbsp. olive oil; 1/2 block firm tofu, crumbled; 1/4 tsp turmeric; 1/2 cup spinach, chopped; 1/4 cup tomatoes, diced; Salt and pepper to taste
DIRECTIONS: Heat olive oil in a pan over medium heat. Add crumbled tofu and turmeric, cook for 5 minutes. Stir in spinach and tomatoes, cook until spinach wilts. Season with salt and pepper. Serve warm.
N.V.: Calories: 150, Fat: 10g, Carbs: 4g, Protein: 12g, Sugar: 2g

RECIPE 4. CHIA SEED PUDDING

PREPARATION TIME: 5 min (plus overnight soaking) - **COOKING TIME:** 0 min **MODE OF COOKING:** Refrigeration - **SERVINGS:** 2
INGREDIENTS: 1/4 cup chia seeds; 1 cup coconut milk; 1 Tbsp. maple syrup; 1/2 tsp vanilla extract; Fresh berries for topping
DIRECTIONS: In a bowl, mix chia seeds, coconut milk, maple syrup, and vanilla extract. Cover and refrigerate overnight. Before serving, stir well and top with fresh berries.
N.V.: Calories: 200, Fat: 12g, Carbs: 18g, Protein: 4g, Sugar: 8g

RECIPE 5. AVOCADO AND EGG WHITE WRAP

PREPARATION TIME: 5 min - **COOKING TIME:** 5 min **MODE OF COOKING:** Griddling - **SERVINGS:** 1
INGREDIENTS: 2 egg whites; 1/2 avocado, sliced; 1 whole wheat tortilla; 1/4 cup spinach; Salt and pepper to taste
DIRECTIONS: Cook egg whites in a non-stick skillet until set. Warm the tortilla on a griddle. Place cooked egg whites on the tortilla, top with avocado slices and spinach. Season with salt and pepper. Roll up the tortilla and serve.
N.V.: Calories: 250, Fat: 11g, Carbs: 27g, Protein: 14g, Sugar: 2g

RECIPE 6. GREEK YOGURT WITH HONEY AND WALNUTS

PREPARATION TIME: 5 min - **COOKING TIME:** 0 min **MODE OF COOKING:** Assembly - **SERVINGS:** 1
INGREDIENTS: 1 cup Greek yogurt; 2 Tbsp. walnuts, chopped; 1 Tbsp. honey
DIRECTIONS: Spoon Greek yogurt into a bowl. Sprinkle with chopped walnuts and drizzle with honey. Serve immediately.
N.V.: Calories: 290, Fat: 15g, Carbs: 24g, Protein: 20g, Sugar: 18g

RECIPE 7. OATMEAL WITH ALMOND BUTTER AND BANANA

PREPARATION TIME: 5 min - **COOKING TIME:** 5 min **MODE OF COOKING:** Boiling - **SERVINGS:** 1
INGREDIENTS: 1/2 cup rolled oats; 1 cup water; 1 Tbsp. almond butter; 1 banana, sliced; 1 tsp chia seeds
DIRECTIONS: In a saucepan, bring water to a boil. Add rolled oats and cook over medium heat until thickened. Stir in almond butter. Top with banana slices and chia seeds. Serve warm.
N.V.: Calories: 350, Fat: 14g, Carbs: 50g, Protein: 10g, Sugar: 12g

RECIPE 8. BERRY SPIRALIZED CUCUMBER SALAD

PREPARATION TIME: 10 min - **COOKING TIME:** 0 min
MODE OF COOKING: No cook - **SERVINGS:** 4
INGREDIENTS: 2 large cucumbers, spiralized; 1 cup mixed berries (strawberries, blueberries, raspberries); 1/4 cup feta cheese, crumbled; 2 Tbsp. fresh mint, chopped; 2 Tbsp. olive oil; 1 Tbsp. apple cider vinegar; Salt and pepper to taste
DIRECTIONS: In a large bowl, combine spiralized cucumbers and mixed berries. Gently toss with feta cheese and fresh mint. Whisk together olive oil and apple cider vinegar, drizzle over salad. Season with salt and pepper, serve immediately.
N.V.: Calories: 150, Fat: 10g, Carbs: 12g, Protein: 3g, Sugar: 7g

RECIPE 9. AVOCADO CITRUS BREAKFAST SALAD

PREPARATION TIME: 15 min - **COOKING TIME:** 0 min
MODE OF COOKING: No cook - **SERVINGS:** 4
INGREDIENTS: 4 cups mixed greens (spinach, arugula, kale); 2 oranges, segmented; 1 grapefruit, segmented; 1 avocado, sliced; 1/4 cup almonds, toasted and chopped; 2 Tbsp. olive oil; 1 Tbsp. lemon juice; Salt and pepper to taste
DIRECTIONS: Arrange mixed greens on plates. Top with citrus segments and avocado slices. Sprinkle with toasted almonds. Whisk together olive oil and lemon juice, season with salt and pepper. Drizzle dressing over salads before serving.
N.V.: Calories: 220, Fat: 15g, Carbs: 20g, Protein: 4g, Sugar: 12g

RECIPE 10. GREEN SMOOTHIE BOWL

PREPARATION TIME: 5 min - **COOKING TIME:** 0 min
MODE OF COOKING: Blending - **SERVINGS:** 2
INGREDIENTS: 2 bananas, frozen; 1 cup spinach; 1/2 avocado; 1 cup unsweetened almond milk; 1 Tbsp. chia seeds; 1 Tbsp. flaxseed meal; Toppings: sliced bananas, blueberries, granola, coconut flakes
DIRECTIONS: Blend bananas, spinach, avocado, almond milk, chia seeds, and flaxseed meal until smooth. Pour into bowls and top with sliced bananas, blueberries, granola, and coconut flakes.
N.V.: Calories: 300, Fat: 14g, Carbs: 40g, Protein: 6g, Sugar: 18g

RECIPE 11. TOFU AND VEGETABLE BREAKFAST SCRAMBLE

PREPARATION TIME: 10 min - **COOKING TIME:** 15 min
MODE OF COOKING: Sautéing - **SERVINGS:** 4

INGREDIENTS: 14 oz firm tofu, crumbled; 1 Tbsp. olive oil; 1/2 tsp turmeric; 1/2 cup cherry tomatoes, halved; 1 cup spinach, chopped; 1/4 cup red bell pepper, diced; 1/4 cup yellow bell pepper, diced; Salt and pepper to taste; 1/4 cup fresh cilantro, chopped

DIRECTIONS: Heat olive oil in a skillet over medium heat. Add crumbled tofu and turmeric, cook for 5 minutes. Stir in cherry tomatoes, spinach, and bell peppers. Cook until vegetables are tender. Season with salt and pepper. Garnish with fresh cilantro before serving.

N.V.: Calories: 180, Fat: 11g, Carbs: 8g, Protein: 12g, Sugar: 3g

CHAPTER 9: THE ULTIMATE BURGERS AND SANDWICHES

In the grand tapestry of culinary arts, burgers and sandwiches stand out as quintessential icons of comfort food. Yet, beneath their humble appearance lies a canvas ripe for innovation and mastery. Chapter 9, "The Ultimate Burgers and Sandwiches," is a homage to these beloved staples, inviting you on a gastronomic journey that redefines what you thought possible between two slices of bread or within a bun.

This chapter is not just about assembling ingredients; it's about elevating every component to create a symphony of flavors and textures. From the succulent, perfectly grilled patties that form the heart of our burgers to the artisanal breads that do more than just hold everything together, each element is a testament to the joy of cooking and the art of layering flavors.

We'll explore the classics, paying homage to the timeless combinations that have captured hearts around the globe, and then venture into the uncharted territories of gourmet and avant-garde, where innovation knows no bounds. This is where the familiar comfort of a burger or sandwich meets the thrill of culinary exploration—where aged cheeses, exotic condiments, and unconventional fillings come together in a celebration of taste.

Prepare to push the boundaries of what you thought possible, to blend tradition with innovation, and to discover the endless possibilities that await within the realm of burgers and sandwiches. Welcome to a chapter that promises not just meals but experiences, crafting memories one bite at a time.

CRAFTING THE ULTIMATE PATTIES

RECIPE 1. CLASSIC BEEF BURGER PATTY

PREPARATION TIME: 15 min - **COOKING TIME:** 10 min **MODE OF COOKING:** Grilling - **SERVINGS:** 4
INGREDIENTS: 1 lb. ground beef (80/20 mix); 1 tsp salt; 1/2 tsp ground black pepper; 1 Tbsp. Worcestershire sauce; 4 hamburger buns
DIRECTIONS: In a bowl, mix ground beef with salt, pepper, and Worcestershire sauce gently. Form into 4 equal-sized patties. Preheat grill to medium-high heat. Grill patties for about 5 minutes per side for medium-rare. Serve on buns with desired toppings.
N.V.: Calories: 290, Fat: 15g, Carbs: 20g, Protein: 20g, Sugar: 3g

RECIPE 2. TURKEY AND SAGE BURGER PATTY

PREPARATION TIME: 20 min - **COOKING TIME:** 10 min **MODE OF COOKING:** Grilling - **SERVINGS:** 4
INGREDIENTS: 1 lb. ground turkey; 2 Tbsp. fresh sage, finely chopped; 1/4 cup breadcrumbs; 1 egg, beaten; 1 tsp salt; 1/2 tsp black pepper; 4 whole wheat buns
DIRECTIONS: Combine turkey, sage, breadcrumbs, egg, salt, and pepper in a bowl. Form into 4 patties. Preheat grill to medium heat. Cook patties for 5 minutes on each side or until fully cooked. Serve on whole wheat buns with your choice of toppings.

N.V.: Calories: 250, Fat: 6g, Carbs: 18g, Protein: 30g, Sugar: 2g

RECIPE 3. SPICY BLACK BEAN VEGGIE BURGER PATTY

PREPARATION TIME: 25 min - **COOKING TIME:** 8 min **MODE OF COOKING:** Grilling - **SERVINGS:** 4

INGREDIENTS: 2 cans black beans, drained and rinsed; 1/2 cup breadcrumbs; 1 egg; 1 Tbsp. chili powder; 1/2 tsp cumin; 1/4 cup cilantro, chopped; Salt and pepper to taste; 4 whole grain buns

DIRECTIONS: Mash black beans in a bowl. Mix in breadcrumbs, egg, chili powder, cumin, cilantro, salt, and pepper. Form into 4 patties. Grill over medium heat for 4 minutes on each side. Serve on whole grain buns with avocado and salsa.

N.V.: Calories: 320, Fat: 3g, Carbs: 52g, Protein: 18g, Sugar: 3g

RECIPE 4. SALMON AND DILL BURGER PATTY

PREPARATION TIME: 20 min - **COOKING TIME:** 6 min **MODE OF COOKING:** Grilling - **SERVINGS:** 4

INGREDIENTS: 1 lb. fresh salmon, finely chopped; 2 Tbsp. fresh dill, chopped; 1 egg, beaten; 1/4 cup panko breadcrumbs; 1 lemon, zest only; Salt and pepper to taste; 4 brioche buns

DIRECTIONS: Combine salmon, dill, egg, breadcrumbs, lemon zest, salt, and pepper. Form into 4 patties. Preheat grill to medium-high. Grill patties for 3 minutes per side. Serve on brioche buns with yogurt-dill sauce.

N.V.: Calories: 310, Fat: 12g, Carbs: 23g, Protein: 25g, Sugar: 3g

RECIPE 5. CHICKPEA AND QUINOA VEGGIE BURGER PATTY

PREPARATION TIME: 30 min - **COOKING TIME:** 10 min **MODE OF COOKING:** Grilling - **SERVINGS:** 4

INGREDIENTS: 1 can chickpeas, drained and rinsed; 1/2 cup cooked quinoa; 1/4 cup red onion, finely chopped; 1/4 cup carrots, grated; 2 Tbsp. parsley, chopped; 1 egg; 1/2 tsp garlic powder; Salt and pepper to taste; 4 multigrain buns

DIRECTIONS: Mash chickpeas in a bowl. Mix in quinoa, onion, carrots, parsley, egg, garlic powder, salt, and pepper. Form into 4 patties. Preheat grill to medium. Grill patties for 5 minutes on each side. Serve on multigrain buns with lettuce and tomato.

N.V.: Calories: 270, Fat: 4g, Carbs: 45g, Protein: 12g, Sugar: 5g

RECIPE 6. PORTOBELLO MUSHROOM BURGER PATTY

PREPARATION TIME: 10 min - **COOKING TIME:** 8 min **MODE OF COOKING:** Grilling - **SERVINGS:** 4

INGREDIENTS: 4 large portobello mushroom caps; 2 Tbsp. balsamic vinegar; 1 Tbsp. olive oil; 1 tsp garlic, minced; Salt and pepper to taste; 4 ciabatta rolls

DIRECTIONS: In a small bowl, whisk together balsamic vinegar, olive oil, garlic, salt, and pepper. Brush mixture over both sides of mushrooms. Preheat grill to medium-high. Grill mushrooms 4 minutes per side. Serve on toasted ciabatta rolls with arugula and red onion.

N.V.: Calories: 220, Fat: 7g, Carbs: 32g, Protein: 8g, Sugar: 6g

RECIPE 7. LENTIL AND WALNUT BURGER PATTY

PREPARATION TIME: 30 min - **COOKING TIME:** 10 min **MODE OF COOKING:** Grilling - **SERVINGS:** 4

INGREDIENTS: 1 cup cooked lentils; 1/2 cup walnuts, finely chopped; 1/4 cup mushrooms, finely chopped; 1 egg; 1/4 cup breadcrumbs; 1 tsp smoked paprika; Salt and pepper to taste; 4 whole grain buns

DIRECTIONS: In a bowl, mash lentils. Mix in walnuts, mushrooms, egg, breadcrumbs, smoked paprika, salt, and pepper. Form into 4 patties. Grill over medium heat for 5 minutes on each side. Serve on whole grain buns with spinach and tzatziki sauce.

N.V.: Calories: 330, Fat: 15g, Carbs: 37g, Protein: 15g, Sugar: 4g

RECIPE 8. SMOKED PAPRIKA CHICKPEA PATTIES

PREPARATION TIME: 15 min - **COOKING TIME:** 10 min
MODE OF COOKING: Pan-frying - **SERVINGS:** 4
INGREDIENTS: 2 cans chickpeas, drained and rinsed; 1 large egg; 2 cloves garlic, minced; 1/2 cup breadcrumbs; 2 Tbsp. smoked paprika; 1 tsp cumin; Salt and pepper to taste; 2 Tbsp. olive oil for cooking

DIRECTIONS: Mash chickpeas in a bowl until mostly smooth. Mix in egg, garlic, breadcrumbs, smoked paprika, cumin, salt, and pepper until well combined. Form into 4 patties. Heat olive oil in a skillet over medium heat. Cook patties until golden brown on each side, about 5 min per side.

N.V.: Calories: 260, Fat: 8g, Carbs: 38g, Protein: 12g, Sugar: 6g

RECIPE 9. HERBED TURKEY AND QUINOA PATTIES

PREPARATION TIME: 20 min - **COOKING TIME:** 15 min
MODE OF COOKING: Grilling - **SERVINGS:** 4
INGREDIENTS: 1 lb ground turkey; 1/2 cup cooked quinoa; 1/4 cup fresh parsley, finely chopped; 1/4 cup fresh chives, finely chopped; 2 tsp Worcestershire sauce; Salt and pepper to taste; 1 Tbsp. olive oil

DIRECTIONS: Combine ground turkey, quinoa, parsley, chives, Worcestershire sauce, salt, and pepper in a bowl. Mix thoroughly and form into 4 patties. Brush each patty with olive oil. Preheat grill to medium-high heat. Grill patties for about 7-8 min on each side or until fully cooked.

N.V.: Calories: 240, Fat: 11g, Carbs: 10g, Protein: 26g, Sugar: 1g

RECIPE 10. SPICY BLACK BEAN AND SWEET POTATO PATTIES

PREPARATION TIME: 25 min - **COOKING TIME:** 8 min
MODE OF COOKING: Pan-frying - **SERVINGS:** 4
INGREDIENTS: 1 large sweet potato, cooked and mashed; 1 can black beans, drained and rinsed; 1/2 cup corn; 1 jalapeño, finely chopped; 1 tsp chili powder; 1/2 tsp garlic powder; Salt to taste; 1/4 cup breadcrumbs; 2 Tbsp. vegetable oil for cooking

DIRECTIONS: In a large bowl, combine mashed sweet potato, black beans, corn, jalapeño, chili powder, garlic powder, and salt. Mash together and mix in breadcrumbs until the mixture can be formed into patties. Heat vegetable oil in a skillet over medium heat. Cook patties until crispy and heated through, about 4 min per side.

N.V.: Calories: 270, Fat: 7g, Carbs: 42g, Protein: 10g, Sugar: 5g

RECIPE 11. MEDITERRANEAN LENTIL PATTIES

PREPARATION TIME: 30 min (includes cooking lentils) - **COOKING TIME:** 10 min
MODE OF COOKING: Pan-frying - **SERVINGS:** 4

INGREDIENTS: 1 cup green lentils, cooked; 1/4 cup red onion, finely chopped; 1/4 cup Kalamata olives, chopped; 2 Tbsp. sun-dried tomatoes, chopped; 2 Tbsp. feta cheese, crumbled; 1 egg; 1/2 tsp oregano; Salt and pepper to taste; 1/4 cup breadcrumbs; 2 Tbsp. olive oil for cooking
DIRECTIONS: Pulse cooked lentils in a food processor until partially mashed. Transfer to a bowl and add red onion, olives, sun-dried tomatoes, feta cheese, egg, oregano, salt, and pepper. Mix well. Stir in breadcrumbs until the mixture holds together. Form into 4 patties. Heat olive oil in a skillet over medium heat. Cook patties until golden brown, about 5 min on each side.
N.V.: Calories: 310, Fat: 12g, Carbs: 38g, Protein: 14g

SANDWICH CREATIONS AND INNOVATIONS

RECIPE 1. GRILLED CHICKEN AND AVOCADO CLUB

PREPARATION TIME: 20 min - **COOKING TIME:** 10 min **MODE OF COOKING:** Grilling - **SERVINGS:** 4
INGREDIENTS: 4 chicken breast fillets; 1 tsp olive oil; Salt and pepper to taste; 8 slices whole grain bread; 1 avocado, sliced; 4 lettuce leaves; 2 tomatoes, sliced; 4 Tbsp. mayonnaise; 8 slices bacon, cooked
DIRECTIONS: Preheat grill to medium-high. Brush chicken with olive oil, season with salt and pepper. Grill for 5 minutes each side or until cooked through. Toast bread slices. Spread mayonnaise on 4 slices. Layer chicken, bacon, avocado, lettuce, and tomato. Top with remaining bread slices. Cut and serve.
N.V.: Calories: 650, Fat: 30g, Carbs: 45g, Protein: 50g, Sugar: 5g

RECIPE 2. ROASTED VEGETABLE AND HUMMUS PITA POCKET

PREPARATION TIME: 15 min - **COOKING TIME:** 20 min **MODE OF COOKING:** Roasting - **SERVINGS:** 4
INGREDIENTS: 1 zucchini, sliced; 1 bell pepper, sliced; 1 red onion, sliced; 2 Tbsp. olive oil; Salt and pepper to taste; 4 pita bread pockets; 1 cup hummus; 1 cup spinach leaves
DIRECTIONS: Preheat oven to 425°F (220°C). Toss zucchini, bell pepper, and onion with olive oil, salt, and pepper. Roast for 20 minutes. Warm pita pockets in oven last 5 minutes. Spread hummus inside pitas, fill with roasted vegetables and spinach. Serve immediately.
N.V.: Calories: 310, Fat: 14g, Carbs: 40g, Protein: 10g, Sugar: 5g

RECIPE 3. APPLE, BRIE, AND WALNUT SANDWICH

PREPARATION TIME: 5 min - **COOKING TIME:** 5 min **MODE OF COOKING:** Griddling - **SERVINGS:** 4
INGREDIENTS: 8 slices sourdough bread; 1 apple, thinly sliced; 8 oz. Brie cheese, sliced; 1/2 cup walnuts, chopped; 4 Tbsp. honey
DIRECTIONS: Heat a griddle over medium heat. Assemble sandwiches with bread, apple slices, Brie, and walnuts. Drizzle honey over filling. Cook on griddle until bread is golden and cheese melts. Flip carefully. Serve warm.
N.V.: Calories: 520, Fat: 24g, Carbs: 62g, Protein: 20g, Sugar: 22g

RECIPE 4. SPICY TUNA AND CUCUMBER WRAP

PREPARATION TIME: 10 min - **COOKING TIME:** 0 min **MODE OF COOKING:** Assembly - **SERVINGS:** 4
INGREDIENTS: 2 cans tuna in water, drained; 1/4 cup mayonnaise; 2 Tbsp. sriracha sauce; 1 cucumber, thinly sliced; 4 large flour tortillas; 1 avocado, sliced; Salt and pepper to taste
DIRECTIONS: In a bowl, mix tuna, mayonnaise, and sriracha. Season with salt and pepper. Lay out tortillas, spread tuna mixture, top with cucumber and avocado slices. Roll tightly, slice in half, and serve.
N.V.: Calories: 420, Fat: 20g, Carbs: 34g, Protein: 25g, Sugar: 2g

RECIPE 5. MEDITERRANEAN VEGGIE SANDWICH

PREPARATION TIME: 15 min - **COOKING TIME:** 0 min **MODE OF COOKING:** Assembly - **SERVINGS:** 4
INGREDIENTS: 1 cup roasted red peppers; 1 cup artichoke hearts, chopped; 1/2 cup olives, sliced; 4 Tbsp. pesto; 4 ciabatta rolls; 1 cup arugula; 4 slices provolone cheese
DIRECTIONS: Spread pesto on ciabatta rolls. Layer with roasted red peppers, artichoke hearts, olives, arugula, and provolone cheese. Press sandwiches lightly. Serve at room temperature or slightly warmed.
N.V.: Calories: 450, Fat: 22g, Carbs: 48g, Protein: 18g, Sugar: 3g

RECIPE 6. BUFFALO CHICKEN WRAP

PREPARATION TIME: 20 min - **COOKING TIME:** 10 min **MODE OF COOKING:** Griddling - **SERVINGS:** 4
INGREDIENTS: 1 lb. chicken breast, cooked and shredded; 1/2 cup buffalo sauce; 4 large flour tortillas; 1 cup lettuce, shredded; 1/2 cup blue cheese, crumbled; 1/4 cup ranch dressing; 1 carrot, shredded
DIRECTIONS: Toss shredded chicken with buffalo sauce. Lay tortillas flat, divide chicken among them. Top with lettuce, blue cheese, carrot, and a drizzle of ranch dressing. Roll tightly, slice in half, and serve.
N.V.: Calories: 530, Fat: 28g, Carbs: 38g, Protein: 35g, Sugar: 3g

RECIPE 7. PESTO CHICKPEA SALAD SANDWICH

PREPARATION TIME: 15 min - **COOKING TIME:** 0 min **MODE OF COOKING:** Assembly - **SERVINGS:** 4
INGREDIENTS: 1 can chickpeas, drained and mashed; 1/4 cup pesto; 2 Tbsp. mayonnaise; 1/2 cup sun-dried tomatoes, chopped; 8 slices multigrain bread; 1 cup baby spinach leaves
DIRECTIONS: In a bowl, mix mashed chickpeas, pesto, mayonnaise, and sun-dried tomatoes. Spread on 4 bread slices, top with spinach, cover with remaining bread. Serve immediately.
N.V.: Calories: 380, Fat: 18g, Carbs: 45g, Protein: 12g, Sugar: 8g

RECIPE 8. ROASTED VEGETABLE AND HUMMUS GRILLED SANDWICH

PREPARATION TIME: 20 min - **COOKING TIME:** 10 min
MODE OF COOKING: Grilling - **SERVINGS:** 4
INGREDIENTS: 8 slices whole grain bread; 1 zucchini, sliced; 1 red bell pepper, sliced; 1 yellow bell pepper, sliced; 1 eggplant, sliced; 1 cup hummus; 2 Tbsp. olive oil; Salt and pepper to taste
DIRECTIONS: Preheat grill to medium-high heat. Toss zucchini, bell peppers, and eggplant in olive oil, salt, and pepper. Grill vegetables until tender and charred, about 5 min on each side.

Spread hummus on one side of each bread slice. Layer grilled vegetables on 4 bread slices, top with remaining bread. Grill sandwiches for 2-3 min on each side until crispy.

N.V.: Calories: 320, Fat: 14g, Carbs: 42g, Protein: 12g, Sugar: 6g

RECIPE 9. CHIPOTLE CHICKEN AVOCADO WRAP

PREPARATION TIME: 15 min - **COOKING TIME:** 10 min
MODE OF COOKING: Pan-frying - **SERVINGS:** 4
INGREDIENTS: 2 chicken breasts, thinly sliced; 4 large whole wheat wraps; 1 avocado, sliced; 1 cup lettuce, shredded; 1/2 cup cherry tomatoes, halved; 1/4 cup Greek yogurt; 1 Tbsp. chipotle paste; 1 Tbsp. olive oil; Salt and pepper to taste
DIRECTIONS: Heat olive oil in a pan over medium heat. Cook chicken with salt, pepper, and chipotle paste until browned and cooked through. Mix Greek yogurt with remaining chipotle paste for sauce. Lay wraps flat, spread a layer of chipotle yogurt sauce, then top with lettuce, tomato, avocado, and cooked chicken. Roll wraps tightly and cut in half.
N.V.: Calories: 400, Fat: 14g, Carbs: 42g, Protein: 30g, Sugar: 3g

RECIPE 10. MEDITERRANEAN EGGPLANT PANINI

PREPARATION TIME: 20 min - **COOKING TIME:** 5 min
MODE OF COOKING: Panini press - **SERVINGS:** 4
INGREDIENTS: 1 large eggplant, sliced into 1/2-inch rounds; 8 slices ciabatta bread; 1/2 cup pesto; 1 tomato, sliced; 1 cup spinach leaves; 1/2 cup feta cheese, crumbled; 2 Tbsp. olive oil; Salt and pepper to taste
DIRECTIONS: Preheat panini press. Brush eggplant slices with olive oil, season with salt and pepper. Grill eggplant on press until tender. Spread pesto on one side of each bread slice. Assemble sandwiches with grilled eggplant, tomato slices, spinach, and feta. Grill in panini press until bread is toasted and contents are warmed through.
N.V.: Calories: 450, Fat: 25g, Carbs: 48g, Protein: 15g, Sugar: 5g

RECIPE 11. SMOKED SALMON AND CREAM CHEESE BAGEL

PREPARATION TIME: 5 min - **COOKING TIME:** 0 min
MODE OF COOKING: No cook - **SERVINGS:** 4
INGREDIENTS: 4 whole wheat bagels, halved; 8 oz smoked salmon; 1/2 cup cream cheese, softened; 1/4 red onion, thinly sliced; 2 Tbsp. capers; 1 cucumber, thinly sliced; Fresh dill for garnish; Pepper to taste
DIRECTIONS: Spread cream cheese evenly over each bagel half. Layer smoked salmon, cucumber slices, and red onion on 4 bagel halves. Sprinkle with capers and fresh dill. Season with pepper. Top with remaining bagel halves to form sandwiches.
N.V.: Calories: 360, Fat: 12g, Carbs: 44g, Protein: 22g, Sugar: 6g

VEGETARIAN DELIGHTS BETWEEN THE BUNS

RECIPE 1. GRILLED PORTOBELLO MUSHROOM BURGER

PREPARATION TIME: 15 min - **COOKING TIME:** 8 min **MODE OF COOKING:** Grilling - **SERVINGS:** 4

INGREDIENTS: 4 large portobello mushroom caps; 2 Tbsp. soy sauce; 2 Tbsp. balsamic vinegar; 1 Tbsp. olive oil; 1 garlic clove, minced; Salt and pepper to taste; 4 whole grain buns; Lettuce, tomato, and red onion for topping

DIRECTIONS: In a bowl, whisk together soy sauce, balsamic vinegar, olive oil, garlic, salt, and pepper. Marinate mushrooms for 10 minutes. Grill over medium heat for 4 minutes per side. Serve on buns with lettuce, tomato, and onion.

N.V.: Calories: 300, Fat: 9g, Carbs: 45g, Protein: 10g, Sugar: 8g

RECIPE 2. SWEET POTATO AND BLACK BEAN BURGER

PREPARATION TIME: 30 min - **COOKING TIME:** 40 min **MODE OF COOKING:** Baking & Grilling - **SERVINGS:** 4

INGREDIENTS: 2 medium sweet potatoes, roasted and mashed; 1 can black beans, drained and rinsed; 1/2 cup quinoa, cooked; 1 tsp cumin; 1/2 tsp smoked paprika; Salt and pepper to taste; 4 whole wheat buns; Avocado slices and sprouts for topping

DIRECTIONS: Mix sweet potatoes, black beans, quinoa, cumin, paprika, salt, and pepper. Form into patties and chill for 30 minutes. Bake at 375°F (190°C) for 30 minutes, flipping halfway. Serve on buns with avocado and sprouts.

N.V.: Calories: 350, Fat: 3g, Carbs: 67g, Protein: 14g, Sugar: 8g

RECIPE 3. FALAFEL PITA SANDWICH

PREPARATION TIME: 20 min - **COOKING TIME:** 10 min **MODE OF COOKING:** Frying - **SERVINGS:** 4

INGREDIENTS: 16 falafel balls (pre-made or homemade); 4 pita bread; 1 cup tzatziki sauce; 1 cup lettuce, chopped; 1 tomato, diced; 1/2 cucumber, sliced; 1/4 red onion, sliced

DIRECTIONS: Heat falafel balls as directed on package or recipe. Warm pita bread. Cut pitas in half and open pockets. Fill with falafel balls, tzatziki sauce, lettuce, tomato, cucumber, and red onion. Serve immediately.

N.V.: Calories: 450, Fat: 18g, Carbs: 58g, Protein: 14g, Sugar: 5g

RECIPE 4. CAPRESE GRILLED CHEESE SANDWICH

PREPARATION TIME: 5 min - **COOKING TIME:** 10 min **MODE OF COOKING:** Griddling - **SERVINGS:** 4

INGREDIENTS: 8 slices sourdough bread; 1 ball fresh mozzarella, sliced; 2 tomatoes, sliced; 1/4 cup basil leaves; Balsamic glaze for drizzling; Salt and pepper to taste; 2 Tbsp. olive oil

DIRECTIONS: Assemble sandwiches with bread, mozzarella, tomato slices, and basil. Season with salt and pepper. Drizzle with balsamic glaze. Brush outside of sandwiches with olive oil. Griddle until golden and cheese melts. Serve warm.

N.V.: Calories: 400, Fat: 20g, Carbs: 40g, Protein: 18g, Sugar: 4g

RECIPE 5. AVOCADO AND SPINACH PANINI

PREPARATION TIME: 10 min - **COOKING TIME:** 5 min **MODE OF COOKING:** Panini Press - **SERVINGS:** 4

INGREDIENTS: 8 slices ciabatta bread; 2 avocados, mashed; 1 cup baby spinach; 1/2 cup sun-dried tomatoes, chopped; 1/4 red onion, thinly sliced; Salt and pepper to taste
DIRECTIONS: Spread mashed avocado on 4 bread slices. Top with spinach, sun-dried tomatoes, and onion. Season with salt and pepper. Cover with remaining bread slices. Grill in panini press until crispy. Serve hot.
N.V.: Calories: 310, Fat: 15g, Carbs: 36g, Protein: 8g, Sugar: 5g

RECIPE 6. EGGPLANT AND ROASTED PEPPER BURGER

PREPARATION TIME: 20 min - **COOKING TIME:** 25 min **MODE OF COOKING:** Grilling & Roasting - **SERVINGS:** 4
INGREDIENTS: 1 large eggplant, sliced into 1/2-inch rounds; 2 red bell peppers, halved and seeded; 4 whole grain buns; 1/4 cup hummus; 1 cup arugula; 1 Tbsp. olive oil; Salt and pepper to taste
DIRECTIONS: Brush eggplant and bell peppers with olive oil, season with salt and pepper. Grill until tender. Roast peppers until charred, peel off skin. Assemble burgers on buns with hummus, eggplant, pepper, and arugula.
N.V.: Calories: 290, Fat: 9g, Carbs: 46g, Protein: 9g, Sugar: 13g

RECIPE 7. ZUCCHINI AND GOAT CHEESE CIABATTA

PREPARATION TIME: 15 min - **COOKING TIME:** 10 min **MODE OF COOKING:** Grilling - **SERVINGS:** 4
INGREDIENTS: 2 zucchinis, sliced lengthwise; 1 log goat cheese, softened; 4 ciabatta rolls, split; 1/4 cup pesto; 2 tomatoes, sliced; Salt and pepper to taste; 1 Tbsp. olive oil
DIRECTIONS: Brush zucchini slices with olive oil, season with salt and pepper. Grill until tender and marked. Spread goat cheese on ciabatta bottoms, top with grilled zucchini, tomato slices, and a dollop of pesto. Cover with ciabatta tops. Serve immediately.
N.V.: Calories: 370, Fat: 15g, Carbs: 45g, Protein: 14g, Sugar: 6g

RECIPE 8. CHICKPEA AND AVOCADO SMASH SANDWICH

PREPARATION TIME: 10 min - **COOKING TIME:** 0 min
MODE OF COOKING: No cook - **SERVINGS:** 4
INGREDIENTS: 1 can chickpeas, drained and mashed; 2 avocados, mashed; Juice of 1 lemon; Salt and pepper to taste; 8 slices whole grain bread; 1/2 cucumber, sliced; 1/4 red onion, thinly sliced
DIRECTIONS: In a bowl, combine mashed chickpeas, avocados, lemon juice, salt, and pepper. Spread mixture on 4 bread slices. Top with cucumber and red onion slices. Cover with remaining bread slices. Cut and serve.
N.V.: Calories: 320, Fat: 12g, Carbs: 44g, Protein: 12g, Sugar: 6g

RECIPE 9. BEETROOT AND GOAT CHEESE GRILLED CHEESE

PREPARATION TIME: 15 min - **COOKING TIME:** 5 min
MODE OF COOKING: Pan-frying - **SERVINGS:** 4
INGREDIENTS: 8 slices sourdough bread; 1 cup roasted beetroot, sliced; 4 oz goat cheese, softened; 2 Tbsp. honey; 1/2 tsp thyme leaves; Butter for grilling
DIRECTIONS: Spread goat cheese on 4 bread slices. Top with beetroot slices, drizzle with honey, and sprinkle thyme. Cover with remaining bread slices. Butter the outside of each sandwich. Grill on a hot pan until golden brown on both sides.

N.V.: Calories: 380, Fat: 14g, Carbs: 52g, Protein: 14g, Sugar: 12g

CHAPTER 10: REINVENTING SIDES AND VEGETABLES

Chapter 10, "Reinventing Sides and Vegetables," invites you on a culinary journey to elevate the often-understated role of sides and vegetables in our meals. Moving beyond the traditional steamed broccoli or mashed potatoes, this chapter unveils a world where sides are not just accompaniments but stars in their own right. From the smoky allure of grilled vegetables to the comforting warmth of innovative casseroles, each recipe is designed to challenge your perceptions and enhance your dining experience.

In the pages that follow, you'll discover how simple ingredients can be transformed with a touch of creativity and the right techniques. Whether it's roasting, grilling, sautéing, or even raw preparations, the methods explored here promise to unlock flavors and textures you never knew existed in the humble vegetable.

Not only are these dishes meant to complement any main course, but they also stand proudly on their own, offering satisfying and wholesome options for vegetarians and veggie-lovers alike. From vibrant salads bursting with color and life to hearty grains and legumes that provide both comfort and nutrition, this chapter is a testament to the versatility and boundless potential of plant-based cuisine.

As we delve into "Reinventing Sides and Vegetables," let's embrace the opportunity to give these unsung heroes of the dining table their moment in the spotlight. Prepare to be inspired, surprised, and, most importantly, delighted by the depth of flavors that awaits.

VEGETABLE DISHES REIMAGINED

RECIPE 1. SMOKY CAULIFLOWER STEAKS

PREPARATION TIME: 10 min - **COOKING TIME:** 25 min **MODE OF COOKING:** Roasting - **SERVINGS:** 4
INGREDIENTS: 2 large cauliflowers, sliced into 1-inch steaks; 3 Tbsp. olive oil; 1 tsp smoked paprika; 1/2 tsp garlic powder; Salt and pepper to taste
DIRECTIONS: Preheat oven to 400°F (200°C). Brush cauliflower steaks with olive oil and season with smoked paprika, garlic powder, salt, and pepper. Roast on a baking sheet for 25 minutes, flipping halfway through, until tender and edges are crispy.
N.V.: Calories: 120, Fat: 10g, Carbs: 8g, Protein: 3g, Sugar: 3g

RECIPE 2. HERBED ZUCCHINI RIBBONS

PREPARATION TIME: 15 min - **COOKING TIME:** 5 min **MODE OF COOKING:** Sautéing - **SERVINGS:** 4
INGREDIENTS: 4 zucchinis, thinly sliced lengthwise; 2 Tbsp. olive oil; 1 Tbsp. mixed fresh herbs (basil, thyme, oregano), chopped; Salt and pepper to taste; 1/4 cup grated Parmesan cheese

DIRECTIONS: Heat olive oil in a pan over medium heat. Add zucchini ribbons, sauté for 3-5 minutes until tender. Stir in fresh herbs, season with salt and pepper. Serve topped with grated Parmesan.
N.V.: Calories: 100, Fat: 7g, Carbs: 6g, Protein: 4g, Sugar: 3g

RECIPE 3. BALSAMIC BRUSSELS SPROUTS

PREPARATION TIME: 10 min - **COOKING TIME:** 20 min **MODE OF COOKING:** Roasting - **SERVINGS:** 4
INGREDIENTS: 1 lb. Brussels sprouts, halved; 2 Tbsp. olive oil; 3 Tbsp. balsamic vinegar; Salt and pepper to taste; 1 Tbsp. honey
DIRECTIONS: Preheat oven to 425°F (220°C). Toss Brussels sprouts with olive oil, balsamic vinegar, and honey. Season with salt and pepper. Roast on a baking sheet for 20 minutes, until caramelized and tender.
N.V.: Calories: 130, Fat: 7g, Carbs: 15g, Protein: 4g, Sugar: 7g

RECIPE 4. SPICED SWEET POTATO WEDGES

PREPARATION TIME: 10 min - **COOKING TIME:** 30 min **MODE OF COOKING:** Roasting - **SERVINGS:** 4
INGREDIENTS: 2 large sweet potatoes, cut into wedges; 2 Tbsp. olive oil; 1 tsp cumin; 1/2 tsp smoked paprika; Salt and pepper to taste
DIRECTIONS: Preheat oven to 400°F (200°C). Toss sweet potato wedges with olive oil, cumin, smoked paprika, salt, and pepper. Roast on a baking sheet for 30 minutes, turning halfway through, until crispy and golden.
N.V.: Calories: 200, Fat: 7g, Carbs: 33g, Protein: 2g, Sugar: 7g

RECIPE 5. GARLIC ROASTED GREEN BEANS

PREPARATION TIME: 10 min - **COOKING TIME:** 15 min **MODE OF COOKING:** Roasting - **SERVINGS:** 4
INGREDIENTS: 1 lb. green beans, trimmed; 3 Tbsp. olive oil; 3 garlic cloves, minced; Salt and pepper to taste; Lemon zest from 1 lemon
DIRECTIONS: Preheat oven to 425°F (220°C). Toss green beans with olive oil, minced garlic, salt, and pepper. Roast on a baking sheet for 15 minutes. Sprinkle with lemon zest before serving.
N.V.: Calories: 110, Fat: 7g, Carbs: 10g, Protein: 2g, Sugar: 4g

RECIPE 6. MEDITERRANEAN STUFFED BELL PEPPERS

PREPARATION TIME: 20 min - **COOKING TIME:** 25 min **MODE OF COOKING:** Baking - **SERVINGS:** 4
INGREDIENTS: 4 bell peppers, halved and seeded; 1 cup cooked quinoa; 1 cup spinach, chopped; 1/2 cup feta cheese, crumbled; 1/4 cup olives, sliced; 2 Tbsp. pine nuts; 1 tsp oregano; Salt and pepper to taste; Olive oil for drizzling
DIRECTIONS: Preheat oven to 375°F (190°C). Mix quinoa, spinach, feta, olives, pine nuts, oregano, salt, and pepper. Stuff bell peppers with the mixture, drizzle with olive oil. Bake for 25 minutes or until peppers are tender.
N.V.: Calories: 220, Fat: 12g, Carbs: 24g, Protein: 7g, Sugar: 5g

RECIPE 7. CURRIED CAULIFLOWER RICE

PREPARATION TIME: 10 min - **COOKING TIME:** 15 min **MODE OF COOKING:** Sautéing - **SERVINGS:** 4

INGREDIENTS: 1 large cauliflower, grated into rice-size pieces; 2 Tbsp. coconut oil; 1 onion, diced; 1 tsp curry powder; 1/2 cup peas; 1/2 cup carrots, diced; Salt to taste
DIRECTIONS: Heat coconut oil in a large pan over medium heat. Sauté onion until translucent. Add curry powder, stirring for 1 minute. Add cauliflower rice, peas, and carrots. Cook for 15 minutes, stirring occasionally. Season with salt.
N.V.: Calories: 120, Fat: 7g, Carbs: 13g, Protein: 3g, Sugar: 5g

RECIPE 8. CHARRED BROCCOLINI WITH LEMON TAHINI DRIZZLE

PREPARATION TIME: 10 min - **COOKING TIME:** 10 min
MODE OF COOKING: Grilling - **SERVINGS:** 4
INGREDIENTS: 2 bunches broccolini, trimmed; 2 Tbsp. olive oil; Salt and pepper to taste; **For the Lemon Tahini Drizzle:** 1/4 cup tahini; Juice of 1 lemon; 1 clove garlic, minced; 2-4 Tbsp. water; Salt to taste
DIRECTIONS: Preheat grill to medium-high heat. Toss broccolini in olive oil, salt, and pepper. Grill until charred, about 5 min per side. For the drizzle, whisk together tahini, lemon juice, garlic, and water until smooth, adding more water as needed for consistency. Season with salt. Serve broccolini with tahini drizzle.
N.V.: Calories: 180, Fat: 14g, Carbs: 10g, Protein: 5g, Sugar: 3g

RECIPE 9. SPICED CAULIFLOWER STEAKS

PREPARATION TIME: 5 min - **COOKING TIME:** 25 min
MODE OF COOKING: Roasting - **SERVINGS:** 4
INGREDIENTS: 2 large heads cauliflower, sliced into 1-inch steaks; 3 Tbsp. olive oil; 1 tsp smoked paprika; 1/2 tsp cumin; 1/4 tsp turmeric; Salt and pepper to taste
DIRECTIONS: Preheat oven to 425°F (218°C). Mix olive oil, smoked paprika, cumin, turmeric, salt, and pepper. Brush mixture onto both sides of cauliflower steaks. Roast on a lined baking sheet until tender and golden, about 12-15 min per side.
N.V.: Calories: 150, Fat: 10g, Carbs: 14g, Protein: 5g, Sugar: 5g

RECIPE 10. BALSAMIC GLAZED BRUSSELS SPROUTS WITH WALNUTS

PREPARATION TIME: 10 min - **COOKING TIME:** 20 min
MODE OF COOKING: Sautéing - **SERVINGS:** 4
INGREDIENTS: 1 lb Brussels sprouts, halved; 2 Tbsp. olive oil; 1/4 cup balsamic vinegar; 2 Tbsp. honey; 1/2 cup walnuts, chopped; Salt and pepper to taste
DIRECTIONS: Heat olive oil in a large skillet over medium heat. Add Brussels sprouts, salt, and pepper, cook until browned, about 10 min. Reduce heat, add balsamic vinegar and honey, cook until sprouts are glazed, about 10 min. Stir in walnuts before serving.
N.V.: Calories: 220, Fat: 14g, Carbs: 22g, Protein: 6g, Sugar: 11g

RECIPE 11. GRILLED ZUCCHINI RIBBONS WITH PINE NUT PESTO

PREPARATION TIME: 15 min - **COOKING TIME:** 5 min
MODE OF COOKING: Grilling - **SERVINGS:** 4
INGREDIENTS: 4 zucchinis, sliced into long ribbons; 2 Tbsp. olive oil; Salt and pepper to taste; **For the Pine Nut Pesto:** 1/2 cup pine nuts, toasted; 1 cup basil leaves; 1/4 cup Parmesan cheese, grated; 1 clove garlic; 1/4 cup olive oil; Salt to taste
DIRECTIONS: Preheat grill to high. Toss zucchini ribbons with olive oil, salt, and pepper. Grill until tender, about 2-3 min per side. For the pesto, blend pine nuts, basil, Parmesan, garlic, and

olive oil in a food processor until smooth. Season with salt. Serve zucchini with a dollop of pine nut pesto.
N.V.: Calories: 290, Fat: 25g, Carbs: 12g, Protein: 6g, Sugar: 4g

SIDE DISHES TO COMPLEMENT ANY MEAL

RECIPE 1. LEMON HERB QUINOA

PREPARATION TIME: 5 min - **COOKING TIME:** 20 min **MODE OF COOKING:** Simmering - **SERVINGS:** 4
INGREDIENTS: 1 cup quinoa, rinsed; 2 cups vegetable broth; Zest and juice of 1 lemon; 1 Tbsp. olive oil; 1/4 cup fresh parsley, chopped; 1/4 cup fresh basil, chopped; Salt and pepper to taste
DIRECTIONS: In a saucepan, bring vegetable broth to a boil. Add quinoa, reduce heat to low, cover, and simmer for 15 minutes until liquid is absorbed. Stir in lemon zest, lemon juice, olive oil, parsley, basil, salt, and pepper. Serve warm or at room temperature.
N.V.: Calories: 210, Fat: 5g, Carbs: 35g, Protein: 7g, Sugar: 1g

RECIPE 2. ROASTED GARLIC MASHED POTATOES

PREPARATION TIME: 10 min - **COOKING TIME:** 45 min **MODE OF COOKING:** Boiling & Roasting - **SERVINGS:** 4
INGREDIENTS: 2 lbs. Yukon Gold potatoes, peeled and quartered; 1 head garlic; 1 Tbsp. olive oil; 1/2 cup milk; 2 Tbsp. unsalted butter; Salt and pepper to taste
DIRECTIONS: Preheat oven to 400°F (200°C). Cut top off garlic head, drizzle with olive oil, wrap in foil, and roast for 45 minutes. Boil potatoes until tender, drain. Squeeze roasted garlic into potatoes, add milk and butter, mash until smooth. Season with salt and pepper.
N.V.: Calories: 250, Fat: 8g, Carbs: 40g, Protein: 5g, Sugar: 2g

RECIPE 3. CRISPY PARMESAN ASPARAGUS STICKS

PREPARATION TIME: 15 min - **COOKING TIME:** 10 min **MODE OF COOKING:** Baking - **SERVINGS:** 4
INGREDIENTS: 1 lb. asparagus, trimmed; 1/2 cup flour; 2 eggs, beaten; 1 cup Panko breadcrumbs; 1/2 cup grated Parmesan cheese; Salt and pepper to taste
DIRECTIONS: Preheat oven to 425°F (220°C). Dredge asparagus in flour, dip in eggs, then coat in Panko mixed with Parmesan, salt, and pepper. Bake on a wire rack for 10 minutes until golden and crispy.
N.V.: Calories: 220, Fat: 9g, Carbs: 26g, Protein: 13g, Sugar: 3g

RECIPE 4. SWEET AND SPICY ROASTED CARROTS

PREPARATION TIME: 10 min - **COOKING TIME:** 25 min **MODE OF COOKING:** Roasting - **SERVINGS:** 4
INGREDIENTS: 1 lb. carrots, peeled and sliced; 2 Tbsp. olive oil; 2 Tbsp. honey; 1 tsp chili powder; Salt and pepper to taste
DIRECTIONS: Preheat oven to 400°F (200°C). Toss carrots with olive oil, honey, chili powder, salt, and pepper. Roast for 25 minutes, stirring once, until caramelized and tender.
N.V.: Calories: 160, Fat: 7g, Carbs: 24g, Protein: 1g, Sugar: 17g

Recipe 5. Grilled Corn with Cilantro Lime Butter

PREPARATION TIME: 5 min - **COOKING TIME:** 10 min **MODE OF COOKING:** Grilling - **SERVINGS:** 4
INGREDIENTS: 4 ears corn, husks removed; 4 Tbsp. unsalted butter, softened; 1 lime, zest and juice; 1/4 cup cilantro, chopped; Salt and chili powder to taste
DIRECTIONS: Preheat grill to medium-high. Grill corn, turning occasionally, until charred and tender, about 10 minutes. Mix butter with lime zest, juice, cilantro, salt, and chili powder. Spread over warm corn.
N.V.: Calories: 200, Fat: 11g, Carbs: 27g, Protein: 4g, Sugar: 6g

Recipe 6. Baked Zucchini Fries

PREPARATION TIME: 15 min - **COOKING TIME:** 20 min **MODE OF COOKING:** Baking - **SERVINGS:** 4
INGREDIENTS: 2 zucchinis, cut into fries; 1/2 cup flour; 2 eggs, beaten; 1 cup Panko breadcrumbs; 1/4 cup grated Parmesan cheese; 1 tsp garlic powder; Salt and pepper to taste
DIRECTIONS: Preheat oven to 425°F (220°C). Dredge zucchini in flour, dip in eggs, then coat in mixture of Panko, Parmesan, garlic powder, salt, and pepper. Bake on a greased sheet for 20 minutes until crispy.
N.V.: Calories: 220, Fat: 8g, Carbs: 28g, Protein: 10g, Sugar: 4g

Recipe 7. Cucumber and Dill Salad

PREPARATION TIME: 10 min - **COOKING TIME:** 0 min **MODE OF COOKING:** Mixing - **SERVINGS:** 4
INGREDIENTS: 2 cucumbers, thinly sliced; 1/4 cup red onion, thinly sliced; 1/4 cup white wine vinegar; 1 Tbsp. olive oil; 2 Tbsp. fresh dill, chopped; Salt and pepper to taste
DIRECTIONS: In a bowl, mix cucumbers and onion. In another bowl, whisk together vinegar, olive oil, dill, salt, and pepper. Pour over cucumbers and onions, toss to coat. Chill before serving.
N.V.: Calories: 70, Fat: 3.5g, Carbs: 9g, Protein: 1g, Sugar: 4g

Recipe 8. Charred Brussels Sprouts with Lemon Aioli

PREPARATION TIME: 10 min - **COOKING TIME:** 15 min
MODE OF COOKING: Grilling - **SERVINGS:** 4
INGREDIENTS: 1 lb Brussels sprouts, halved; 2 Tbsp. olive oil; Salt and pepper to taste; **For the aioli:** 1/2 cup mayonnaise; 1 clove garlic, minced; 1 Tbsp. lemon juice; Zest of 1 lemon; Salt to taste
DIRECTIONS: Preheat grill to medium-high heat. Toss Brussels sprouts with olive oil, salt, and pepper. Grill until charred and tender, about 7-8 min per side. For the aioli, whisk together mayonnaise, garlic, lemon juice, lemon zest, and salt. Serve Brussels sprouts with lemon aioli on the side.
N.V.: Calories: 220, Fat: 18g, Carbs: 12g, Protein: 4g, Sugar: 3g

Recipe 9. Roasted Sweet Potato Wedges with Cinnamon Dip

PREPARATION TIME: 15 min - **COOKING TIME:** 25 min
MODE OF COOKING: Roasting - **SERVINGS:** 4
INGREDIENTS: 2 large sweet potatoes, cut into wedges; 2 Tbsp. olive oil; 1 tsp smoked paprika; Salt to taste; **For the dip:** 1/2 cup Greek yogurt; 1 Tbsp. honey; 1/2 tsp cinnamon; Pinch of salt

DIRECTIONS: Preheat oven to 425°F (218°C). Toss sweet potato wedges with olive oil, smoked paprika, and salt. Arrange on a baking sheet and roast until crispy, about 25 min. Mix Greek yogurt, honey, cinnamon, and a pinch of salt for the dip. Serve wedges with cinnamon dip.
N.V.: Calories: 210, Fat: 7g, Carbs: 33g, Protein: 4g, Sugar: 10g

RECIPE 10. GRILLED CORN WITH COTIJA CHEESE AND LIME

PREPARATION TIME: 5 min - **COOKING TIME:** 10 min
MODE OF COOKING: Grilling - **SERVINGS:** 4
INGREDIENTS: 4 ears of corn, husks removed; 2 Tbsp. melted butter; 1/2 cup Cotija cheese, crumbled; 1 lime, cut into wedges; Chili powder to taste; Salt to taste
DIRECTIONS: Preheat grill to high heat. Brush corn with melted butter and season with salt. Grill until kernels are slightly charred and tender, turning occasionally, about 10 min. Sprinkle grilled corn with Cotija cheese and chili powder. Serve with lime wedges.
N.V.: Calories: 180, Fat: 11g, Carbs: 18g, Protein: 5g, Sugar: 6g

RECIPE 11. BALSAMIC ROASTED CARROT SALAD

PREPARATION TIME: 10 min - **COOKING TIME:** 20 min
MODE OF COOKING: Roasting - **SERVINGS:** 4
INGREDIENTS: 1 lb carrots, peeled and sliced; 2 Tbsp. olive oil; 3 Tbsp. balsamic vinegar; 1 Tbsp. honey; Salt and pepper to taste; 1/4 cup goat cheese, crumbled; 1/4 cup walnuts, chopped; 2 Tbsp. fresh parsley, chopped
DIRECTIONS: Preheat oven to 400°F (204°C). Toss carrots with olive oil, 2 Tbsp. balsamic vinegar, honey, salt, and pepper. Roast until tender and caramelized, about 20 min. Drizzle with remaining balsamic vinegar. Top with goat cheese, walnuts, and parsley before serving.
N.V.: Calories: 220, Fat: 14g, Carbs: 22g, Protein: 4g, Sugar: 12g

CREATIVE SALADS AND SLAWS

RECIPE 1. CRUNCHY APPLE AND FENNEL SLAW

PREPARATION TIME: 15 min - **COOKING TIME:** 0 min **MODE OF COOKING:** Mixing - **SERVINGS:** 4
INGREDIENTS: 2 apples, julienned; 1 fennel bulb, julienned; 1/4 cup walnuts, chopped; 2 Tbsp. lemon juice; 1 Tbsp. olive oil; 1 tsp honey; Salt and pepper to taste
DIRECTIONS: In a large bowl, combine apples, fennel, and walnuts. In a small bowl, whisk together lemon juice, olive oil, honey, salt, and pepper. Pour dressing over apple mixture and toss to coat evenly. Chill before serving.
N.V.: Calories: 150, Fat: 9g, Carbs: 18g, Protein: 2g, Sugar: 12g

RECIPE 2. KALE AND QUINOA SALAD WITH AVOCADO DRESSING

PREPARATION TIME: 20 min - **COOKING TIME:** 15 min **MODE OF COOKING:** Boiling & Blending - **SERVINGS:** 4

INGREDIENTS: 1 cup quinoa, cooked; 2 cups kale, chopped; 1 avocado; 1 lemon, juiced; 1 garlic clove; 2 Tbsp. olive oil; Salt and pepper to taste; 1/4 cup pumpkin seeds

DIRECTIONS: Blend avocado, lemon juice, garlic, olive oil, salt, and pepper until smooth for dressing. In a large bowl, mix cooked quinoa and kale. Add dressing and toss until well coated. Garnish with pumpkin seeds.

N.V.: Calories: 320, Fat: 18g, Carbs: 36g, Protein: 9g, Sugar: 2g

RECIPE 3. BEETROOT AND GOAT CHEESE SALAD

PREPARATION TIME: 15 min - **COOKING TIME:** 1 hr (for roasting beets) **MODE OF COOKING:** Roasting & Mixing - **SERVINGS:** 4

INGREDIENTS: 4 medium beets, roasted and sliced; 1/4 cup goat cheese, crumbled; 2 Tbsp. walnuts, toasted and chopped; 2 cups mixed salad greens; For dressing: 2 Tbsp. balsamic vinegar, 1 Tbsp. olive oil, 1 tsp honey, Salt and pepper

DIRECTIONS: Whisk together balsamic vinegar, olive oil, honey, salt, and pepper for dressing. Toss mixed greens in half the dressing and arrange on plates. Top with sliced beets, goat cheese, and walnuts. Drizzle with remaining dressing.

N.V.: Calories: 200, Fat: 12g, Carbs: 16g, Protein: 6g, Sugar: 12g

RECIPE 4. SPICY SOUTHWESTERN SLAW

PREPARATION TIME: 20 min - **COOKING TIME:** 0 min **MODE OF COOKING:** Mixing - **SERVINGS:** 4

INGREDIENTS: 1/2 head cabbage, shredded; 1 carrot, julienned; 1/2 red onion, thinly sliced; 1/2 cup corn kernels; 1/2 cup black beans, rinsed and drained; 1/4 cup cilantro, chopped; For dressing: 2 Tbsp. lime juice, 1 Tbsp. honey, 1 tsp chipotle chili powder, 1/4 cup olive oil, Salt and pepper

DIRECTIONS: In a large bowl, combine cabbage, carrot, red onion, corn, black beans, and cilantro. In a small bowl, whisk together lime juice, honey, chipotle chili powder, olive oil, salt, and pepper. Pour dressing over slaw and toss to combine.

N.V.: Calories: 220, Fat: 14g, Carbs: 24g, Protein: 4g, Sugar: 8g

RECIPE 5. MEDITERRANEAN CHICKPEA SALAD

PREPARATION TIME: 15 min - **COOKING TIME:** 0 min **MODE OF COOKING:** Mixing - **SERVINGS:** 4

INGREDIENTS: 1 can chickpeas, drained and rinsed; 1 cucumber, diced; 1 bell pepper, diced; 1/4 cup red onion, finely chopped; 1/4 cup kalamata olives, sliced; 1/4 cup feta cheese, crumbled; For dressing: 3 Tbsp. olive oil, 1 Tbsp. red wine vinegar, 1 tsp oregano, Salt and pepper

DIRECTIONS: In a large bowl, combine chickpeas, cucumber, bell pepper, red onion, olives, and feta cheese. In a small bowl, whisk together olive oil, red wine vinegar, oregano, salt, and pepper. Pour dressing over salad and toss to combine.

N.V.: Calories: 250, Fat: 15g, Carbs: 22g, Protein: 8g, Sugar: 5g

RECIPE 6. ASIAN SESAME BROCCOLI SALAD

PREPARATION TIME: 15 min - **COOKING TIME:** 0 min **MODE OF COOKING:** Blending & Tossing - **SERVINGS:** 4

INGREDIENTS: 4 cups broccoli florets; 1/4 cup sliced almonds; 1/4 cup dried cranberries; For dressing: 2 Tbsp. soy sauce, 1 Tbsp. sesame oil, 1 Tbsp. honey, 1 tsp grated ginger, 1 Tbsp. rice vinegar, 1 tsp sesame seeds

DIRECTIONS: Steam broccoli until just tender, then cool. Toast almonds. Whisk together soy sauce, sesame oil, honey, ginger, rice vinegar, and sesame seeds for dressing. Toss broccoli with almonds, cranberries, and dressing.

N.V.: Calories: 180, Fat: 9g, Carbs: 23g, Protein: 5g, Sugar: 12g

RECIPE 7. PEAR AND WALNUT ARUGULA SALAD

PREPARATION TIME: 10 min - **COOKING TIME:** 0 min **MODE OF COOKING:** Tossing - **SERVINGS:** 4

INGREDIENTS: 4 cups arugula; 1 pear, thinly sliced; 1/4 cup walnuts, toasted and chopped; 1/4 cup blue cheese, crumbled; For dressing: 2 Tbsp. balsamic vinegar, 1 Tbsp. olive oil, 1 tsp honey, Salt and pepper

DIRECTIONS: In a large bowl, toss arugula with pear slices, walnuts, and blue cheese. In a small bowl, whisk together balsamic vinegar, olive oil, honey, salt, and pepper. Drizzle dressing over

RECIPE 8. POMEGRANATE PEARL COUSCOUS SALAD

PREPARATION TIME: 15 min - **COOKING TIME:** 10 min
MODE OF COOKING: Boiling - **SERVINGS:** 4

INGREDIENTS: 1 cup pearl couscous; 2 cups water; 1 cup pomegranate seeds; 1/2 cup cucumber, diced; 1/2 cup cherry tomatoes, halved; 1/4 cup red onion, finely chopped; 1/4 cup feta cheese, crumbled; 2 Tbsp. fresh mint, chopped; **For the dressing:** 3 Tbsp. olive oil; 1 Tbsp. lemon juice; 1 tsp honey; Salt and pepper to taste

DIRECTIONS: Cook couscous in boiling water until tender, about 10 min. Drain and let cool. In a large bowl, combine couscous with pomegranate seeds, cucumber, cherry tomatoes, red onion, feta cheese, and mint. Whisk together olive oil, lemon juice, honey, salt, and pepper for the dressing. Drizzle over salad, toss to combine.

N.V.: Calories: 280, Fat: 10g, Carbs: 42g, Protein: 8g, Sugar: 8g

RECIPE 9. CRUNCHY ASIAN RAMEN NOODLE SLAW

PREPARATION TIME: 20 min - **COOKING TIME:** 0 min
MODE OF COOKING: No cook - **SERVINGS:** 4

INGREDIENTS: 2 cups shredded cabbage; 1 cup shredded carrots; 1/2 cup green onions, sliced; 1/2 cup cilantro, chopped; 1 cup cooked and cooled ramen noodles, roughly chopped; 1/2 cup toasted almonds, sliced; **For the dressing:** 3 Tbsp. soy sauce; 2 Tbsp. rice vinegar; 1 Tbsp. sesame oil; 2 tsp honey; 1 clove garlic, minced; 1 tsp ginger, grated

DIRECTIONS: In a large bowl, mix cabbage, carrots, green onions, cilantro, ramen noodles, and toasted almonds. For the dressing, whisk together soy sauce, rice vinegar, sesame oil, honey, garlic, and ginger. Pour dressing over the slaw mixture, toss until evenly coated. Serve chilled.

N.V.: Calories: 210, Fat: 12g, Carbs: 22g, Protein: 5g, Sugar: 6g

RECIPE 10. WATERMELON FETA MINT SALAD

PREPARATION TIME: 10 min - **COOKING TIME:** 0 min
MODE OF COOKING: No cook - **SERVINGS:** 4

INGREDIENTS: 4 cups watermelon, cubed; 1/2 cup feta cheese, crumbled; 1/4 cup fresh mint, chopped; **For the dressing:** 2 Tbsp. olive oil; 1 Tbsp. balsamic glaze; Salt and pepper to taste

DIRECTIONS: In a large bowl, combine watermelon cubes with crumbled feta cheese and chopped mint. In a small bowl, whisk together olive oil and balsamic glaze, season with salt and pepper. Drizzle the dressing over the watermelon mixture, gently toss to coat. Serve chilled.

N.V.: Calories: 180, Fat: 9g, Carbs: 22g, Protein: 4g, Sugar: 18g

RECIPE 11. GRILLED ZUCCHINI RIBBON SALAD

PREPARATION TIME: 15 min - **COOKING TIME:** 5 min
MODE OF COOKING: Grilling - **SERVINGS:** 4
INGREDIENTS: 2 large zucchinis, thinly sliced lengthwise; 2 Tbsp. olive oil; Salt and pepper to taste; 1/4 cup pine nuts, toasted; 1/4 cup Parmesan cheese, shaved; **For the dressing:** 3 Tbsp. lemon juice; 1 Tbsp. olive oil; 1 tsp Dijon mustard; 1 clove garlic, minced
DIRECTIONS: Preheat grill to medium-high heat. Brush zucchini ribbons with olive oil, season with salt and pepper. Grill until tender and slightly charred, about 2-3 min per side. Whisk together lemon juice, olive oil, Dijon mustard, and garlic for the dressing. Arrange zucchini on a platter, sprinkle with pine nuts and Parmesan cheese, drizzle with dressing.
N.V.: Calories: 190, Fat: 15g, Carbs: 8g, Protein: 5g, Sugar: 4g

CHAPTER 11: CELEBRATING BEEF

In the realm of culinary arts, beef stands as a testament to the rich tapestry of flavors and textures that chefs and home cooks alike have celebrated through generations. Chapter 11 delves into the heart of beef's culinary significance, exploring the myriad ways this versatile ingredient can transform a meal from the ordinary to the extraordinary. Here, we journey through the lush pastures of tradition to the cutting-edge techniques that redefine what beef can be on our plates. This chapter is not merely a collection of recipes; it's an homage to the robust, earthy flavors of beef that have been the cornerstone of memorable meals around the globe. From the rustic charm of a perfectly seared steak to the complex layers of flavors in a slow-cooked beef stew, we explore the spectrum of dishes that celebrate beef in all its glory.

We pay tribute to the classics, dishes that have stood the test of time and continue to evoke nostalgia and comfort with every bite. Yet, we also venture into contemporary interpretations, where innovation and tradition collide to create new classics. Whether it's the art of choosing the right cut, mastering the perfect cooking method, or pairing flavors that enhance the natural richness of beef, this chapter is your guide to celebrating beef in your culinary creations.

Join us as we embark on this flavorful journey, where every recipe is a celebration of beef's enduring legacy and its endless potential to delight our senses.

MASTERING STEAKS AND RIBS

RECIPE 1. RUSTIC HERB CRUSTED RIB EYE

PREPARATION TIME: 20 min - **COOKING TIME:** 40 min
MODE OF COOKING: Grilling - **SERVINGS:** 4
INGREDIENTS: 2 lb. rib eye steaks (about 2 inches thick); 2 Tbsp. olive oil; 1 Tbsp. coarse sea salt; 2 tsp cracked black pepper; 1 Tbsp. fresh rosemary, finely chopped; 1 Tbsp. fresh thyme, finely chopped; 4 cloves garlic, minced.
DIRECTIONS: Preheat your Pit Boss grill to 450°F (232°C). Rub steaks with olive oil, then season with salt, pepper, rosemary, thyme, and garlic. Let rest for 15 minutes. Grill steaks for 20 minutes per side for medium-rare, or until desired doneness. Rest for 10 minutes before slicing.
N.V.: Calories: 540, Fat: 38g, Carbs: 1g, Protein: 48g, Sugar: 0g

RECIPE 2. SMOKEY BOURBON BBQ RIBS

PREPARATION TIME: 15 min - **COOKING TIME:** 4 hr
MODE OF COOKING: Smoking - **SERVINGS:** 6
INGREDIENTS: 3 lb. baby back ribs; 1 cup bourbon; 1 cup BBQ sauce; 2 Tbsp. brown sugar; 1 Tbsp. smoked paprika; 1 tsp garlic powder; 1 tsp onion powder; Salt and pepper to taste.

DIRECTIONS: Remove the membrane from ribs. Mix bourbon, BBQ sauce, brown sugar, paprika, garlic and onion powder, salt, and pepper. Marinate ribs for at least 2 hours. Preheat your Pit Boss to 225°F (107°C). Smoke ribs, covered, for 4 hours, basting with the marinade every hour.
N.V.: Calories: 580, Fat: 35g, Carbs: 15g, Protein: 40g, Sugar: 12g

RECIPE 3. CHARRED CHIMICHURRI STEAK SKEWERS

PREPARATION TIME: 25 min - **COOKING TIME:** 10 min
MODE OF COOKING: Grilling - **SERVINGS:** 4
INGREDIENTS: 2 lb. sirloin steak, cut into 1-inch cubes; 1 cup fresh parsley; 1/2 cup olive oil; 1/4 cup red wine vinegar; 3 cloves garlic; 1 tsp red pepper flakes; Salt and pepper to taste.
DIRECTIONS: Puree parsley, olive oil, vinegar, garlic, red pepper flakes, salt, and pepper to make chimichurri. Marinate steak cubes in half the chimichurri for 1 hour. Thread steak onto skewers. Grill over high heat for 5 minutes per side. Serve with remaining chimichurri.
N.V.: Calories: 498, Fat: 34g, Carbs: 3g, Protein: 44g, Sugar: 1g

RECIPE 4. PEPPER CRUSTED T-BONE WITH GARLIC HERB BUTTER

PREPARATION TIME: 15 min - **COOKING TIME:** 15 min
MODE OF COOKING: Grilling - **SERVINGS:** 2
INGREDIENTS: 2 T-bone steaks; 2 Tbsp. coarse black pepper; 2 Tbsp. Sea salt; 4 Tbsp. unsalted butter, softened; 1 Tbsp. chopped parsley; 2 cloves garlic, minced.
DIRECTIONS: Preheat grill to 450°F (232°C). Season steaks with salt and press in black pepper. Grill for 7 minutes per side for medium-rare. Mix butter, parsley, and garlic. Top steaks with garlic herb butter before serving.
N.V.: Calories: 720, Fat: 60g, Carbs: 1g, Protein: 48g, Sugar: 0g

RECIPE 5. SWEET AND SPICY ASIAN BEEF SHORT RIBS

PREPARATION TIME: 20 min - **COOKING TIME:** 3 hr
MODE OF COOKING: Smoking - **SERVINGS:** 4
INGREDIENTS: 2 lb. beef short ribs; 1/2 cup soy sauce; 1/4 cup honey; 2 Tbsp. rice vinegar; 1 Tbsp. sesame oil; 1 Tbsp. ginger, minced; 3 cloves garlic, minced; 1 tsp red pepper flakes.
DIRECTIONS: Whisk together soy sauce, honey, vinegar, sesame oil, ginger, garlic, and red pepper flakes. Marinate ribs for 4 hours. Preheat your Pit Boss to 275°F (135°C). Smoke ribs for 3 hours, basting with marinade occasionally.
N.V.: Calories: 622, Fat: 48g, Carbs: 22g, Protein: 30g, Sugar: 18g

RECIPE 6. GARLIC LOVER'S GRILLED FLANK STEAK

PREPARATION TIME: 10 min - **COOKING TIME:** 10 min
MODE OF COOKING: Grilling - **SERVINGS:** 4
INGREDIENTS: 1.5 lb. flank steak; 1/4 cup olive oil; 8 cloves garlic, minced; 2 Tbsp. balsamic vinegar; 1 tsp honey; Salt and pepper to taste.
DIRECTIONS: Whisk together olive oil, garlic, vinegar, honey, salt, and pepper. Marinate steak for 30 minutes. Preheat grill to high. Grill steak for 5 minutes per side. Let rest, then slice against the grain.
N.V.: Calories: 375, Fat: 25g, Carbs: 5g, Protein: 32g, Sugar: 3g

RECIPE 7. BALSAMIC GLAZED BEEF RIBS

PREPARATION TIME: 15 min - **COOKING TIME:** 4 hr
MODE OF COOKING: Smoking - **SERVINGS:** 4

INGREDIENTS: 4 lb. beef ribs; 1 cup balsamic vinegar; 1/2 cup brown sugar; 2 Tbsp. Worcestershire sauce; 1 Tbsp. garlic powder; 1 tsp black pepper; Salt to taste.
DIRECTIONS: Mix balsamic vinegar, brown sugar, Worcestershire sauce, garlic powder, pepper, and salt. Brush ribs with half the glaze. Smoke at 225°F (107°C) for 4 hours, applying remaining glaze in the last hour.
N.V.: Calories: 650, Fat: 42g, Carbs: 22g, Protein: 52g, Sugar: 20g

RECIPE 8. HERB-CRUSTED RIB-EYE STEAK

PREPARATION TIME: 10 min - **COOKING TIME:** 6 min
MODE OF COOKING: Grilling - **SERVINGS:** 4
INGREDIENTS: 4 rib-eye steaks, 1-inch thick; 2 Tbsp. olive oil; 1 Tbsp. fresh rosemary, minced; 1 Tbsp. fresh thyme, minced; 2 cloves garlic, minced; Salt and pepper to taste
DIRECTIONS: Preheat grill to high heat. Rub each steak with olive oil. Combine rosemary, thyme, garlic, salt, and pepper in a bowl. Press herb mixture onto both sides of the steaks. Grill steaks for 3 min per side for medium-rare. Let rest for 5 min before serving.
N.V.: Calories: 480, Fat: 34g, Carbs: 1g, Protein: 46g, Sugar: 0g

RECIPE 9. SMOKEY BBQ BEEF RIBS

PREPARATION TIME: 15 min - **COOKING TIME:** 3 hr
MODE OF COOKING: Smoking - **SERVINGS:** 4
INGREDIENTS: 2 lb beef ribs; 1/4 cup BBQ rub; 1/2 cup BBQ sauce; 2 Tbsp. apple cider vinegar; 2 Tbsp. brown sugar; 1 tsp smoked paprika; 1/2 tsp garlic powder; 1/2 tsp onion powder
DIRECTIONS: Preheat smoker to 225°F (107°C). Mix BBQ rub, smoked paprika, garlic powder, and onion powder. Rub mixture onto ribs. Combine BBQ sauce, apple cider vinegar, and brown sugar for basting. Smoke ribs for 3 hr, basting every hour. Serve with remaining BBQ sauce.
N.V.: Calories: 560, Fat: 42g, Carbs: 18g, Protein: 34g, Sugar: 15g

RECIPE 10. GARLIC BUTTER FILET MIGNON

PREPARATION TIME: 10 min - **COOKING TIME:** 12 min
MODE OF COOKING: Pan-searing - **SERVINGS:** 4
INGREDIENTS: 4 filet mignon steaks, 1.5 inches thick; 2 Tbsp. unsalted butter; 4 cloves garlic, minced; 1 Tbsp. olive oil; Salt and pepper to taste; Fresh parsley, chopped for garnish
DIRECTIONS: Season steaks with salt and pepper. Heat olive oil in a skillet over medium-high heat. Sear steaks for 4-5 min per side for medium-rare. Reduce heat to low, add butter and garlic to the pan. Baste steaks with garlic butter for 2 min. Garnish with parsley before serving.
N.V.: Calories: 410, Fat: 28g, Carbs: 1g, Protein: 38g, Sugar: 0g

RECIPE 11. BALSAMIC GLAZED FLANK STEAK

PREPARATION TIME: 20 min (includes marinating) - **COOKING TIME:** 10 min
MODE OF COOKING: Grilling - **SERVINGS:** 4
INGREDIENTS: 1.5 lb flank steak; 1/2 cup balsamic vinegar; 1/4 cup soy sauce; 2 Tbsp. honey; 3 cloves garlic, minced; 1 Tbsp. olive oil; 1 tsp rosemary, chopped; Salt and pepper to taste
DIRECTIONS: Whisk together balsamic vinegar, soy sauce, honey, garlic, and rosemary for marinade. Marinate steak for at least 15 min. Preheat grill to medium-high heat. Remove steak from marinade, season with salt and pepper. Grill for 5 min per side for medium-rare. Let rest, then slice against the grain.
N.V.: Calories: 320, Fat: 14g, Carbs: 12g, Protein: 36g, Sugar: 10g

BEEF SKEWERS AND MORE

RECIPE 1. MEDITERRANEAN BEEF KEBABS

PREPARATION TIME: 30 min - **COOKING TIME:** 10 min
MODE OF COOKING: Grilling - **SERVINGS:** 4
INGREDIENTS: 2 lb. beef sirloin, cut into 1-inch cubes; 2 Tbsp. olive oil; 1 Tbsp. lemon juice; 2 cloves garlic, minced; 1 tsp dried oregano; 1 tsp cumin; 1/2 tsp salt; 1/4 tsp black pepper; 1 bell pepper, cut into 1-inch pieces; 1 red onion, cut into 1-inch pieces.
DIRECTIONS: In a bowl, combine olive oil, lemon juice, garlic, oregano, cumin, salt, and pepper. Add beef and marinate for at least 20 min. Thread beef, bell pepper, and onion alternately onto skewers. Preheat grill to medium-high heat. Grill kebabs, turning occasionally, until beef is cooked to desired doneness, about 10 min.
N.V.: Calories: 380, Fat: 18g, Carbs: 5g, Protein: 48g, Sugar: 2g

RECIPE 2. ASIAN-INSPIRED BEEF SATAY

PREPARATION TIME: 40 min - **COOKING TIME:** 10 min
MODE OF COOKING: Grilling - **SERVINGS:** 4
INGREDIENTS: 1.5 lb. flank steak, thinly sliced; 1/4 cup soy sauce; 2 Tbsp. honey; 1 Tbsp. lime juice; 1 Tbsp. ginger, grated; 2 cloves garlic, minced; 1 tsp sesame oil; 1 tsp crushed red pepper flakes; Peanut sauce for serving.
DIRECTIONS: Whisk together soy sauce, honey, lime juice, ginger, garlic, sesame oil, and red pepper flakes. Marinate the steak slices for at least 30 min. Thread the marinated steak onto skewers. Preheat grill to high. Grill satay, turning once, until slightly charred and cooked through, about 5 min per side. Serve with peanut sauce.
N.V.: Calories: 295, Fat: 13g, Carbs: 12g, Protein: 34g, Sugar: 9g

RECIPE 3. TEX-MEX BEEF SKEWERS

PREPARATION TIME: 20 min - **COOKING TIME:** 8 min
MODE OF COOKING: Grilling - **SERVINGS:** 4
INGREDIENTS: 2 lb. chuck steak, cut into 1-inch cubes; 1 Tbsp. chili powder; 2 tsp cumin; 1 tsp smoked paprika; 1/2 tsp garlic powder; 1/2 tsp onion powder; Salt and pepper to taste; 1 lime, juiced; 2 Tbsp. olive oil; 1 large bell pepper, diced; 1 large onion, diced.
DIRECTIONS: In a bowl, mix chili powder, cumin, paprika, garlic powder, onion powder, salt, and pepper. Add lime juice and olive oil to create a marinade. Toss beef cubes in the marinade and let sit for 15 min. Thread beef, bell pepper, and onion onto skewers. Grill over medium-high heat, turning occasionally, until beef is browned and vegetables are tender, about 8 min.
N.V.: Calories: 430, Fat: 27g, Carbs: 6g, Protein: 44g, Sugar: 2g

RECIPE 4. BALSAMIC GLAZED STEAK ROLLS

PREPARATION TIME: 25 min - **COOKING TIME:** 10 min
MODE OF COOKING: Grilling - **SERVINGS:** 4
INGREDIENTS: 1.5 lb. flank steak, thinly sliced; Salt and pepper to taste; 1/4 cup balsamic vinegar; 2 Tbsp. brown sugar; 1 Tbsp. olive oil; 1 bell pepper, thinly sliced; 1 zucchini, thinly sliced; 1 small red onion, thinly sliced.
DIRECTIONS: Season steak slices with salt and pepper. Simmer balsamic vinegar and brown sugar in a saucepan over medium heat until reduced by half. Brush steak slices with balsamic

glaze, then top with bell pepper, zucchini, and onion slices. Roll up and secure with a toothpick. Grill rolls over medium-high heat, turning occasionally, until browned outside and cooked to desired doneness, about 10 min. Drizzle with remaining glaze before serving.
N.V.: Calories: 310, Fat: 14g, Carbs: 15g, Protein: 34g, Sugar: 12g

RECIPE 5. HERB MARINATED BEEF KABOBS

PREPARATION TIME: 30 min - **COOKING TIME:** 15 min
MODE OF COOKING: Grilling - **SERVINGS:** 4
INGREDIENTS: 2 lb. top sirloin, cut into 1-inch cubes; 1/4 cup olive oil; 3 Tbsp. lemon juice; 2 Tbsp. fresh parsley, chopped; 1 Tbsp. fresh rosemary, chopped; 2 cloves garlic, minced; Salt and pepper to taste; 2 bell peppers, cut into 1-inch pieces; 1 large red onion, cut into 1-inch pieces.
DIRECTIONS: Whisk together olive oil, lemon juice, parsley, rosemary, garlic, salt, and pepper. Marinate beef cubes for at least 20 min. Thread beef, bell peppers, and onion alternately onto skewers. Grill over medium-high heat, turning occasionally, until beef is cooked to desired doneness and vegetables are tender, about 15 min.
N.V.: Calories: 410, Fat: 24g, Carbs: 9g, Protein: 44g, Sugar: 5g

RECIPE 6. SPICY CAJUN BEEF STICKS

PREPARATION TIME: 15 min - **COOKING TIME:** 10 min
MODE OF COOKING: Grilling - **SERVINGS:** 4
INGREDIENTS: 2 lb. round steak, cut into 1/2-inch strips; 2 Tbsp. Cajun seasoning; 1 Tbsp. olive oil; 1 tsp hot sauce; Salt to taste.
DIRECTIONS: In a bowl, combine Cajun seasoning, olive oil, hot sauce, and salt. Add beef strips and toss to coat evenly. Thread the beef onto skewers. Preheat grill to high. Grill skewers, turning occasionally, until charred and cooked through, about 10 min.
N.V.: Calories: 300, Fat: 15g, Carbs: 1g, Protein: 38g, Sugar: 0g

RECIPE 7. GREEK-STYLE BEEF SKEWERS

PREPARATION TIME: 25 min - **COOKING TIME:** 10 min
MODE OF COOKING: Grilling - **SERVINGS:** 4
INGREDIENTS: 2 lb. beef tenderloin, cut into 1-inch cubes; 1/4 cup olive oil; 2 Tbsp. lemon juice; 1 Tbsp. fresh oregano, chopped; 3 cloves garlic, minced; 1 tsp salt; 1/2 tsp black pepper; 1 large red onion, cut into 1-inch pieces; 1 cup cherry tomatoes.
DIRECTIONS: In a bowl, whisk together olive oil, lemon juice, oregano, garlic, salt, and pepper. Marinate beef cubes for at least 30 min. Thread beef, onion, and cherry tomatoes alternately onto skewers. Preheat grill to medium-high. Grill skewers, turning occasionally, until beef is cooked to desired doneness, about 10 min.
N.V.: Calories: 390, Fat: 22g, Carbs: 6g, Protein: 42g, Sugar: 3g

RECIPE 8. ASIAN-STYLE BEEF SKEWERS

PREPARATION TIME: 30 min (includes marinating) - **COOKING TIME:** 10 min
MODE OF COOKING: Grilling - **SERVINGS:** 4
INGREDIENTS: 1 lb sirloin beef, cut into 1-inch cubes; 1/4 cup soy sauce; 2 Tbsp. brown sugar; 1 Tbsp. sesame oil; 2 cloves garlic, minced; 1 tsp ginger, minced; 1 tsp chili flakes; 8 skewers, soaked in water

DIRECTIONS: Whisk together soy sauce, brown sugar, sesame oil, garlic, ginger, and chili flakes in a bowl. Add beef cubes, marinate for at least 20 min. Thread beef onto skewers. Preheat grill to medium-high heat. Grill skewers, turning occasionally, until charred and cooked to desired doneness, about 8-10 min.

N.V.: Calories: 280, Fat: 14g, Carbs: 10g, Protein: 28g, Sugar: 6g

RECIPE 9. ARGENTINIAN CHIMICHURRI BEEF SKEWERS

PREPARATION TIME: 15 min (plus marinating) - **COOKING TIME:** 10 min
MODE OF COOKING: Grilling - **SERVINGS:** 4
INGREDIENTS: 1 lb beef sirloin, cut into 1-inch cubes; **For the chimichurri:** 1/2 cup parsley, finely chopped; 1/2 cup cilantro, finely chopped; 1/4 cup olive oil; 3 Tbsp. red wine vinegar; 2 cloves garlic, minced; 1 tsp red chili flakes; Salt and pepper to taste; 8 skewers, soaked in water
DIRECTIONS: For the chimichurri, mix parsley, cilantro, olive oil, vinegar, garlic, chili flakes, salt, and pepper in a bowl. Reserve half for serving. Marinate beef cubes in the remaining chimichurri for at least 30 min. Thread beef onto skewers. Grill over medium-high heat, turning occasionally, until charred and cooked to desired doneness, about 8-10 min. Serve with reserved chimichurri.

N.V.: Calories: 290, Fat: 20g, Carbs: 2g, Protein: 24g, Sugar: 0g

INNOVATIVE BEEF DISHES

RECIPE 1. BEEF AND QUINOA STUFFED BELL PEPPERS

PREPARATION TIME: 20 min - **COOKING TIME:** 35 min
MODE OF COOKING: Baking - **SERVINGS:** 4
INGREDIENTS: 4 large bell peppers, halved and seeded; 1 lb. ground beef; 1 cup quinoa, cooked; 1 can (14.5 oz) diced tomatoes, drained; 1 onion, diced; 2 cloves garlic, minced; 1 tsp cumin; 1 tsp smoked paprika; Salt and pepper to taste; 1 cup shredded cheddar cheese.
DIRECTIONS: Preheat oven to 375°F (190°C). In a skillet, cook ground beef, onion, and garlic until beef is browned. Drain excess fat. Stir in cooked quinoa, diced tomatoes, cumin, smoked paprika, salt, and pepper. Fill bell pepper halves with beef mixture. Place in a baking dish and cover with foil. Bake for 25 min. Uncover, top with cheese, and bake for another 10 min.
N.V.: Calories: 450, Fat: 22g, Carbs: 35g, Protein: 28g, Sugar: 8g

RECIPE 2. SLOW-COOKED BEEF RAGU OVER POLENTA

PREPARATION TIME: 15 min - **COOKING TIME:** 6 hr
MODE OF COOKING: Slow Cooking - **SERVINGS:** 6
INGREDIENTS: 2 lb. beef chuck roast; 1 can (28 oz) crushed tomatoes; 1 carrot, diced; 1 celery stalk, diced; 1 onion, diced; 3 cloves garlic, minced; 1 tsp rosemary, chopped; 1 tsp thyme, chopped; Salt and pepper to taste; 3 cups water; 1 cup polenta; 1/4 cup Parmesan cheese, grated.
DIRECTIONS: Place beef, tomatoes, carrot, celery, onion, garlic, rosemary, thyme, salt, and pepper in a slow cooker. Cook on low for 6 hr. Shred beef with forks. Bring water to a boil, gradually whisk in polenta, reduce heat to low, and cook until thickened, stirring frequently. Serve ragu over polenta, topped with Parmesan.
N.V.: Calories: 510, Fat: 25g, Carbs: 40g, Protein: 35g, Sugar: 8g

RECIPE 3. BEEF BRISKET PHO

PREPARATION TIME: 30 min - **COOKING TIME:** 8 hr
MODE OF COOKING: Slow Cooking - **SERVINGS:** 8
INGREDIENTS: 2 lb. beef brisket; 1 onion, charred; 4 cloves garlic, charred; 1 ginger piece, charred; 4-star anise; 2 cinnamon sticks; 4 cloves; 8 cups beef broth; 1 Tbsp. fish sauce; Salt to taste; Rice noodles, cooked; Toppings: bean sprouts, basil, lime wedges, sliced jalapenos, hoisin sauce, sriracha.
DIRECTIONS: In a slow cooker, combine brisket, charred onion, garlic, ginger, star anise, cinnamon, cloves, beef broth, fish sauce, and salt. Cook on low for 8 hr. Slice brisket. Strain broth, return to pot, and heat. Place noodles in bowls, top with brisket slices, pour hot broth over, and serve with toppings.
N.V.: Calories: 340, Fat: 11g, Carbs: 30g, Protein: 32g, Sugar: 3g

RECIPE 4. BEEF STUFFED ACORN SQUASH

PREPARATION TIME: 20 min - **COOKING TIME:** 1 hr
MODE OF COOKING: Baking/Roasting - **SERVINGS:** 4

INGREDIENTS: 2 acorn squash, halved and seeded; 1 lb. ground beef; 1 apple, diced; 1 onion, diced; 1/2 cup walnuts, chopped; 1/2 tsp cinnamon; 1/4 tsp nutmeg; Salt and pepper to taste; 2 Tbsp. maple syrup.

DIRECTIONS: Preheat oven to 400°F (204°C). Place squash halves cut-side down on a baking sheet. Bake for 30 min. Meanwhile, cook beef, apple, onion, walnuts, cinnamon, nutmeg, salt, and pepper in a skillet. Fill roasted squash halves with beef mixture, drizzle with maple syrup, and bake for another 30 min.

N.V.: Calories: 485, Fat: 27g, Carbs: 45g, Protein: 24g, Sugar: 18g

RECIPE 5. BEEF AND SWEET POTATO CURRY

PREPARATION TIME: 20 min - **COOKING TIME:** 40 min
MODE OF COOKING: Simmering - **SERVINGS:** 6
INGREDIENTS: 2 lb. stew beef, cubed; 1 large sweet potato, cubed; 1 onion, diced; 2 cloves garlic, minced; 1 Tbsp. ginger, minced; 1 can (14 oz) coconut milk; 2 Tbsp. curry powder; 1 tsp turmeric; 1/2 tsp cayenne pepper; Salt to taste; 2 cups spinach; 1 Tbsp. lime juice.

DIRECTIONS: In a large pot, sauté onion, garlic, and ginger. Add beef and brown. Stir in sweet potato, coconut milk, curry powder, turmeric, cayenne, and salt. Simmer until beef and sweet potato are tender, about 40 min. Stir in spinach until wilted. Finish with lime juice.

N.V.: Calories: 420, Fat: 22g, Carbs: 22g, Protein: 36g, Sugar: 5g

RECIPE 6. KOREAN BEEF BOWL WITH KIMCHI

PREPARATION TIME: 15 min - **COOKING TIME:** 20 min
MODE OF COOKING: Sautéing - **SERVINGS:** 4
INGREDIENTS: 1 lb. ground beef; 1/4 cup soy sauce; 2 Tbsp. brown sugar; 1 Tbsp. sesame oil; 2 cloves garlic, minced; 1 tsp ginger, minced; 1/4 tsp crushed red pepper flakes; 2 cups cooked rice; 1 cup kimchi; 4 green onions, sliced; Sesame seeds for garnish.

DIRECTIONS: In a skillet, brown ground beef. Drain excess fat. Stir in soy sauce, brown sugar, sesame oil, garlic, ginger, and red pepper flakes. Cook for 5 min. Serve beef over rice, topped with kimchi, green onions, and sesame seeds.

N.V.: Calories: 460, Fat: 24g, Carbs: 35g, Protein: 28g, Sugar: 9g

RECIPE 7. ARGENTINIAN BEEF EMPANADAS

PREPARATION TIME: 30 min - **COOKING TIME:** 25 min
MODE OF COOKING: Baking - **SERVINGS:** 12 empanadas
INGREDIENTS: 1 lb. ground beef; 1 onion, finely chopped; 1 red bell pepper, finely chopped; 2 cloves garlic, minced; 1 tsp cumin; 1/2 tsp paprika; Salt and pepper to taste; 1/2 cup green olives, chopped; 1/4 cup raisins; 2 hard-boiled eggs, chopped; 1 package empanada dough rounds; 1 egg, beaten for egg wash.

DIRECTIONS: Preheat oven to 375°F (190°C). In a skillet, cook beef, onion, bell pepper, and garlic. Season with cumin, paprika, salt, and pepper. Stir in olives, raisins, and eggs. Spoon mixture onto empanada dough, fold, and seal edges. Brush with egg wash. Bake for 25 min.

N.V.: Calories: 250, Fat: 15g, Carbs: 15g, Protein: 12g, Sugar: 2g

RECIPE 8. BEEF AND MUSHROOM BOURGUIGNON

PREPARATION TIME: 15 min - **COOKING TIME:** 1 hr 30 min
MODE OF COOKING: Simmering - **SERVINGS:** 4

INGREDIENTS: 2 lbs beef chuck, cut into cubes; 3 Tbsp. flour; 2 Tbsp. olive oil; 1 onion, chopped; 2 carrots, sliced; 2 cloves garlic, minced; 1 lb mushrooms, quartered; 2 cups red wine; 2 cups beef broth; 2 Tbsp. tomato paste; 1 tsp thyme; Salt and pepper to taste
DIRECTIONS: Dredge beef in flour. Heat olive oil in a large pot, brown beef on all sides. Remove beef, add onion, carrots, and garlic to the pot, cook until softened. Add mushrooms, cook for 5 min. Return beef to the pot, add red wine, beef broth, tomato paste, and thyme. Bring to a boil, then simmer covered for 1.5 hr until beef is tender. Season with salt and pepper.
N.V.: Calories: 560, Fat: 22g, Carbs: 24g, Protein: 48g, Sugar: 6g

RECIPE 9. SPICY BEEF LETTUCE WRAPS

PREPARATION TIME: 15 min - **COOKING TIME:** 10 min
MODE OF COOKING: Sautéing - **SERVINGS:** 4
INGREDIENTS: 1 lb ground beef; 1 Tbsp. sesame oil; 2 cloves garlic, minced; 1 Tbsp. ginger, minced; 1/4 cup soy sauce; 1 Tbsp. hoisin sauce; 1 tsp chili sauce; 1 cup water chestnuts, diced; 4 green onions, sliced; 1 head iceberg lettuce, separated into leaves
DIRECTIONS: Heat sesame oil in a skillet over medium heat. Add garlic and ginger, sauté for 1 min. Add ground beef, cook until browned. Stir in soy sauce, hoisin sauce, chili sauce, and cook for 3 min. Add water chestnuts and green onions, cook for 2 more min. Serve beef mixture in lettuce leaves.
N.V.: Calories: 310, Fat: 18g, Carbs: 12g, Protein: 26g, Sugar: 4g

RECIPE 10. BEEF STROGANOFF WITH SPIRALIZED ZUCCHINI

PREPARATION TIME: 15 min - **COOKING TIME:** 20 min
MODE OF COOKING: Sautéing - **SERVINGS:** 4
INGREDIENTS: 1 lb sirloin steak, thinly sliced; 2 Tbsp. butter; 1 onion, thinly sliced; 2 cloves garlic, minced; 8 oz mushrooms, sliced; 1 cup beef broth; 1/2 cup sour cream; 2 Tbsp. Dijon mustard; 4 zucchinis, spiralized; Salt and pepper to taste; Fresh parsley, chopped for garnish
DIRECTIONS: Melt butter in a large skillet over medium-high heat. Add sirloin steak, cook until browned. Remove steak, add onion, garlic, mushrooms, cook until soft. Stir in beef broth, bring to a simmer. Reduce heat, stir in sour cream, Dijon mustard, and return beef to the skillet. Cook for 5 min. Season spiralized zucchini with salt, serve beef stroganoff over zucchini. Garnish with parsley.
N.V.: Calories: 400, Fat: 24g, Carbs: 14g, Protein: 34g, Sugar: 8g

CHAPTER 12: EXPLORING PORK AND LAMB

As we turn the page to Chapter 12: Exploring Pork and Lamb, we delve into the rich and varied universe of these two versatile meats. Pork and lamb, each with its distinct taste and texture, offer an array of culinary possibilities that extend far beyond the traditional cuts and preparations. This chapter is a journey through the myriad ways to bring out the best in pork and lamb, from the tenderness of a slow-roasted leg of lamb to the crisp, flavorful exterior of perfectly grilled pork chops.

Pork, often celebrated as the "other white meat," presents a canvas for a spectrum of flavors, influenced by its fat content and tenderness. We'll explore how different cuts of pork can be transformed with the right techniques and flavors, embodying the essence of global cuisines. From succulent pulled pork that melts in your mouth to spicy, charred skewers that tantalize the taste buds, pork's versatility will be showcased in all its glory.

Lamb, with its distinctive rich flavor, is a meat that demands respect and a careful approach to highlight its unique qualities. Whether you're preparing a rack of lamb as the centerpiece of a special meal or incorporating ground lamb into casual, spicy kebabs, this section will guide you through enhancing lamb's natural flavors while introducing complementary herbs and spices.

In this chapter, we aim not only to educate but also to inspire you to embrace the diversity of pork and lamb dishes. Through understanding the nuances of each meat, from marbling to muscle structure, you'll be equipped to select the perfect cut for your next culinary adventure, ensuring every meal is not just cooked but crafted with passion and precision.

FLAVORFUL PORK PREPARATIONS

RECIPE 1. HONEY GLAZED PORK TENDERLOIN

PREPARATION TIME: 15 min - **COOKING TIME:** 30 min
MODE OF COOKING: Roasting - **SERVINGS:** 4
INGREDIENTS: 1.5 lb. pork tenderloin; 1/4 cup honey; 2 Tbsp. soy sauce; 1 Tbsp. olive oil; 2 cloves garlic, minced; 1 tsp rosemary, chopped; Salt and pepper to taste.
DIRECTIONS: Preheat oven to 375°F (190°C). In a bowl, mix honey, soy sauce, olive oil, garlic, rosemary, salt, and pepper. Place pork in a roasting pan and brush with the glaze. Roast for 25-30 min, basting occasionally, until the internal temperature reaches 145°F (63°C). Let rest before slicing.
N.V.: Calories: 310, Fat: 8g, Carbs: 18g, Protein: 40g, Sugar: 17g

RECIPE 2. SPICY PORK BELLY TACOS

PREPARATION TIME: 20 min - **COOKING TIME:** 3 hr
MODE OF COOKING: Braising - **SERVINGS:** 6
INGREDIENTS: 2 lb. pork belly, sliced; 1/4 cup apple cider vinegar; 2 Tbsp. brown sugar; 1 Tbsp. chili powder; 1 tsp cumin; 1/2 tsp smoked paprika; Salt and pepper to taste; Corn tortillas; Toppings: diced onions, cilantro, lime wedges.

DIRECTIONS: Preheat oven to 300°F (150°C). Combine vinegar, brown sugar, chili powder, cumin, paprika, salt, and pepper. Toss pork belly slices in the mixture. Place in a baking dish, cover with foil, and braise for 3 hr until tender. Shred pork, serve on tortillas with toppings.
N.V.: Calories: 580, Fat: 44g, Carbs: 20g, Protein: 24g, Sugar: 6g

RECIPE 3. HERB CRUSTED PORK CHOPS

PREPARATION TIME: 10 min - **COOKING TIME:** 15 min
MODE OF COOKING: Grilling - **SERVINGS:** 4
INGREDIENTS: 4 pork chops; 1/4 cup breadcrumbs; 2 Tbsp. grated Parmesan cheese; 1 Tbsp. fresh thyme, chopped; 1 Tbsp. fresh rosemary, chopped; 1 clove garlic, minced; Salt and pepper to taste; 2 Tbsp. olive oil.
DIRECTIONS: Preheat grill to medium-high. Mix breadcrumbs, Parmesan, thyme, rosemary, garlic, salt, and pepper. Brush pork chops with olive oil, coat with breadcrumb mixture. Grill for 7-8 min per side, or until cooked through.
N.V.: Calories: 370, Fat: 18g, Carbs: 9g, Protein: 42g, Sugar: 1g

RECIPE 4. PORK LOIN WITH APPLE CIDER GLAZE

PREPARATION TIME: 20 min - **COOKING TIME:** 1 hr
MODE OF COOKING: Roasting - **SERVINGS:** 6
INGREDIENTS: 3 lb. pork loin; 1 cup apple cider; 2 Tbsp. honey; 1 tsp cinnamon; 1/2 tsp ground ginger; Salt and pepper to taste; 2 apples, sliced.
DIRECTIONS: Preheat oven to 350°F (175°C). Season pork with salt and pepper. Roast for 40 min. Simmer apple cider, honey, cinnamon, and ginger in a saucepan until reduced by half. Baste pork with glaze, add apple slices around the pork, and roast for another 20 min.
N.V.: Calories: 350, Fat: 10g, Carbs: 18g, Protein: 48g, Sugar: 16g

RECIPE 5. SMOKED PORK SHOULDER WITH BBQ RUB

PREPARATION TIME: 30 min - **COOKING TIME:** 8 hr
MODE OF COOKING: Smoking - **SERVINGS:** 8
INGREDIENTS: 5 lb. pork shoulder; 1/4 cup paprika; 1 Tbsp. brown sugar; 1 Tbsp. salt; 1 Tbsp. ground black pepper; 1 tsp garlic powder; 1 tsp onion powder; 1 tsp cayenne pepper.
DIRECTIONS: Mix paprika, brown sugar, salt, pepper, garlic powder, onion powder, and cayenne. Rub mixture all over the pork shoulder. Preheat smoker to 225°F (107°C). Smoke pork for 8 hr, or until internal temperature reaches 195°F (90°C). Rest before shredding.
N.V.: Calories: 510, Fat: 35g, Carbs: 2g, Protein: 48g, Sugar: 1g

RECIPE 6. PORK AND PINEAPPLE KEBABS

PREPARATION TIME: 20 min - **COOKING TIME:** 10 min
MODE OF COOKING: Grilling - **SERVINGS:** 4
INGREDIENTS: 2 lb. pork tenderloin, cubed; 1 pineapple, cubed; 1/4 cup soy sauce; 2 Tbsp. honey; 1 Tbsp. lime juice; 1 tsp garlic, minced; 1 tsp ginger, minced; Salt and pepper to taste.
DIRECTIONS: Whisk together soy sauce, honey, lime juice, garlic, ginger, salt, and pepper. Marinate pork and pineapple cubes for at least 1 hr. Thread pork and pineapple onto skewers. Grill over medium-high heat, turning occasionally, until pork is cooked through, about 10 min.
N.V.: Calories: 390, Fat: 8g, Carbs: 30g, Protein: 48g, Sugar: 24g

Recipe 7. Slow Cooker Pork Ragout

PREPARATION TIME: 15 min - **COOKING TIME:** 6 hr
MODE OF COOKING: Slow Cooking - **SERVINGS:** 6
INGREDIENTS: 2 lb. pork stew meat; 1 can (28 oz) crushed tomatoes; 1 onion, chopped; 2 carrots, chopped; 2 celery stalks, chopped; 2 cloves garlic, minced; 1 tsp rosemary, minced; 1 tsp thyme, minced; Salt and pepper to taste.
DIRECTIONS: Place all ingredients in a slow cooker. Cook on low for 6 hr, or until pork is tender. Serve over cooked pasta or rice.
N.V.: Calories: 320, Fat: 8g, Carbs: 15g, Protein: 44g, Sugar: 8g

Recipe 8. Herb-Encrusted Pork Tenderloin

PREPARATION TIME: 15 min - **COOKING TIME:** 25 min
MODE OF COOKING: Roasting - **SERVINGS:** 4
INGREDIENTS: 1 pork tenderloin (about 1 lb); 2 Tbsp. olive oil; 1 Tbsp. rosemary, finely chopped; 1 Tbsp. thyme, finely chopped; 2 cloves garlic, minced; Salt and pepper to taste
DIRECTIONS: Preheat oven to 375°F (190°C). Rub pork tenderloin with olive oil. Mix rosemary, thyme, garlic, salt, and pepper in a bowl, then coat the pork evenly with the herb mixture. Place in a roasting pan and bake until the internal temperature reaches 145°F (63°C), about 25 min. Let rest for 5 min before slicing.
N.V.: Calories: 220, Fat: 10g, Carbs: 1g, Protein: 31g, Sugar: 0g

Recipe 9. Spicy Maple Glazed Pork Chops

PREPARATION TIME: 10 min - **COOKING TIME:** 15 min
MODE OF COOKING: Pan-frying - **SERVINGS:** 4
INGREDIENTS: 4 pork chops, 1-inch thick; 2 Tbsp. olive oil; 1/4 cup maple syrup; 2 Tbsp. apple cider vinegar; 1 tsp chili flakes; Salt and pepper to taste
DIRECTIONS: Season pork chops with salt and pepper. Heat olive oil in a skillet over medium-high heat, cook pork chops until golden brown, about 5 min per side. Remove pork chops and set aside. Add maple syrup, apple cider vinegar, and chili flakes to the skillet, simmer until thickened. Return pork chops to the skillet, coat with the glaze, and cook for an additional 2 min. Serve glazed pork chops hot.
N.V.: Calories: 340, Fat: 14g, Carbs: 18g, Protein: 35g, Sugar: 15g

Recipe 10. Pork Belly with Crispy Skin

PREPARATION TIME: 10 min - **COOKING TIME:** 2 hr
MODE OF COOKING: Roasting - **SERVINGS:** 4
INGREDIENTS: 1 lb pork belly; 1 Tbsp. Sea salt; 1 tsp black pepper; 1 tsp smoked paprika; 2 cloves garlic, minced
DIRECTIONS: Preheat oven to 350°F (177°C). Score the skin of the pork belly in a diamond pattern. Rub the entire piece with salt, pepper, smoked paprika, and garlic. Place on a rack in a roasting tray, skin-side up, and roast for 2 hr until the skin is crispy and the meat is tender. Let rest before slicing.
N.V.: Calories: 580, Fat: 55g, Carbs: 2g, Protein: 22g, Sugar: 0g

RECIPE 11. SMOKED PORK RIBS WITH APPLE BBQ SAUCE

PREPARATION TIME: 20 min (plus overnight marinating) - **COOKING TIME:** 4 hr
MODE OF COOKING: Smoking - **SERVINGS:** 4
INGREDIENTS: 2 lb pork ribs; **For the rub:** 2 Tbsp. brown sugar; 1 Tbsp. paprika; 1 tsp garlic powder; 1 tsp onion powder; Salt and pepper to taste; **For the sauce:** 1 cup apple cider vinegar; 1/2 cup ketchup; 1/4 cup apple sauce; 2 Tbsp. honey; 1 Tbsp. mustard; 1 tsp chili powder
DIRECTIONS: Mix rub ingredients and apply to ribs. Let marinate overnight. Preheat smoker to 225°F (107°C). Smoke ribs for about 4 hr until tender. For the sauce, combine all ingredients in a saucepan, simmer until thickened. Brush sauce on ribs in the last 30 min of cooking. Serve ribs with remaining sauce.
N.V.: Calories: 710, Fat: 42g, Carbs: 42g, Protein: 46g, Sugar: 36g

LAMB: TECHNIQUES AND TASTES

RECIPE 1. ROSEMARY AND GARLIC LAMB CHOPS

PREPARATION TIME: 15 min - **COOKING TIME:** 10 min
MODE OF COOKING: Grilling - **SERVINGS:** 4
INGREDIENTS: 8 lamb chops; 2 Tbsp. olive oil; 4 cloves garlic, minced; 2 Tbsp. fresh rosemary, chopped; Salt and pepper to taste.
DIRECTIONS: Preheat grill to high. Mix olive oil, garlic, rosemary, salt, and pepper in a bowl. Rub mixture onto lamb chops. Grill chops for 5 minutes each side or until desired doneness.
N.V.: Calories: 410, Fat: 34g, Carbs: 1g, Protein: 24g, Sugar: 0g

RECIPE 2. MINTED LAMB BURGERS

PREPARATION TIME: 20 min - **COOKING TIME:** 10 min
MODE OF COOKING: Grilling - **SERVINGS:** 4
INGREDIENTS: 1 lb. ground lamb; 2 Tbsp. fresh mint, chopped; 2 cloves garlic, minced; 1/2 tsp cumin; Salt and pepper to taste; 4 hamburger buns; Toppings: lettuce, tomato, red onion, tzatziki sauce.
DIRECTIONS: Preheat grill to medium-high. In a bowl, mix ground lamb, mint, garlic, cumin, salt, and pepper. Form into 4 patties. Grill patties for 5 minutes each side. Serve on buns with toppings.
N.V.: Calories: 550, Fat: 30g, Carbs: 40g, Protein: 30g, Sugar: 6g

RECIPE 3. SLOW-ROASTED LAMB SHOULDER WITH ROOT VEGETABLES

PREPARATION TIME: 20 min - **COOKING TIME:** 4 hr
MODE OF COOKING: Roasting - **SERVINGS:** 6
INGREDIENTS: 4 lb. lamb shoulder; 2 Tbsp. olive oil; 1 Tbsp. rosemary, chopped; 1 Tbsp. thyme, chopped; 3 cloves garlic, minced; Salt and pepper to taste; 3 carrots, chopped; 2 parsnips, chopped; 1 onion, quartered.

DIRECTIONS: Preheat oven to 325°F (163°C). Rub lamb with olive oil, rosemary, thyme, garlic, salt, and pepper. Place in a roasting pan with vegetables. Roast for 4 hours or until tender.
N.V.: Calories: 690, Fat: 48g, Carbs: 18g, Protein: 46g, Sugar: 5g

RECIPE 4. GRILLED LAMB SKEWERS WITH YOGURT SAUCE

PREPARATION TIME: 30 min (plus marinating) - **COOKING TIME:** 10 min
MODE OF COOKING: Grilling - **SERVINGS:** 4
INGREDIENTS: 2 lb. lamb leg, cubed; 1/4 cup olive oil; 2 Tbsp. lemon juice; 2 cloves garlic, minced; 1 tsp paprika; Salt and pepper to taste; 1 cup Greek yogurt; 1 cucumber, diced; 2 Tbsp. mint, chopped.
DIRECTIONS: Mix olive oil, lemon juice, garlic, paprika, salt, and pepper. Marinate lamb for 2 hours. Thread onto skewers. Grill over medium-high heat for 10 minutes. Mix yogurt, cucumber, mint for sauce. Serve skewers with sauce.
N.V.: Calories: 520, Fat: 32g, Carbs: 8g, Protein: 52g, Sugar: 5g

RECIPE 5. LAMB TAGINE WITH APRICOTS

PREPARATION TIME: 20 min - **COOKING TIME:** 2 hr
MODE OF COOKING: Simmering - **SERVINGS:** 6
INGREDIENTS: 2 lb. lamb stew meat; 2 Tbsp. olive oil; 1 onion, chopped; 2 cloves garlic, minced; 1 tsp cinnamon; 1/2 tsp ginger; 1/2 tsp turmeric; 1 cup dried apricots; 3 cups beef broth; Salt and pepper to taste; 2 Tbsp. almond slivers, toasted.
DIRECTIONS: In a large pot, brown lamb in olive oil. Add onion, garlic, spices, and cook for 2 min. Add apricots and broth. Simmer for 2 hours. Garnish with almonds.
N.V.: Calories: 420, Fat: 18g, Carbs: 32g, Protein: 34g, Sugar: 20g

RECIPE 6. LAMB AND FETA STUFFED PEPPERS

PREPARATION TIME: 15 min - **COOKING TIME:** 45 min
MODE OF COOKING: Baking - **SERVINGS:** 4
INGREDIENTS: 4 bell peppers, halved; 1 lb. ground lamb; 1 cup cooked quinoa; 1/2 cup feta cheese, crumbled; 1 onion, diced; 2 cloves garlic, minced; 1 tsp oregano; Salt and pepper to taste; 1 can (14 oz) diced tomatoes.
DIRECTIONS: Preheat oven to 375°F (190°C). In a skillet, cook lamb, onion, and garlic. Mix in quinoa, feta, oregano, salt, pepper, and tomatoes. Stuff peppers, bake for 45 min.
N.V.: Calories: 410, Fat: 24g, Carbs: 25g, Protein: 26g, Sugar: 8g

RECIPE 7. ROASTED LAMB RACK WITH MINT PESTO

PREPARATION TIME: 20 min - **COOKING TIME:** 25 min
MODE OF COOKING: Roasting - **SERVINGS:** 4
INGREDIENTS: 2 racks of lamb; Salt and pepper to taste; 1 cup fresh mint leaves; 1/2 cup olive oil; 1/4 cup Parmesan cheese, grated; 2 cloves garlic; 1/4 cup pine nuts.
DIRECTIONS: Preheat oven to 400°F (204°C). Season lamb with salt and pepper. Roast for 25 min. Blend mint, olive oil, Parmesan, garlic, and pine nuts for pesto. Serve lamb with pesto.
N.V.: Calories: 560, Fat: 42g, Carbs: 4g, Protein: 42g, Sugar: 1g

RECIPE 8. ROSEMARY AND GARLIC ROAST LAMB

PREPARATION TIME: 20 min - **COOKING TIME:** 1 hr 30 min
MODE OF COOKING: Roasting - **SERVINGS:** 4

INGREDIENTS: 2 lb leg of lamb; 4 cloves garlic, minced; 2 Tbsp. fresh rosemary, chopped; 3 Tbsp. olive oil; Salt and pepper to taste; 1 cup red wine; 1 cup chicken broth
DIRECTIONS: Preheat oven to 375°F (190°C). Mix garlic, rosemary, olive oil, salt, and pepper in a bowl. Rub the mixture over the lamb. Place lamb in a roasting pan, pour red wine and chicken broth into the pan. Roast for about 1 hr 30 min, or until the internal temperature reaches 145°F (63°C) for medium-rare. Let rest before slicing. Serve with pan juices as a sauce.
N.V.: Calories: 410, Fat: 24g, Carbs: 2g, Protein: 45g, Sugar: 0g

RECIPE 9. LAMB SHANKS BRAISED IN RED WINE

PREPARATION TIME: 15 min - **COOKING TIME:** 2 hr 30 min
MODE OF COOKING: Braising - **SERVINGS:** 4
INGREDIENTS: 4 lamb shanks; 2 Tbsp. olive oil; Salt and pepper to taste; 1 onion, chopped; 2 carrots, chopped; 2 stalks celery, chopped; 4 cloves garlic, minced; 2 cups red wine; 2 cups beef stock; 1 Tbsp. tomato paste; 2 tsp thyme; 2 bay leaves
DIRECTIONS: Season lamb shanks with salt and pepper. Heat olive oil in a large pot over medium-high heat. Brown shanks on all sides, then remove. Add onion, carrots, celery, and garlic to the pot, cook until softened. Return shanks to the pot, add red wine, beef stock, tomato paste, thyme, and bay leaves. Bring to a boil, then cover and simmer on low heat for 2 hr 30 min, until meat is tender. Serve shanks with vegetables and sauce.
N.V.: Calories: 530, Fat: 28g, Carbs: 15g, Protein: 48g, Sugar: 5g

RECIPE 10. GRILLED LAMB KEBABS WITH MINT YOGURT SAUCE

PREPARATION TIME: 25 min (includes marinating) - **COOKING TIME:** 10 min
MODE OF COOKING: Grilling - **SERVINGS:** 4
INGREDIENTS: 1 lb lamb, cut into cubes; 2 Tbsp. olive oil; 1 tsp cumin; 1 tsp paprika; Salt and pepper to taste; **For the sauce:** 1 cup Greek yogurt; 2 Tbsp. mint, finely chopped; 1 clove garlic, minced; Juice of 1 lemon; Salt to taste
DIRECTIONS: Mix lamb with olive oil, cumin, paprika, salt, and pepper. Marinate for at least 20 min. Thread lamb onto skewers. Preheat grill to medium-high heat. Grill lamb kebabs, turning occasionally, until browned and cooked to desired doneness, about 10 min. For the sauce, combine Greek yogurt, mint, garlic, lemon juice, and salt. Serve kebabs with mint yogurt sauce.
N.V.: Calories: 320, Fat: 18g, Carbs: 6g, Protein: 34g, Sugar: 3g

RECIPE 11. MOROCCAN SPICED LAMB MEATBALLS

PREPARATION TIME: 20 min - **COOKING TIME:** 30 min
MODE OF COOKING: Baking - **SERVINGS:** 4
INGREDIENTS: 1 lb ground lamb; 1 egg; 1/4 cup breadcrumbs; 2 cloves garlic, minced; 1 tsp ground cumin; 1 tsp paprika; 1/2 tsp cinnamon; 1/4 tsp cayenne pepper; Salt and pepper to taste; 1/4 cup fresh cilantro, chopped; 1/4 cup fresh parsley, chopped
DIRECTIONS: Preheat oven to 375°F (190°C). In a bowl, combine ground lamb, egg, breadcrumbs, garlic, cumin, paprika, cinnamon, cayenne, salt, pepper, cilantro, and parsley. Mix well and form into 1-inch meatballs. Place meatballs on a baking sheet and bake for 30 min, or until cooked through. Serve hot.
N.V.: Calories: 340, Fat: 22g, Carbs: 9g, Protein: 26g, Sugar: 2g

FUSION DISHES FEATURING PORK AND LAMB

RECIPE 1. SICILIAN PORK AND LAMB INVOLTINI

PREPARATION TIME: 30 min - **COOKING TIME:** 20 min **MODE OF COOKING:** Sautéing - **SERVINGS:** 4
INGREDIENTS: 8 thin slices pork loin; 8 thin slices lamb shoulder; 1/2 cup breadcrumbs; 1/4 cup grated Pecorino cheese; 2 Tbsp pine nuts; 2 Tbsp raisins; 1 egg; 1/2 tsp dried oregano; Salt and pepper to taste; 2 Tbsp olive oil; 1 cup white wine
PROCEDURE: In a bowl, mix breadcrumbs, Pecorino, pine nuts, raisins, egg, oregano, salt, and pepper. Place a spoonful of filling on each slice of meat, roll tightly, and secure with toothpicks. Heat olive oil in a pan, brown the rolls on all sides. Add white wine, reduce heat, cover, and simmer for 20 min. Remove toothpicks before serving.
N.V.: Calories: 450, Fat: 20g, Carbs: 18g, Protein: 40g, Sugar: 4g

RECIPE 2. KOREAN BBQ PORK AND LAMB WRAPS

PREPARATION TIME: 25 min - **COOKING TIME:** 10 min **MODE OF COOKING:** Grilling - **SERVINGS:** 4
INGREDIENTS: 1/2 lb pork belly, thinly sliced; 1/2 lb lamb loin, thinly sliced; 1/4 cup soy sauce; 2 Tbsp sesame oil; 1 Tbsp gochujang; 2 garlic cloves, minced; 1 tsp ginger, grated; 1 Tbsp honey; Lettuce leaves for wrapping; 1/4 cup kimchi, for serving
PROCEDURE: Combine soy sauce, sesame oil, gochujang, garlic, ginger, and honey in a bowl. Marinate pork and lamb slices for at least 1 hr. Preheat grill to high. Grill meat until charred and cooked through, about 3-5 min per side. Serve in lettuce leaves, topped with kimchi.
N.V.: Calories: 520, Fat: 40g, Carbs: 10g, Protein: 30g, Sugar: 6g

RECIPE 3. MEDITERRANEAN STUFFED PORK AND LAMB CHOPS

PREPARATION TIME: 20 min - **COOKING TIME:** 25 min **MODE OF COOKING:** Roasting - **SERVINGS:** 4
INGREDIENTS: 4 pork chops; 4 lamb chops; 1 cup spinach, chopped; 1/2 cup feta cheese, crumbled; 2 Tbsp sun-dried tomatoes, chopped; 1 Tbsp olives, chopped; 2 garlic cloves, minced; Salt and pepper to taste; 2 Tbsp olive oil
PROCEDURE: Preheat oven to 375°F (190°C). Make a pocket in each chop by cutting into the side. Mix spinach, feta, sun-dried tomatoes, olives, and garlic. Stuff mixture into each chop, season with salt and pepper. Heat olive oil in a pan, sear chops on both sides. Transfer to oven, roast until cooked, about 20 min.
N.V.: Calories: 470, Fat: 30g, Carbs: 5g, Protein: 45g, Sugar: 2g

RECIPE 4. ARGENTINIAN PORK AND LAMB CHIMICHURRI SKEWERS

PREPARATION TIME: 15 min (plus marinating) - **COOKING TIME:** 10 min **MODE OF COOKING:** Grilling - **SERVINGS:** 4

INGREDIENTS: 1/2 lb pork tenderloin, cubed; 1/2 lb lamb shoulder, cubed; 1 cup parsley, finely chopped; 3 cloves garlic, minced; 1/2 cup olive oil; 2 Tbsp red wine vinegar; 1 tsp red chili flakes; Salt and pepper to taste

PROCEDURE: Mix parsley, garlic, olive oil, vinegar, chili flakes, salt, and pepper to create chimichurri sauce. Marinate pork and lamb cubes in half the sauce for at least 2 hr. Thread meat onto skewers. Grill over medium-high heat until charred and cooked through, about 5 min per side. Serve with remaining chimichurri sauce.

N.V.: Calories: 400, Fat: 30g, Carbs: 2g, Protein: 30g, Sugar: 0g

RECIPE 5. ITALIAN HERB CRUSTED PORK AND LAMB RACK

PREPARATION TIME: 20 min - **COOKING TIME:** 1 hr **MODE OF COOKING:** Roasting - **SERVINGS:** 6

INGREDIENTS: 1 rack of pork ribs; 1 rack of lamb; 1/4 cup olive oil; 2 Tbsp rosemary, minced; 2 Tbsp thyme, minced; 4 cloves garlic, minced; Salt and pepper to taste; 1/2 cup breadcrumbs

PROCEDURE: Preheat oven to 375°F (190°C). Mix olive oil, rosemary, thyme, garlic, salt, and pepper. Rub mixture onto both racks. Press breadcrumbs onto the meat. Place racks in a roasting pan, bone-side down. Roast until crust is golden and meat is cooked to desired doneness, about 1 hr for medium-rare. Let rest before slicing.

N.V.: Calories: 560, Fat: 40g, Carbs: 12g, Protein: 40g, Sugar: 1g

RECIPE 6. LAMB AND PORK BELLY VINDALOO

PREPARATION TIME: 20 min - **COOKING TIME:** 2 hr **MODE OF COOKING:** Slow Cooking - **SERVINGS:** 6

INGREDIENTS: 1/2 lb pork belly, cut into chunks; 1/2 lb lamb shoulder, cut into chunks; 2 Tbsp vindaloo paste; 1 can (14 oz.) diced tomatoes; 1 onion, chopped; 2 cloves garlic, minced; 1 tsp ginger, minced; 1 cup chicken stock; Salt to taste

PROCEDURE: Brown pork belly and lamb chunks in a large pot. Remove meat, sauté onion, garlic, and ginger until soft. Add vindaloo paste, cooking for 1 min. Return meat to pot, add tomatoes and chicken stock. Bring to a boil, then simmer covered on low heat until meat is tender, about 2 hr. Season with salt.

N.V.: Calories: 520, Fat: 40g, Carbs: 8g, Protein: 35g, Sugar: 4g

RECIPE 8. PORK GYOZA WITH LAMB BROTH

PREPARATION TIME: 45 min - **COOKING TIME:** 2 hr
MODE OF COOKING: Steaming and Simmering - **SERVINGS:** 4
INGREDIENTS:
- **For Gyoza:** 1 lb ground pork; 2 Tbsp. soy sauce; 1 Tbsp. sesame oil; 1/4 cup green onions, chopped; 2 cloves garlic, minced; 1 tsp ginger, minced; 30 gyoza wrappers
- **For Lamb Broth:** 2 lb lamb bones; 1 onion, quartered; 2 carrots, chopped; 2 stalks celery, chopped; 10 cups water; Salt to taste

DIRECTIONS:
- **For the Broth:** Place lamb bones, onion, carrots, and celery in a large pot. Cover with water and simmer for 2 hr. Strain the broth, season with salt.
- **For Gyoza:** Mix ground pork, soy sauce, sesame oil, green onions, garlic, and ginger. Place a teaspoon of filling in the center of each gyoza wrapper, wet edges, and fold, pressing to seal. Steam gyoza for about 10 min.
- Serve hot gyoza in lamb broth.

N.V.: Calories: 580, Fat: 30g, Carbs: 40g, Protein: 38g, Sugar: 4g

RECIPE 9. LAMB AND PORK BELLY BAO BUNS

PREPARATION TIME: 3 hr (includes dough rising) - **COOKING TIME:** 1 hr
MODE OF COOKING: Steaming - **SERVINGS:** 4
INGREDIENTS:
- **For Bao Buns:** 2 cups all-purpose flour; 1/2 cup warm water; 1 tsp yeast; 2 Tbsp. sugar; 1 Tbsp. vegetable oil
- **For Filling:** 1/2 lb ground lamb; 1/2 lb pork belly, thinly sliced; 2 Tbsp. hoisin sauce; 1 Tbsp. soy sauce; 1 tsp five-spice powder; 1/4 cup green onions, chopped

DIRECTIONS:
- **For Bao Buns:** Dissolve yeast and sugar in warm water. Mix in flour and oil until a dough forms. Let rise for 2 hr. Divide into small balls, roll out, and fold over to form bun shapes.
- **For Filling:** Cook ground lamb and pork belly with hoisin sauce, soy sauce, and five-spice powder until well done. Stir in green onions.
- Steam bao buns for 15 min. Fill with the meat mixture and serve.

N.V.: Calories: 660, Fat: 35g, Carbs: 52g, Protein: 32g, Sugar: 8g

RECIPE 10. SPICED LAMB AND PORK RAGOUT WITH POLENTA

PREPARATION TIME: 15 min - **COOKING TIME:** 1 hr
MODE OF COOKING: Simmering - **SERVINGS:** 4
INGREDIENTS:
- **For Ragout:** 1/2 lb ground lamb; 1/2 lb ground pork; 1 onion, diced; 2 cloves garlic, minced; 1 can diced tomatoes; 1 tsp cumin; 1 tsp coriander; 1 tsp smoked paprika; Salt and pepper to taste
- **For Polenta:** 1 cup polenta; 4 cups water; Salt to taste; 1/4 cup grated Parmesan cheese

DIRECTIONS:
- **For Ragout:** In a pot, sauté onion and garlic. Add ground lamb and pork, cook until browned. Add tomatoes, cumin, coriander, paprika, salt, and pepper. Simmer for 45 min.
- **For Polenta:** Bring water to a boil, whisk in polenta and salt. Reduce heat, cook until thickened, stirring frequently. Stir in Parmesan.
- Serve ragout over polenta.

N.V.: Calories: 510, Fat: 30g, Carbs: 34g, Protein: 28g, Sugar: 6g

RECIPE 11. CURRIED LAMB AND PORK STUFFED PEPPERS

PREPARATION TIME: 20 min - **COOKING TIME:** 40 min
MODE OF COOKING: Baking - **SERVINGS:** 4
INGREDIENTS: 4 large bell peppers, halved and seeded; 1/2 lb ground lamb; 1/2 lb ground pork; 1 onion, chopped; 2 cloves garlic, minced; 2 Tbsp. curry powder; 1 cup cooked rice; 1/2 cup raisins; Salt and pepper to taste; 1/2 cup chicken broth

DIRECTIONS:

Preheat oven to 375°F (190°C). In a skillet, cook onion, garlic, lamb, and pork with curry powder until meat is browned. Stir in cooked rice, raisins, salt, and pepper.
Stuff bell pepper halves with the meat mixture. Place in a baking dish, pour chicken broth around peppers. Cover with foil, bake for 40 min until peppers are tender.

N.V.: Calories: 460, Fat: 22g, Carbs: 42g, Protein: 24g, Sugar: 16g

CHAPTER 13: POULTRY PERFECTION

Embarking on Chapter 13, we delve into the realm of "Poultry Perfection," a chapter dedicated to the art and science of cooking with chicken, turkey, duck, and more. Poultry, with its versatility and wide appeal, serves as a canvas for a range of flavors and techniques, from the simplest of preparations to the most complex and nuanced dishes. This chapter aims not only to master the basics of poultry cooking but also to explore innovative ways to bring out the best in each bird, ensuring every meal is a celebration of texture and taste.

In the journey through poultry perfection, we'll explore the fundamentals of selecting quality poultry, understanding the importance of proper preparation and marination, and mastering various cooking methods that elevate poultry from the ordinary to the extraordinary. Whether it's achieving the perfect roast chicken with golden, crispy skin and juicy, flavorful meat, grilling succulent turkey burgers, or crafting a decadently rich duck confit, this chapter is designed to inspire confidence and creativity in the kitchen.

Through a collection of carefully curated recipes, we'll navigate the diverse world of poultry, showcasing traditional favorites alongside unexpected, bold flavor pairings. Each recipe is crafted with the home cook in mind, emphasizing clear, straightforward instructions and tips for success. From weekday dinners to special occasion feasts, "Poultry Perfection" is your guide to unlocking the full potential of poultry, transforming everyday meals into memorable culinary experiences that delight and inspire.

BEYOND THE BASICS WITH CHICKEN

RECIPE 1. CHICKEN CONFIT WITH GARLIC AND THYME

PREPARATION TIME: 10 min - **COOKING TIME:** 2 hr 30 min **MODE OF COOKING:** Slow Cooking - **SERVINGS:** 4

INGREDIENTS: 4 chicken thighs, skin-on; 2 cups olive oil; 6 cloves garlic, smashed; 4 sprigs fresh thyme; 1 tsp salt; 1/2 tsp black pepper

PROCEDURE: Preheat your oven to 275°F (135°C). Season chicken thighs with salt and pepper. Place chicken in a single layer in a baking dish. Add garlic and thyme, then pour olive oil over chicken until completely submerged. Cover and bake until chicken is very tender, about 2 hours 30 minutes. Allow to cool in the oil. Serve chicken warm, drizzled with some of the cooking oil.

N.V.: Calories: 500, Fat: 45g, Carbs: 1g, Protein: 25g, Sugar: 0g

RECIPE 2. SMOKED PAPRIKA AND HONEY GLAZED CHICKEN

PREPARATION TIME: 15 min - **COOKING TIME:** 45 min **MODE OF COOKING:** Roasting - **SERVINGS:** 4

INGREDIENTS: 4 chicken breasts; 2 Tbsp olive oil; 2 Tbsp honey; 1 Tbsp smoked paprika; 1 tsp garlic powder; Salt and pepper to taste

PROCEDURE: Preheat oven to 375°F (190°C). In a bowl, whisk together olive oil, honey, smoked paprika, garlic powder, salt, and pepper. Place chicken breasts in a baking dish and coat evenly with the honey-paprika mixture. Roast until chicken is cooked through and glaze is caramelized, about 45 minutes.

N.V.: Calories: 320, Fat: 9g, Carbs: 12g, Protein: 47g, Sugar: 11g

RECIPE 3. LEMON AND HERB ROASTED CHICKEN DRUMSTICKS

PREPARATION TIME: 10 min - **COOKING TIME:** 40 min **MODE OF COOKING:** Roasting - **SERVINGS:** 4

INGREDIENTS: 8 chicken drumsticks; 2 Tbsp olive oil; 1 lemon, juiced and zested; 2 tsp rosemary, chopped; 2 tsp thyme, chopped; 1 garlic clove, minced; Salt and pepper to taste

PROCEDURE: Preheat oven to 400°F (204°C). In a bowl, mix together olive oil, lemon juice and zest, rosemary, thyme, garlic, salt, and pepper. Toss drumsticks in the mixture until well coated. Arrange on a baking sheet and roast until golden brown and cooked through, about 40 minutes, turning halfway through.

N.V.: Calories: 290, Fat: 15g, Carbs: 2g, Protein: 37g, Sugar: 1g

RECIPE 4. CHICKEN TIKKA SKEWERS

PREPARATION TIME: 20 min (plus marinating) - **COOKING TIME:** 15 min **MODE OF COOKING:** Grilling - **SERVINGS:** 4

INGREDIENTS: 2 lb chicken breast, cubed; 1/2 cup yogurt; 2 Tbsp lemon juice; 2 tsp garam masala; 1 tsp turmeric; 1 tsp cumin; 1/2 tsp chili powder; 1/2 tsp garlic, minced; Salt to taste

PROCEDURE: Mix yogurt, lemon juice, garam masala, turmeric, cumin, chili powder, garlic, and salt in a bowl. Add chicken cubes, marinate for at least 1 hour. Thread chicken onto skewers. Preheat grill to medium-high heat (375°F/190°C). Grill skewers, turning occasionally, until chicken is charred and cooked through, about 15 minutes.

N.V.: Calories: 260, Fat: 3g, Carbs: 5g, Protein: 50g, Sugar: 3g

RECIPE 5. ASIAN-STYLE CHICKEN LETTUCE WRAPS

PREPARATION TIME: 15 min - **COOKING TIME:** 10 min **MODE OF COOKING:** Sautéing - **SERVINGS:** 4

INGREDIENTS: 1 lb ground chicken; 1 Tbsp sesame oil; 2 cloves garlic, minced; 1 Tbsp ginger, minced; 1/4 cup soy sauce; 2 Tbsp hoisin sauce; 1 Tbsp rice vinegar; 1 tsp chili sauce; 1 cup water chestnuts, diced; 4 green onions, sliced; 1 head iceberg lettuce, leaves separated

PROCEDURE: Heat sesame oil in a skillet over medium heat. Add garlic and ginger, sauté until fragrant. Add ground chicken, cook until browned. Stir in soy sauce, hoisin sauce, rice vinegar, chili sauce, water chestnuts, and half of the green onions, cooking for a few more minutes. Serve the chicken mixture in lettuce leaves, topped with remaining green onions.

N.V.: Calories: 235, Fat: 11g, Carbs: 12g, Protein: 23g, Sugar: 5g

RECIPE 6. BALSAMIC-GLAZED CHICKEN WITH ROASTED VEGETABLES

PREPARATION TIME: 15 min - **COOKING TIME:** 30 min **MODE OF COOKING:** Roasting - **SERVINGS:** 4

INGREDIENTS: 4 chicken thighs; 2 Tbsp balsamic vinegar; 1 Tbsp honey; 1 Tbsp olive oil; 1 tsp rosemary, minced; 2 carrots, sliced; 2 parsnips, sliced; 1 red onion, quartered; Salt and pepper to taste

PROCEDURE: Preheat oven to 425°F (220°C). Whisk together balsamic vinegar, honey, olive oil, rosemary, salt, and pepper. Toss chicken and vegetables in the balsamic mixture. Arrange on a baking sheet and roast until chicken is cooked through and vegetables are tender, about 30 minutes.

N.V.: Calories: 350, Fat: 20g, Carbs: 18g, Protein: 27g, Sugar: 10g

RECIPE 7. SZECHUAN PEPPER CHICKEN STIR-FRY

PREPARATION TIME: 10 min - **COOKING TIME:** 20 min **MODE OF COOKING:** Stir-Frying - **SERVINGS:** 4

INGREDIENTS: 1 lb chicken breast, thinly sliced; 2 Tbsp vegetable oil; 1 bell pepper, sliced; 1/2 cup snap peas; 3 green onions, sliced; 2 cloves garlic, minced; 1 Tbsp ginger, minced; 2 Tbsp soy sauce; 1 Tbsp hoisin sauce; 1 tsp Szechuan pepper, crushed; 1 tsp cornstarch dissolved in 2 Tbsp water

PROCEDURE: Heat oil in a large skillet over high heat. Add chicken, stir-fry until browned. Remove chicken and set aside. In the same skillet, add bell pepper, snap peas, green onions, garlic, and ginger, stir-fry for a few minutes. Return chicken to skillet. Add soy sauce, hoisin sauce, Szechuan pepper, and cornstarch mixture. Cook until sauce thickens and chicken is cooked through.

N.V.: Calories: 225, Fat: 8g, Carbs: 10g, Protein: 29g, Sugar: 4g

RECIPE 8. LEMON AND HERB ROASTED CHICKEN

PREPARATION TIME: 20 min - **COOKING TIME:** 1 hr 10 min
MODE OF COOKING: Roasting - **SERVINGS:** 4

INGREDIENTS: 1 whole chicken (about 4 lbs); 2 lemons, quartered; 4 garlic cloves, minced; 2 Tbsp. fresh rosemary, chopped; 2 Tbsp. fresh thyme, chopped; 2 Tbsp. olive oil; Salt and pepper to taste

DIRECTIONS: Preheat oven to 425°F (220°C). Stuff chicken cavity with lemon quarters. Mix garlic, rosemary, thyme, salt, and pepper in a bowl. Rub the chicken with olive oil, then coat evenly with the herb mixture. Place chicken in a roasting pan, breast side up. Roast for 1 hr 10 min, or until juices run clear. Let rest before carving.

N.V.: Calories: 450, Fat: 25g, Carbs: 5g, Protein: 50g, Sugar: 1g

RECIPE 9. SPICY CHICKEN TIKKA KEBABS

PREPARATION TIME: 30 min (includes marinating) - **COOKING TIME:** 15 min
MODE OF COOKING: Grilling - **SERVINGS:** 4

INGREDIENTS: 2 lbs chicken breast, cubed; 1 cup plain yogurt; 2 Tbsp. tikka masala paste; 1 tsp cumin; 1 tsp paprika; Salt to taste; 1 lime, for garnish; Fresh cilantro, for garnish

DIRECTIONS: Mix yogurt, tikka masala paste, cumin, paprika, and salt in a bowl. Add chicken, marinate for at least 20 min. Thread chicken onto skewers. Preheat grill to medium-high. Grill kebabs, turning occasionally, until charred and cooked through, about 15 min. Serve with lime wedges and cilantro.

N.V.: Calories: 310, Fat: 6g, Carbs: 8g, Protein: 54g, Sugar: 5g

RECIPE 10. CHICKEN AND ASPARAGUS LEMON STIR-FRY

PREPARATION TIME: 15 min - **COOKING TIME:** 20 min
MODE OF COOKING: Stir-frying - **SERVINGS:** 4
INGREDIENTS: 1 lb chicken breast, thinly sliced; 1 lb asparagus, trimmed and cut; 2 Tbsp. olive oil; 2 cloves garlic, minced; 1 Tbsp. ginger, minced; 3 Tbsp. soy sauce; Juice of 1 lemon; Zest of 1 lemon; 1 tsp honey; Salt and pepper to taste
DIRECTIONS: Heat olive oil in a large skillet over medium-high heat. Add garlic and ginger, sauté for 1 min. Add chicken, cook until no longer pink. Add asparagus, cook until tender. Mix soy sauce, lemon juice, lemon zest, honey, salt, and pepper. Pour over chicken and asparagus, stir well to coat. Cook for another 2 min. Serve hot.
N.V.: Calories: 220, Fat: 9g, Carbs: 10g, Protein: 29g, Sugar: 4g

RECIPE 11. SMOKED PAPRIKA CHICKEN THIGHS

PREPARATION TIME: 10 min - **COOKING TIME:** 40 min
MODE OF COOKING: Baking - **SERVINGS:** 4
INGREDIENTS: 8 chicken thighs, skin on; 2 Tbsp. smoked paprika; 1 tsp garlic powder; 1 tsp onion powder; 1/2 tsp cayenne pepper; 2 Tbsp. olive oil; Salt and pepper to taste
DIRECTIONS: Preheat oven to 400°F (200°C). Mix smoked paprika, garlic powder, onion powder, cayenne, salt, and pepper in a bowl. Rub chicken thighs with olive oil, then coat with the spice mixture. Place thighs on a baking sheet. Bake for 40 min, or until the skin is crispy and the chicken is cooked through.
N.V.: Calories: 340, Fat: 22g, Carbs: 2g, Protein: 32g, Sugar: 0g

TURKEY, DUCK, AND MORE POULTRY DISHES

RECIPE 1. TURKEY BREAST WITH MAPLE-MUSTARD GLAZE

PREPARATION TIME: 15 min - **COOKING TIME:** 1 hr 30 min **MODE OF COOKING:** Roasting - **SERVINGS:** 6
INGREDIENTS: 3 lb turkey breast; 1/4 cup maple syrup; 2 Tbsp Dijon mustard; 1 Tbsp olive oil; 1 tsp thyme, dried; Salt and pepper to taste
PROCEDURE: Preheat oven to 325°F (163°C). In a bowl, mix maple syrup, Dijon mustard, olive oil, thyme, salt, and pepper. Place turkey breast in a roasting pan, brush with the maple-mustard mixture. Roast until the internal temperature reaches 165°F (74°C), about 1 hr 30 min, basting every 30 min. Let rest before slicing.
N.V.: Calories: 330, Fat: 6g, Carbs: 12g, Protein: 55g, Sugar: 10g

RECIPE 2. DUCK BREAST WITH CHERRY SAUCE

PREPARATION TIME: 20 min - **COOKING TIME:** 25 min **MODE OF COOKING:** Pan-searing - **SERVINGS:** 4
INGREDIENTS: 4 duck breasts; Salt and pepper to taste; 1 cup cherries, pitted; 1/2 cup red wine; 2 Tbsp honey; 1 tsp balsamic vinegar; 1 shallot, minced
PROCEDURE: Score duck breast skin, season with salt and pepper. Cook skin-side down in a cold pan over medium heat until fat renders and skin crisps, about 10 min. Flip, cook to desired

doneness, about 5 min for medium-rare. Remove, rest. For sauce, sauté shallot, add cherries, wine, honey, vinegar, simmer until thickened. Serve over sliced duck.

N.V.: Calories: 410, Fat: 18g, Carbs: 18g, Protein: 38g, Sugar: 16g

RECIPE 3. QUAIL STUFFED WITH WILD RICE AND MUSHROOMS

PREPARATION TIME: 30 min - **COOKING TIME:** 40 min **MODE OF COOKING:** Roasting - **SERVINGS:** 4

INGREDIENTS: 4 quails; 1 cup wild rice, cooked; 1/2 cup mushrooms, diced; 1 shallot, minced; 2 Tbsp parsley, chopped; 2 Tbsp olive oil; Salt and pepper to taste

PROCEDURE: Preheat oven to 375°F (190°C). Sauté shallot and mushrooms in 1 Tbsp olive oil, mix with wild rice, parsley, salt, pepper. Stuff quails with mixture, truss legs. Place in a roasting pan, drizzle with remaining oil, season. Roast until golden and cooked through, about 40 min. Rest before serving.

N.V.: Calories: 290, Fat: 12g, Carbs: 22g, Protein: 24g, Sugar: 2g

RECIPE 4. ROASTED PHEASANT WITH APPLES AND CIDER

PREPARATION TIME: 20 min - **COOKING TIME:** 1 hr **MODE OF COOKING:** Roasting - **SERVINGS:** 2

INGREDIENTS: 1 pheasant; 2 apples, cored and quartered; 1 cup apple cider; 2 Tbsp butter, melted; 1 tsp sage, dried; Salt and pepper to taste

PROCEDURE: Preheat oven to 350°F (177°C). Season pheasant inside and out with salt, pepper, sage. Place apples inside cavity. Place in a roasting pan, pour cider over, brush with butter. Roast, basting occasionally, until cooked through, about 1 hr. Let rest, serve with roasted apples.

N.V.: Calories: 510, Fat: 22g, Carbs: 34g, Protein: 42g, Sugar: 28g

RECIPE 5. GRILLED CORNISH HEN WITH LEMON AND HERBS

PREPARATION TIME: 15 min - **COOKING TIME:** 45 min **MODE OF COOKING:** Grilling - **SERVINGS:** 4

INGREDIENTS: 2 Cornish hens, halved; 2 lemons, quartered; 2 Tbsp olive oil; 1 Tbsp rosemary, chopped; 1 Tbsp thyme, chopped; Salt and pepper to taste

PROCEDURE: Preheat grill to medium-high. Squeeze lemon over hens, rub with olive oil, rosemary, thyme, salt, pepper. Place skin-side up on grill, cover, cook for 20 min. Flip, grill until skin crisps, about 25 min. Serve with additional lemon.

N.V.: Calories: 360, Fat: 24g, Carbs: 6g, Protein: 30g, Sugar: 1g

RECIPE 6. TURDUCKEN ROLLS WITH CRANBERRY GLAZE

PREPARATION TIME: 1 hr - **COOKING TIME:** 2 hr **MODE OF COOKING:** Roasting - **SERVINGS:** 8

INGREDIENTS: 1 duck breast, flattened; 1 turkey breast, flattened; 1 chicken breast, flattened; Salt and pepper to taste; 2 cups stuffing; 1 cup cranberries; 1/2 cup orange juice; 2 Tbsp honey; 1 tsp cinnamon

PROCEDURE: Preheat oven to 325°F (163°C). Season poultry layers with salt, pepper. Layer turkey, duck, chicken with stuffing in between each layer. Roll tightly, tie with kitchen twine. Roast until internal temperature reaches 165°F (74°C), about 2 hr. For glaze, simmer cranberries, orange juice, honey, cinnamon until thickened. Brush over rolls during last 30 min of roasting.

N.V.: Calories: 450, Fat: 12g, Carbs: 32g, Protein: 58g, Sugar: 20g

Recipe 7. Spiced Goose with Red Wine Poached Pears

PREPARATION TIME: 30 min - **COOKING TIME:** 3 hr **MODE OF COOKING:** Roasting - **SERVINGS:** 6

INGREDIENTS: 1 whole goose; 1 bottle red wine; 4 pears, peeled; 1 cup sugar; 2 cinnamon sticks; 4 cloves; 1 star anise; Salt and pepper to taste

PROCEDURE: Preheat oven to 325°F (163°C). Season goose with salt and pepper. Roast, covered, for 2 hr. Meanwhile, in a pot, combine wine, sugar, cinnamon, cloves, star anise, bring to boil. Add pears, simmer until tender. Uncover goose, increase oven to 400°F (204°C), roast until skin crisps, about 1 hr. Serve goose with pears and reduced poaching liquid.

N.V.: Calories: 720, Fat: 48g, Carbs: 40g, Protein: 35g, Sugar: 38g

Recipe 8. Orange and Thyme Roasted Turkey Breast

PREPARATION TIME: 20 min - **COOKING TIME:** 1 hr 30 min
MODE OF COOKING: Roasting - **SERVINGS:** 4

INGREDIENTS: 1 turkey breast (about 3 lbs); 2 oranges, zested and juiced; 2 Tbsp. fresh thyme, chopped; 2 cloves garlic, minced; 3 Tbsp. olive oil; Salt and pepper to taste

DIRECTIONS: Preheat oven to 375°F (190°C). In a bowl, mix orange zest, orange juice, thyme, garlic, olive oil, salt, and pepper. Place turkey breast in a roasting pan, and pour the orange and thyme mixture over it, making sure it's well coated. Roast in the oven for about 1 hr 30 min, or until the internal temperature reaches 165°F (74°C). Baste the turkey with the pan juices halfway through cooking. Let rest before slicing.

N.V.: Calories: 310, Fat: 8g, Carbs: 6g, Protein: 50g, Sugar: 4g

Recipe 9. Crispy Duck Breast with Balsamic Glaze

PREPARATION TIME: 15 min - **COOKING TIME:** 25 min
MODE OF COOKING: Pan-searing and Baking - **SERVINGS:** 4

INGREDIENTS: 4 duck breasts; Salt and pepper to taste; 1/4 cup balsamic vinegar; 2 Tbsp. honey; 1 tsp rosemary, chopped

DIRECTIONS: Preheat oven to 400°F (200°C). Score the duck skin in a diamond pattern, season with salt and pepper. Heat a skillet over medium heat, place duck breasts skin side down, and cook until the skin is golden and crisp, about 6-8 min. Transfer duck, skin side up, to a baking dish. In a saucepan, reduce balsamic vinegar, honey, and rosemary to a glaze. Brush glaze over duck breasts and bake for 10 min for medium-rare. Let rest before slicing.

N.V.: Calories: 380, Fat: 22g, Carbs: 12g, Protein: 34g, Sugar: 11g

Recipe 10. Herbed Cornish Hen with Lemon Butter

PREPARATION TIME: 20 min - **COOKING TIME:** 50 min
MODE OF COOKING: Roasting - **SERVINGS:** 4

INGREDIENTS: 2 Cornish hens, halved; 4 Tbsp. unsalted butter, softened; 1 lemon, zested and juiced; 2 Tbsp. fresh parsley, chopped; 1 Tbsp. fresh thyme, chopped; Salt and pepper to taste

DIRECTIONS: Preheat oven to 375°F (190°C). Mix butter, lemon zest, lemon juice, parsley, thyme, salt, and pepper in a bowl. Rub the herb butter mixture under and over the skin of the Cornish hens. Place hens in a roasting pan and roast for about 50 min, or until golden and the juices run clear. Baste occasionally with pan juices.

N.V.: Calories: 410, Fat: 28g, Carbs: 3g, Protein: 36g, Sugar: 1g

RECIPE 11. SMOKED PAPRIKA CHICKEN QUARTERS

PREPARATION TIME: 10 min - **COOKING TIME:** 45 min
MODE OF COOKING: Baking - **SERVINGS:** 4
INGREDIENTS: 4 chicken leg quarters; 3 Tbsp. olive oil; 2 Tbsp. smoked paprika; 1 tsp garlic powder; 1 tsp onion powder; Salt and pepper to taste
DIRECTIONS: Preheat oven to 400°F (200°C). In a bowl, mix olive oil, smoked paprika, garlic powder, onion powder, salt, and pepper. Rub the spice mixture all over the chicken leg quarters. Place chicken on a baking sheet, and bake for 45 min, or until the skin is crispy and the chicken is cooked through.
N.V.: Calories: 320, Fat: 20g, Carbs: 2g, Protein: 34g, Sugar: 0g

HEALTHFUL AND HEARTY POULTRY RECIPES

RECIPE 1. TURKEY AND QUINOA STUFFED BELL PEPPERS

PREPARATION TIME: 20 min - **COOKING TIME:** 35 min **MODE OF COOKING:** Baking - **SERVINGS:** 4
INGREDIENTS: 4 large bell peppers, halved and seeded; 1 lb ground turkey; 1 cup quinoa, cooked; 1 can (15 oz.) diced tomatoes, drained; 1 onion, chopped; 2 cloves garlic, minced; 1 tsp cumin; 1 tsp chili powder; 1/2 tsp paprika; Salt and pepper to taste; 1/2 cup shredded Monterey Jack cheese
PROCEDURE: Preheat oven to 375°F (190°C). In a skillet, cook turkey, onion, and garlic until turkey is browned. Stir in quinoa, tomatoes, cumin, chili powder, paprika, salt, and pepper. Fill bell pepper halves with turkey-quinoa mixture. Place in a baking dish, cover with foil, bake for 30 min. Uncover, top with cheese, bake until cheese is melted, about 5 min.
N.V.: Calories: 330, Fat: 9g, Carbs: 34g, Protein: 29g, Sugar: 8g

RECIPE 2. CHICKEN AND VEGETABLE STIR-FRY

PREPARATION TIME: 15 min - **COOKING TIME:** 10 min **MODE OF COOKING:** Stir-Frying - **SERVINGS:** 4
INGREDIENTS: 1 lb chicken breast, thinly sliced; 2 Tbsp olive oil; 1 bell pepper, sliced; 1 carrot, julienned; 1 cup broccoli florets; 1/2 cup snap peas; 2 Tbsp soy sauce; 1 Tbsp honey; 1 tsp ginger, grated; 2 cloves garlic, minced; Salt and pepper to taste
PROCEDURE: Heat olive oil in a large skillet over medium-high heat. Add chicken, cook until browned. Remove chicken. Add vegetables, stir-fry until tender-crisp. Return chicken to skillet. Mix soy sauce, honey, ginger, garlic, salt, and pepper; pour over chicken and vegetables. Stir until heated through.
N.V.: Calories: 240, Fat: 8g, Carbs: 14g, Protein: 29g, Sugar: 7g

RECIPE 3. SPICY TURKEY LETTUCE WRAPS

PREPARATION TIME: 10 min - **COOKING TIME:** 15 min **MODE OF COOKING:** Sautéing - **SERVINGS:** 4
INGREDIENTS: 1 lb ground turkey; 1 Tbsp sesame oil; 1 onion, diced; 2 cloves garlic, minced; 1 Tbsp chili paste; 2 tsp soy sauce; 1 tsp rice vinegar; 1/4 cup water chestnuts, diced; 1/4 cup green onions, sliced; 8 lettuce leaves

PROCEDURE: Heat sesame oil in a pan over medium heat. Add turkey, onion, garlic, cook until turkey is browned. Stir in chili paste, soy sauce, rice vinegar. Add water chestnuts, cook for 2 more min. Remove from heat, stir in green onions. Spoon mixture into lettuce leaves to serve.
N.V.: Calories: 220, Fat: 10g, Carbs: 8g, Protein: 25g, Sugar: 3g

RECIPE 4. GRILLED CHICKEN WITH AVOCADO SALSA

PREPARATION TIME: 15 min - **COOKING TIME:** 10 min **MODE OF COOKING:** Grilling - **SERVINGS:** 4
INGREDIENTS: 4 chicken breasts; 1 Tbsp olive oil; 1 tsp cumin; Salt and pepper to taste; 1 avocado, diced; 1 tomato, diced; 1/4 cup red onion, diced; 1 lime, juiced; 2 Tbsp cilantro, chopped
PROCEDURE: Preheat grill to medium-high heat. Rub chicken with olive oil, cumin, salt, and pepper. Grill until cooked through, about 5 min per side. Mix avocado, tomato, red onion, lime juice, cilantro, salt, and pepper to make salsa. Serve grilled chicken topped with avocado salsa.
N.V.: Calories: 290, Fat: 14g, Carbs: 9g, Protein: 34g, Sugar: 2g

RECIPE 5. BAKED LEMON HERB CHICKEN

PREPARATION TIME: 10 min - **COOKING TIME:** 25 min **MODE OF COOKING:** Baking - **SERVINGS:** 4
INGREDIENTS: 4 chicken breasts; 2 lemons, juiced and zested; 2 Tbsp olive oil; 1 tsp rosemary, chopped; 1 tsp thyme, chopped; Salt and pepper to taste
PROCEDURE: Preheat oven to 375°F (190°C). In a bowl, mix lemon juice, zest, olive oil, rosemary, thyme, salt, and pepper. Place chicken in a baking dish, pour lemon herb mixture over. Bake until chicken is cooked through, about 25 min.
N.V.: Calories: 210, Fat: 9g, Carbs: 3g, Protein: 30g, Sugar: 0g

RECIPE 6. TURKEY ZUCCHINI MEATBALLS

PREPARATION TIME: 20 min - **COOKING TIME:** 20 min **MODE OF COOKING:** Baking - **SERVINGS:** 4
INGREDIENTS: 1 lb ground turkey; 1 cup zucchini, grated and squeezed dry; 1/4 cup breadcrumbs; 1 egg; 1/2 tsp garlic powder; 1/2 tsp onion powder; Salt and pepper to taste; 1 cup marinara sauce
PROCEDURE: Preheat oven to 400°F (204°C). Mix turkey, zucchini, breadcrumbs, egg, garlic powder, onion powder, salt, and pepper. Form into meatballs, place on a baking sheet. Bake until browned, about 20 min. Warm marinara sauce, serve meatballs with sauce.
N.V.: Calories: 250, Fat: 11g, Carbs: 10g, Protein: 28g, Sugar: 4g

RECIPE 7. CHICKEN AND SWEET POTATO STEW

PREPARATION TIME: 15 min - **COOKING TIME:** 40 min **MODE OF COOKING:** Simmering - **SERVINGS:** 6
INGREDIENTS: 1 lb chicken breast, cubed; 2 Tbsp olive oil; 1 onion, chopped; 2 cloves garlic, minced; 2 sweet potatoes, peeled and cubed; 4 cups chicken broth; 1 tsp paprika; 1 tsp cumin; Salt and pepper to taste; 2 cups spinach leaves
PROCEDURE: In a large pot, heat olive oil over medium heat. Add chicken, onion, garlic, and sauté until chicken is browned. Add sweet potatoes, chicken broth, paprika, cumin, salt, and pepper. Bring to a boil, then reduce heat and simmer until sweet potatoes are tender, about 30 min. Stir in spinach until wilted. Serve hot.
N.V.: Calories: 220, Fat: 6g, Carbs: 20g, Protein: 22g, Sugar: 5g

Recipe 8. Turkey and Quinoa Stuffed Peppers

PREPARATION TIME: 20 min - **COOKING TIME:** 35 min
MODE OF COOKING: Baking - **SERVINGS:** 4
INGREDIENTS: 4 large bell peppers, halved and deseeded; 1 lb ground turkey; 1 cup quinoa, cooked; 1 onion, diced; 2 cloves garlic, minced; 1 can (15 oz) diced tomatoes, drained; 1 tsp cumin; 1 tsp paprika; Salt and pepper to taste; 1/2 cup shredded low-fat mozzarella cheese
DIRECTIONS: Preheat oven to 375°F (190°C). In a skillet, cook ground turkey, onion, and garlic over medium heat until turkey is browned. Stir in quinoa, diced tomatoes, cumin, paprika, salt, and pepper. Fill bell pepper halves with the turkey mixture. Place in a baking dish, cover with foil, and bake for 30 min. Uncover, top with mozzarella, bake for an additional 5 min until cheese is melted.
N.V.: Calories: 320, Fat: 9g, Carbs: 34g, Protein: 28g, Sugar: 6g

Recipe 9. Grilled Chicken and Vegetable Kebabs

PREPARATION TIME: 15 min (plus marinating) - **COOKING TIME:** 10 min
MODE OF COOKING: Grilling - **SERVINGS:** 4
INGREDIENTS: 2 chicken breasts, cut into cubes; 1 zucchini, sliced; 1 bell pepper, chopped; 1 red onion, chopped; **For the marinade:** 2 Tbsp. olive oil; 2 Tbsp. lemon juice; 1 tsp dried oregano; Salt and pepper to taste
DIRECTIONS: Whisk together olive oil, lemon juice, oregano, salt, and pepper in a bowl. Add chicken and vegetables, toss to coat. Marinate for at least 30 min. Thread chicken and vegetables onto skewers. Preheat grill to medium-high heat. Grill kebabs, turning occasionally, until chicken is cooked through, about 10 min.
N.V.: Calories: 200, Fat: 7g, Carbs: 8g, Protein: 26g, Sugar: 4g

Recipe 10. Duck Breast Salad with Berry Vinaigrette

PREPARATION TIME: 20 min - **COOKING TIME:** 15 min
MODE OF COOKING: Pan-searing - **SERVINGS:** 4
INGREDIENTS: 2 duck breasts; Salt and pepper to taste; 6 cups mixed greens; 1/2 cup mixed berries; **For the vinaigrette:** 1/4 cup berry puree; 2 Tbsp. balsamic vinegar; 1 Tbsp. olive oil; 1 tsp honey; Salt and pepper to taste
DIRECTIONS: Score duck skin, season with salt and pepper. Heat a skillet over medium heat, cook duck skin-side down until crisp, about 8 min. Flip, cook for another 7 min. Let rest, slice thinly. Whisk together vinaigrette ingredients. Toss mixed greens and berries with vinaigrette, top with sliced duck.
N.V.: Calories: 310, Fat: 18g, Carbs: 12g, Protein: 24g, Sugar: 8g

Recipe 11. Spicy Thai Chicken Lettuce Wraps

PREPARATION TIME: 20 min - **COOKING TIME:** 10 min
MODE OF COOKING: Sautéing - **SERVINGS:** 4
INGREDIENTS: 1 lb ground chicken; 1 Tbsp. olive oil; 1 bell pepper, diced; 1 carrot, grated; 2 green onions, sliced; 2 cloves garlic, minced; 1 Tbsp. ginger, minced; 2 Tbsp. soy sauce; 1 Tbsp. hoisin sauce; 1 tsp chili flakes; 1 head of lettuce, leaves separated; Fresh cilantro for garnish
DIRECTIONS: Heat olive oil in a pan over medium heat. Add garlic and ginger, sauté for 1 min. Add ground chicken, cook until browned. Stir in bell pepper, carrot, green onions, soy sauce,

hoisin sauce, and chili flakes. Cook for another 5 min. Spoon chicken mixture into lettuce leaves, garnish with cilantro.
N.V.: Calories: 220, Fat: 9g, Carbs: 10g, Protein: 27g, Sugar: 5g

CHAPTER 14: SEAFOOD ADVENTURES

Embarking on a seafood adventure is akin to setting sail on a vast, uncharted culinary ocean, where each wave brings a new flavor, and every tide uncovers a hidden gem of gastronomic delight. In Chapter 14, we delve deep into the heart of seafood cooking, guiding you through the serene waters of grilling fish to perfection, exploring the mystical depths of shellfish delights, and navigating the bountiful catches of seafood mixes and matches. This chapter is not just a collection of recipes; it's a compass for discovering the soul of seafood, transforming your Pit Boss grill into a vessel that ferries you towards mastery over these aquatic treasures.

Seafood, with its delicate textures and flavors, demands a nuanced approach that respects its integrity while enhancing its natural goodness. We'll explore the finesse required to handle seafood on the grill, ensuring it remains moist and flavorful, imbued with the smoky essence of wood pellets. From the crisp skin of a perfectly grilled fish to the succulent sweetness of grilled shellfish, each recipe is a step in a journey toward seafood sophistication.

Moreover, we're not just cooking seafood; we're embracing the diversity of the sea's bounty. With techniques tailored for everything from hearty salmon steaks to delicate scallops, this chapter serves as your beacon, illuminating the path to a treasure trove of flavors. Whether it's a simple family dinner or a lavish feast for friends, these recipes promise to elevate your outdoor cooking experience, making every meal an adventure worth remembering. Join us, as we cast our nets wide, diving into the art of seafood grilling with the enthusiasm of explorers discovering new worlds.

GRILLING FISH TO PERFECTION

RECIPE 1. CEDAR-PLANKED SALMON WITH LEMON-HERB BUTTER

PREPARATION TIME: 1 hr (includes soaking) - **COOKING TIME:** 20 min **MODE OF COOKING:** Grilling - **SERVINGS:** 4

INGREDIENTS: 1 cedar plank; 4 salmon fillets (6 oz. each); 2 Tbsp unsalted butter, softened; 1 tsp lemon zest; 1 Tbsp fresh dill, chopped; 1 Tbsp fresh parsley, chopped; Salt and pepper to taste

PROCEDURE: Soak cedar plank in water for 1 hr. Preheat grill to medium-high (375°F/190°C). Mix butter with lemon zest, dill, parsley, salt, and pepper. Place salmon on the plank, season with salt and pepper, and spread lemon-herb butter on top. Grill for 15-20 min, or until salmon is opaque and flakes easily with a fork.

N.V.: Calories: 300, Fat: 18g, Carbs: 1g, Protein: 34g, Sugar: 0g

RECIPE 2. GRILLED TUNA STEAKS WITH AVOCADO SALSA

PREPARATION TIME: 15 min - **COOKING TIME:** 6 min **MODE OF COOKING:** Grilling - **SERVINGS:** 4

INGREDIENTS: 4 tuna steaks (6 oz. each); 2 Tbsp olive oil; Salt and pepper to taste; 1 avocado, diced; 1 tomato, diced; 1/4 cup red onion, diced; 2 Tbsp cilantro, chopped; 1 lime, juiced; Salt to taste
PROCEDURE: Preheat grill to high (400°F/204°C). Brush tuna steaks with olive oil, season with salt and pepper. Grill for 3 min per side for medium-rare. Mix avocado, tomato, red onion, cilantro, lime juice, and salt to make the salsa. Serve tuna steaks topped with avocado salsa.
N.V.: Calories: 290, Fat: 15g, Carbs: 6g, Protein: 34g, Sugar: 2g

RECIPE 3. HERB-CRUSTED GRILLED TROUT

PREPARATION TIME: 10 min - **COOKING TIME:** 8 min **MODE OF COOKING:** Grilling - **SERVINGS:** 4
INGREDIENTS: 4 trout fillets; 2 Tbsp olive oil; 1/4 cup breadcrumbs; 2 Tbsp Parmesan cheese, grated; 1 Tbsp fresh basil, chopped; 1 Tbsp fresh thyme, chopped; Salt and pepper to taste
PROCEDURE: Preheat grill to medium (350°F/177°C). Mix breadcrumbs, Parmesan, basil, thyme, salt, and pepper. Brush trout with olive oil, press breadcrumb mixture onto the skinless side. Grill skin-side down for 4 min, carefully flip, and grill until cooked through, about 4 min.
N.V.: Calories: 250, Fat: 12g, Carbs: 5g, Protein: 31g, Sugar: 0g

RECIPE 4. GRILLED MAHI-MAHI WITH MANGO LIME SAUCE

PREPARATION TIME: 15 min - **COOKING TIME:** 10 min **MODE OF COOKING:** Grilling - **SERVINGS:** 4
INGREDIENTS: 4 mahi-mahi fillets (6 oz. each); 2 Tbsp olive oil; Salt and pepper to taste; 1 mango, peeled and diced; 1/4 cup lime juice; 1 Tbsp honey; 1 jalapeño, seeded and minced; 2 Tbsp cilantro, chopped
PROCEDURE: Preheat grill to medium-high (375°F/190°C). Season mahi-mahi with salt and pepper, brush with olive oil. Grill for 5 min per side. For the sauce, blend mango, lime juice, honey, and jalapeño until smooth. Stir in cilantro. Serve fish with mango lime sauce.
N.V.: Calories: 260, Fat: 9g, Carbs: 15g, Protein: 35g, Sugar: 12g

RECIPE 5. GRILLED SWORDFISH WITH OLIVE TAPENADE

PREPARATION TIME: 20 min - **COOKING TIME:** 10 min **MODE OF COOKING:** Grilling - **SERVINGS:** 4
INGREDIENTS: 4 swordfish steaks (6 oz. each); 2 Tbsp olive oil; Salt and pepper to taste; 1/2 cup olives, pitted and chopped; 2 Tbsp capers, rinsed and chopped; 2 cloves garlic, minced; 1 lemon, zested and juiced; 2 Tbsp parsley, chopped
PROCEDURE: Preheat grill to high (400°F/204°C). Season swordfish with salt and pepper, brush with olive oil. Grill for 5 min per side. Mix olives, capers, garlic, lemon zest, lemon juice, and parsley to make tapenade. Serve swordfish topped with olive tapenade.
N.V.: Calories: 310, Fat: 18g, Carbs: 3g, Protein: 34g, Sugar: 1g

RECIPE 6. SPICY GRILLED SHRIMP WITH GARLIC LIME BUTTER

PREPARATION TIME: 15 min - **COOKING TIME:** 5 min **MODE OF COOKING:** Grilling - **SERVINGS:** 4
INGREDIENTS: 1 lb large shrimp, peeled and deveined; 2 Tbsp olive oil; 1 tsp chili powder; 1/2 tsp garlic powder; Salt and pepper to taste; 4 Tbsp unsalted butter; 1 garlic clove, minced; 1 lime, juiced; 1 Tbsp cilantro, chopped

PROCEDURE: Preheat grill to medium-high (375°F/190°C). Toss shrimp with olive oil, chili powder, garlic powder, salt, and pepper. Grill until pink and opaque, about 2-3 min per side. Melt butter in a pan, add garlic, lime juice, and cilantro. Pour over grilled shrimp.
N.V.: Calories: 290, Fat: 20g, Carbs: 2g, Protein: 24g, Sugar: 0g

RECIPE 7. BLACKENED CATFISH WITH CUCUMBER DILL YOGURT SAUCE

PREPARATION TIME: 10 min - **COOKING TIME:** 8 min **MODE OF COOKING:** Grilling - **SERVINGS:** 4
INGREDIENTS: 4 catfish fillets (6 oz. each); 2 Tbsp blackening seasoning; 2 Tbsp olive oil; 1 cup Greek yogurt; 1/2 cucumber, grated and drained; 1 Tbsp fresh dill, chopped; 1 lemon, zested and juiced; Salt and pepper to taste
PROCEDURE: Preheat grill to medium-high (375°F/190°C). Rub catfish fillets with blackening seasoning and olive oil. Grill for 4 min on each side, or until the fish flakes easily with a fork. For the sauce, combine Greek yogurt, cucumber, dill, lemon zest, lemon juice, salt, and pepper in a bowl. Serve grilled catfish with a dollop of cucumber dill yogurt sauce on the side.
N.V.: Calories: 280, Fat: 15g, Carbs: 3g, Protein: 34g, Sugar: 2g

RECIPE 8. LEMON-HERB GRILLED SALMON

PREPARATION TIME: 15 min - **COOKING TIME:** 10 min
MODE OF COOKING: Grilling - **SERVINGS:** 4
INGREDIENTS: 4 salmon fillets (6 oz each); 2 lemons, one juiced and one sliced; 2 Tbsp. olive oil; 2 Tbsp. fresh dill, chopped; 2 Tbsp. fresh parsley, chopped; Salt and pepper to taste
DIRECTIONS: Preheat grill to medium-high heat. In a small bowl, mix lemon juice, olive oil, dill, parsley, salt, and pepper. Brush this mixture over both sides of the salmon fillets. Place lemon slices on the grill, and lay salmon on top, skin-side down. Grill for about 5 min, then carefully flip over and cook for another 5 min or until salmon is cooked through and flakes easily with a fork. Serve immediately, garnished with grilled lemon slices.
N.V.: Calories: 280, Fat: 16g, Carbs: 2g, Protein: 30g, Sugar: 1g

RECIPE 9. SPICY GRILLED SHRIMP WITH GARLIC LIME SAUCE

PREPARATION TIME: 20 min - **COOKING TIME:** 5 min
MODE OF COOKING: Grilling - **SERVINGS:** 4
INGREDIENTS: 1 lb large shrimp, peeled and deveined; 1 Tbsp. olive oil; 1 tsp chili powder; 1 tsp paprika; Salt and pepper to taste; **For the sauce:** 2 Tbsp. butter; 2 cloves garlic, minced; Juice of 1 lime; 1 tsp honey; 1 Tbsp. fresh cilantro, chopped
DIRECTIONS: Preheat grill to high heat. In a bowl, toss shrimp with olive oil, chili powder, paprika, salt, and pepper. Grill shrimp for 2-3 min on each side or until opaque. For the sauce, melt butter in a small pan over medium heat. Add garlic and cook until fragrant. Remove from heat, stir in lime juice, honey, and cilantro. Drizzle sauce over grilled shrimp before serving.
N.V.: Calories: 200, Fat: 10g, Carbs: 5g, Protein: 24g, Sugar: 2g

RECIPE 10. GRILLED MAHI-MAHI WITH MANGO SALAD

PREPARATION TIME: 15 min - **COOKING TIME:** 8 min
MODE OF COOKING: Grilling - **SERVINGS:** 4
INGREDIENTS: 4 mahi-mahi fillets (6 oz each); 2 Tbsp. olive oil; Salt and pepper to taste; **For the salad:** 1 ripe mango, diced; 1/2 cucumber, diced; 1/4 cup red bell pepper, diced; 1/4 cup red onion, thinly sliced; Juice of 1 lime; 2 Tbsp. fresh mint, chopped; Salt to taste

DIRECTIONS: Preheat grill to medium-high heat. Brush mahi-mahi with olive oil, season with salt and pepper. Grill for 4 min on each side or until fish flakes easily with a fork. For the salad, combine mango, cucumber, bell pepper, red onion, lime juice, mint, and salt in a bowl. Serve grilled mahi-mahi with mango salad on the side.
N.V.: Calories: 240, Fat: 9g, Carbs: 12g, Protein: 29g, Sugar: 9g

SHELLFISH AND BEYOND

RECIPE 1. GRILLED SCALLOPS WITH HERB BUTTER

PREPARATION TIME: 10 min - **COOKING TIME:** 6 min **MODE OF COOKING:** Grilling - **SERVINGS:** 4
INGREDIENTS: 12 large scallops; 2 Tbsp unsalted butter, softened; 1 Tbsp parsley, finely chopped; 1 clove garlic, minced; Zest of 1 lemon; Salt and pepper to taste
PROCEDURE: Preheat grill to high (450°F/232°C). Mix butter, parsley, garlic, lemon zest, salt, and pepper. Thread scallops onto skewers, season with salt and pepper. Grill for 3 min on each side or until opaque and slightly firm. Top scallops with a dollop of herb butter before serving.
N.V.: Calories: 150, Fat: 8g, Carbs: 4g, Protein: 14g, Sugar: 0g

RECIPE 2. LEMON-GRILLED SHRIMP SKEWERS

PREPARATION TIME: 15 min - **COOKING TIME:** 5 min **MODE OF COOKING:** Grilling - **SERVINGS:** 4
INGREDIENTS: 1 lb large shrimp, peeled and deveined; 2 lemons, thinly sliced; 2 Tbsp olive oil; 1 tsp smoked paprika; Salt and pepper to taste
PROCEDURE: Preheat grill to medium-high (375°F/190°C). Thread shrimp and lemon slices alternately onto skewers. Brush with olive oil, sprinkle with smoked paprika, salt, and pepper. Grill for 2-3 min on each side until shrimp are pink and opaque. Serve immediately.
N.V.: Calories: 200, Fat: 8g, Carbs: 3g, Protein: 30g, Sugar: 0g

RECIPE 3. CHAR-GRILLED OYSTERS WITH PARMESAN

PREPARATION TIME: 10 min - **COOKING TIME:** 5 min **MODE OF COOKING:** Grilling - **SERVINGS:** 4
INGREDIENTS: 12 oysters, shucked, on the half shell; 1/4 cup grated Parmesan cheese; 2 Tbsp unsalted butter, melted; 1 clove garlic, minced; 1 tsp parsley, chopped; Lemon wedges, for serving
PROCEDURE: Preheat grill to high (450°F/232°C). Mix Parmesan, butter, garlic, and parsley. Place oysters on the grill, shell side down. Spoon Parmesan mixture onto each oyster. Grill until bubbly and golden, about 5 min. Serve with lemon wedges.
N.V.: Calories: 110, Fat: 9g, Carbs: 2g, Protein: 6g, Sugar: 0g

RECIPE 4. GRILLED CLAMS WITH CHORIZO

PREPARATION TIME: 20 min - **COOKING TIME:** 10 min **MODE OF COOKING:** Grilling - **SERVINGS:** 4
INGREDIENTS: 24 clams, scrubbed; 4 oz chorizo, diced; 1/4 cup white wine; 2 Tbsp parsley, chopped; Bread, for serving
PROCEDURE: Preheat grill to medium (350°F/177°C). Place clams directly on the grill. Cook until they start to open, about 5 min. In a skillet, cook chorizo until crisp. Add white wine, simmer

for 1 min. Spoon chorizo mixture over opened clams, sprinkle with parsley. Serve immediately with bread.
N.V.: Calories: 220, Fat: 12g, Carbs: 10g, Protein: 18g, Sugar: 1g

RECIPE 5. SPICY GRILLED LOBSTER TAILS WITH GARLIC BUTTER

PREPARATION TIME: 15 min - **COOKING TIME:** 8 min **MODE OF COOKING:** Grilling - **SERVINGS:** 4
INGREDIENTS: 4 lobster tails, split; 4 Tbsp unsalted butter, melted; 2 cloves garlic, minced; 1 tsp red pepper flakes; Salt and pepper to taste; Lemon wedges, for serving
PROCEDURE: Preheat grill to medium-high (375°F/190°C). Mix butter, garlic, red pepper flakes, salt, and pepper. Brush mixture over lobster meat. Grill, flesh side down, for 4 min. Flip, grill until meat is opaque and cooked through, about 4 min more. Serve with lemon wedges.
N.V.: Calories: 230, Fat: 15g, Carbs: 2g, Protein: 22g, Sugar: 0g

RECIPE 6. GRILLED MUSSELS WITH HERB CRUMBS

PREPARATION TIME: 15 min - **COOKING TIME:** 6 min **MODE OF COOKING:** Grilling - **SERVINGS:** 4
INGREDIENTS: 2 lbs mussels, cleaned; 1/2 cup breadcrumbs; 1/4 cup Parmesan cheese, grated; 2 Tbsp olive oil; 2 cloves garlic, minced; 1 tsp thyme, chopped; Lemon wedges, for serving
PROCEDURE: Preheat grill to high (450°F/232°C). Mix breadcrumbs, Parmesan, olive oil, garlic, and thyme. Grill mussels until they open, about 5 min. Sprinkle breadcrumb mixture over mussels, grill until golden, about 1 min. Serve with lemon wedges.
N.V.: Calories: 310, Fat: 15g, Carbs: 20g, Protein: 25g, Sugar: 1g

RECIPE 7. CEDAR-PLANKED SCALLOPS WITH SMOKY CHILI SAUCE

PREPARATION TIME: 1 hr (includes soaking) - **COOKING TIME:** 8 min **MODE OF COOKING:** Grilling - **SERVINGS:** 4
INGREDIENTS: 1 cedar plank; 16 large scallops; 2 Tbsp olive oil; 1 Tbsp chili powder; 1 tsp smoked paprika; Salt to taste; 1/4 cup mayonnaise; 1 Tbsp lime juice; 1 tsp chipotle in adobo, minced; Cilantro, for garnish
PROCEDURE: Soak cedar plank in water for 1 hr. Preheat grill to medium-high (375°F/190°C). Mix olive oil, chili powder, smoked paprika, and salt. Toss scallops in the mixture. Place scallops on the plank. Grill for 6-8 min. Mix mayonnaise, lime juice, and chipotle for the sauce. Serve scallops with sauce, garnished with cilantro.
N.V.: Calories: 240, Fat: 18g, Carbs: 5g, Protein: 15g, Sugar: 0g

RECIPE 8. SMOKED SCALLOPS WITH HERB BUTTER

PREPARATION TIME: 10 min - **COOKING TIME:** 15 min
MODE OF COOKING: Smoking - **SERVINGS:** 4
INGREDIENTS: 12 large scallops; 2 Tbsp. unsalted butter, softened; 1 Tbsp. fresh parsley, finely chopped; 1 tsp fresh thyme leaves; 1 clove garlic, minced; Salt and pepper to taste; Lemon wedges for serving
DIRECTIONS: Mix butter with parsley, thyme, garlic, salt, and pepper; Set aside. Season scallops with salt and pepper. Preheat smoker to 225°F (107°C). Place scallops on smoker, cook until opaque, about 15 min. Top each scallop with herb butter before serving with lemon wedges.
N.V.: Calories: 150, Fat: 8g, Carbs: 4g, Protein: 14g, Sugar: 0g

RECIPE 9. CHAR-GRILLED OYSTER MUSHROOMS

PREPARATION TIME: 5 min - **COOKING TIME:** 8 min
MODE OF COOKING: Grilling - **SERVINGS:** 4
INGREDIENTS: 16 large oyster mushrooms; 2 Tbsp. olive oil; 2 Tbsp. soy sauce; 1 Tbsp. balsamic vinegar; 1 tsp smoked paprika; Salt and pepper to taste; Fresh parsley, chopped for garnish
DIRECTIONS: Whisk together olive oil, soy sauce, vinegar, smoked paprika, salt, and pepper. Brush mixture over mushrooms. Preheat grill to high (450°F or 232°C). Grill mushrooms 4 min per side until charred. Garnish with parsley.
N.V.: Calories: 90, Fat: 7g, Carbs: 6g, Protein: 2g, Sugar: 2g

RECIPE 10. LEMON-HERB GRILLED SHRIMP

PREPARATION TIME: 20 min (includes marinating) - **COOKING TIME:** 6 min
MODE OF COOKING: Grilling - **SERVINGS:** 4
INGREDIENTS: 1 lb. large shrimp, peeled and deveined; 1/4 cup olive oil; Juice and zest of 1 lemon; 2 Tbsp. fresh dill, chopped; 2 Tbsp. fresh parsley, chopped; 1 garlic clove, minced; Salt and pepper to taste
DIRECTIONS: Mix olive oil, lemon juice and zest, dill, parsley, garlic, salt, and pepper. Marinate shrimp for 15 min. Preheat grill to medium-high (375°F or 190°C). Grill shrimp 2-3 min per side until pink. Serve immediately.
N.V.: Calories: 200, Fat: 10g, Carbs: 2g, Protein: 24g, Sugar: 0g

RECIPE 11. SPICY GRILLED CRAB LEGS

PREPARATION TIME: 5 min - **COOKING TIME:** 10 min
MODE OF COOKING: Grilling - **SERVINGS:** 4
INGREDIENTS: 2 lbs. crab legs, split; 1/4 cup butter, melted; 1 Tbsp. Cajun seasoning; 1 tsp garlic powder; 1/2 tsp red pepper flakes; Lemon wedges for serving
DIRECTIONS: Preheat grill to medium (350°F or 177°C). Mix melted butter with Cajun seasoning, garlic powder, and red pepper flakes. Brush mixture over crab legs. Grill 5 min per side. Serve with lemon wedges.
N.V.: Calories: 300, Fat: 15g, Carbs: 1g, Protein: 35g, Sugar: 0g

SEAFOOD MIXES AND MATCHES

RECIPE 1. SEAFOOD PAELLA ON THE GRILL

PREPARATION TIME: 30 min - **COOKING TIME:** 40 min **MODE OF COOKING:** Grilling - **SERVINGS:** 6
INGREDIENTS: 2 cups paella rice; 4 cups fish stock; 1 lb mixed seafood (shrimp, mussels, and squid rings); 1/2 lb chicken thighs, cubed; 1/2 cup tomato sauce; 1 bell pepper, sliced; 1 onion, chopped; 2 cloves garlic, minced; 1/2 cup peas; 1 tsp saffron threads; Salt and pepper to taste; 2 Tbsp olive oil; Lemon wedges, for serving
PROCEDURE: Preheat grill to medium-high (375°F/190°C). In a large paella pan, heat olive oil. Sauté onion, garlic, and bell pepper. Add chicken, cook until browned. Stir in rice, tomato sauce,

saffron, salt, and pepper. Pour in fish stock, bring to a simmer. Arrange seafood on top, cover with foil, cook on the grill for 30 min, until rice is tender and seafood is cooked. Serve with lemon wedges.

N.V.: Calories: 450, Fat: 10g, Carbs: 65g, Protein: 30g, Sugar: 3g

Recipe 2. Grilled Seafood and Vegetable Skewers

PREPARATION TIME: 20 min - **COOKING TIME:** 10 min **MODE OF COOKING:** Grilling - **SERVINGS:** 4

INGREDIENTS: 8 large shrimp, peeled and deveined; 8 sea scallops; 1 zucchini, sliced; 1 red onion, cut into chunks; 1 bell pepper, cut into chunks; 2 Tbsp olive oil; 1 lemon, juiced; 1 Tbsp fresh thyme, chopped; Salt and pepper to taste

PROCEDURE: Preheat grill to high (450°F/232°C). Thread shrimp, scallops, zucchini, onion, and bell pepper alternately onto skewers. Mix olive oil, lemon juice, thyme, salt, and pepper. Brush the mixture over skewers. Grill for 5 min on each side, or until seafood is cooked through and vegetables are tender.

N.V.: Calories: 200, Fat: 7g, Carbs: 12g, Protein: 24g, Sugar: 4g

Recipe 3. Spicy Grilled Fish Tacos

PREPARATION TIME: 15 min - **COOKING TIME:** 10 min **MODE OF COOKING:** Grilling - **SERVINGS:** 4

INGREDIENTS: 1 lb white fish fillets (like cod or tilapia); 2 Tbsp olive oil; 1 Tbsp lime juice; 1 Tbsp chili powder; 1 tsp cumin; 1/2 tsp cayenne pepper; Salt to taste; 8 corn tortillas; 1 cup cabbage, shredded; 1 avocado, sliced; 1/4 cup fresh cilantro, chopped; Lime wedges, for serving

PROCEDURE: Preheat grill to medium-high (375°F/190°C). Mix olive oil, lime juice, chili powder, cumin, cayenne pepper, and salt. Marinate fish in mixture for 10 min. Grill fish for 5 min on each side. Break into pieces. Warm tortillas on the grill. Assemble tacos with fish, cabbage, avocado, cilantro. Serve with lime wedges.

N.V.: Calories: 310, Fat: 15g, Carbs: 25g, Protein: 23g, Sugar: 2g

Recipe 4. Grilled Salmon and Shrimp Scampi

PREPARATION TIME: 20 min - **COOKING TIME:** 12 min **MODE OF COOKING:** Grilling - **SERVINGS:** 4

INGREDIENTS: 4 salmon fillets (6 oz. each); 12 large shrimp, peeled and deveined; 4 Tbsp butter; 4 cloves garlic, minced; 1/4 cup white wine; 1 lemon, juiced; 2 Tbsp parsley, chopped; Salt and pepper to taste

PROCEDURE: Preheat grill to medium (350°F/177°C). Season salmon and shrimp with salt and pepper. Grill salmon for 6 min on each side. In a skillet on the grill, melt butter, add garlic, sauté for 1 min. Add shrimp, white wine, and lemon juice, cook until shrimp are pink, about 5 min. Stir in parsley. Serve shrimp scampi over grilled salmon.

N.V.: Calories: 400, Fat: 23g, Carbs: 2g, Protein: 44g, Sugar: 0g

Recipe 5. Mixed Seafood Grill with Garlic Lemon Butter

PREPARATION TIME: 15 min - **COOKING TIME:** 10 min **MODE OF COOKING:** Grilling - **SERVINGS:** 4

INGREDIENTS: 1/2 lb scallops; 1/2 lb large shrimp, peeled and deveined; 1/2 lb salmon, cut into chunks; 4 Tbsp unsalted butter; 2 cloves garlic, minced; 1 lemon, juiced; 2 Tbsp parsley, chopped; Salt and pepper to taste

PROCEDURE: Preheat grill to medium-high (375°F/190°C). Season seafood with salt and pepper. Grill scallops, shrimp, and salmon chunks for 2-3 min on each side. In a skillet on the grill, melt butter, add garlic, cook until fragrant. Remove from heat, stir in lemon juice and parsley. Pour garlic lemon butter over grilled seafood.
N.V.: Calories: 290, Fat: 15g, Carbs: 3g, Protein: 35g, Sugar: 0g

RECIPE 6. GRILLED MEDITERRANEAN SEAFOOD PIZZA

PREPARATION TIME: 20 min - **COOKING TIME:** 15 min **MODE OF COOKING:** Grilling - **SERVINGS:** 4
INGREDIENTS: 1 pre-made pizza dough; 1/2 cup marinara sauce; 1/4 lb shrimp, peeled and deveined; 1/4 lb calamari rings; 1/4 cup olives, sliced; 1/2 cup feta cheese, crumbled; 2 Tbsp olive oil; 1 tsp oregano; Salt and pepper to taste
PROCEDURE: Preheat grill to medium (350°F/177°C). Roll out pizza dough, brush with olive oil. Grill one side until golden, about 5 min. Flip dough, spread marinara sauce, top with shrimp, calamari, olives, feta cheese. Season with oregano, salt, and pepper. Close grill lid, cook until crust is crispy and seafood is cooked, Abou 10 min. Serve immediately.
N.V.: Calories: 390, Fat: 18g, Carbs: 35g, Protein: 22g, Sugar: 3g

RECIPE 7. CIOPPINO-STYLE GRILLED SEAFOOD STEW

PREPARATION TIME: 25 min - **COOKING TIME:** 20 min **MODE OF COOKING:** Grilling and Simmering - **SERVINGS:** 6
INGREDIENTS: 1/2 lb sea bass, cubed; 1/2 lb large shrimp, peeled and deveined; 12 mussels, cleaned; 1/2 lb scallops; 1 can (14 oz.) diced tomatoes; 1 onion, diced; 3 cloves garlic, minced; 1 cup white wine; 2 cups fish stock; 1 tsp dried basil; 1 tsp dried oregano; 1/2 tsp red pepper flakes; 2 Tbsp olive oil; Salt and pepper to taste; Fresh parsley, for garnish
PROCEDURE: Preheat grill to medium-high (375°F/190°C). In a large pot on the grill, heat olive oil. Add onion and garlic, sauté until translucent. Add tomatoes, white wine, fish stock, basil, oregano, red pepper flakes, salt, and pepper. Bring to a simmer. Grill sea bass, shrimp, mussels, and scallops separately until just cooked, about 3-5 min each. Add grilled seafood to the pot, simmer for an additional 5 min. Garnish with fresh parsley before serving.
N.V.: Calories: 310, Fat: 10g, Carbs: 12g, Protein: 36g, Sugar: 3g

RECIPE 8. GRILLED SEAFOOD PAELLA

PREPARATION TIME: 20 min - **COOKING TIME:** 40 min
MODE OF COOKING: Grilling - **SERVINGS:** 6
INGREDIENTS: 1 cup Arborio rice; 2 cups fish stock; 1/2 lb. shrimp, peeled; 1/2 lb. mussels, cleaned; 1/2 lb. squid rings; 1/4 cup olive oil; 1 onion, finely chopped; 2 garlic cloves, minced; 1 red bell pepper, diced; 1/2 cup peas; 1 tsp saffron threads; 1 tsp smoked paprika; Salt and pepper to taste; Lemon wedges for serving
DIRECTIONS: Preheat grill to medium-high (375°F or 190°C). In a large skillet on the grill, heat olive oil; sauté onion, garlic, and bell pepper until soft. Add rice, stirring to coat. Pour in fish stock, add saffron, smoked paprika, salt, and pepper. Bring to a simmer, cover, cook 20 min. Add shrimp, mussels, squid, and peas, cook uncovered 10-15 min until seafood is cooked and rice is tender. Serve with lemon wedges.
N.V.: Calories: 350, Fat: 10g, Carbs: 45g, Protein: 25g, Sugar: 2g

RECIPE 9. CEDAR-PLANKED SALMON AND SCALLOP DUO

PREPARATION TIME: 15 min (plus soaking) - **COOKING TIME:** 20 min
MODE OF COOKING: Grilling - **SERVINGS:** 4
INGREDIENTS: 4 salmon fillets, 6 oz. each; 12 large scallops; 2 cedar planks, soaked; 2 Tbsp. maple syrup; 2 Tbsp. soy sauce; 1 Tbsp. Dijon mustard; 1 garlic clove, minced; Salt and pepper to taste
DIRECTIONS: Preheat grill to medium (350°F or 177°C). Mix maple syrup, soy sauce, mustard, and garlic. Season salmon and scallops with salt and pepper, brush with mixture. Place on soaked planks. Grill covered 15-20 min until salmon is opaque and scallops are firm.
N.V.: Calories: 300, Fat: 12g, Carbs: 15g, Protein: 35g, Sugar: 7g

RECIPE 10. SMOKEY SHRIMP AND CHORIZO SKILLET

PREPARATION TIME: 10 min - **COOKING TIME:** 15 min
MODE OF COOKING: Grilling - **SERVINGS:** 4
INGREDIENTS: 1 lb. shrimp, peeled and deveined; 1/2 lb. chorizo, sliced; 1 onion, chopped; 1 red bell pepper, chopped; 2 garlic cloves, minced; 1 tsp smoked paprika; 1/2 tsp cayenne pepper; Salt and pepper to taste; 2 Tbsp. olive oil; Fresh parsley, chopped for garnish
DIRECTIONS: Preheat grill to medium-high (375°F or 190°C). In a cast-iron skillet on the grill, heat olive oil. Add chorizo, cook 5 min. Add onion, bell pepper, garlic, cook until soft. Add shrimp, smoked paprika, cayenne, salt, and pepper, cook 5-7 min until shrimp are pink. Garnish with parsley.
N.V.: Calories: 400, Fat: 25g, Carbs: 5g, Protein: 35g, Sugar: 2g

RECIPE 11. GRILLED CLAMS AND MUSSELS WITH GARLIC BUTTER

PREPARATION TIME: 10 min - **COOKING TIME:** 10 min
MODE OF COOKING: Grilling - **SERVINGS:** 4
INGREDIENTS: 1 lb. clams, cleaned; 1 lb. mussels, cleaned; 1/4 cup unsalted butter, melted; 3 garlic cloves, minced; 2 Tbsp. parsley, chopped; 1 lemon, juiced; Salt and pepper to taste; Crusty bread for serving
DIRECTIONS: Preheat grill to high (450°F or 232°C). Mix butter, garlic, parsley, lemon juice, salt, and pepper. Place clams and mussels in a grill basket. Grill covered 8-10 min until shells open. Toss with garlic butter. Serve with crusty bread.
N.V.: Calories: 210, Fat: 12g, Carbs: 10g, Protein: 20g, Sugar: 0g

CHAPTER 15: SNACKING AND SHARING

In the heart of every memorable gathering, there lies a table laden with the magic of shared meals — a collection of snacks and small plates that bring people together, igniting conversations and laughter. Chapter 15, "Snacking and Sharing," is dedicated to the art of creating these convivial moments through the warmth of grilled delights. Here, we venture beyond the conventional, exploring an array of quick bites and finger foods that are perfect for any social occasion, from casual backyard get-togethers to elegant outdoor soirees.

This chapter is a treasure trove of recipes designed not just to satiate hunger but to enhance the very experience of companionship. Each recipe, crafted with the same passion and precision as our heartier dishes, is intended to be shared, to circulate among friends and family as easily as the stories and laughter that accompany them. From the smoky allure of grilled skewers to the tantalizing bite of stuffed mushrooms, these dishes are made to traverse the table, inviting everyone to partake in the bounty.

The beauty of these snacks lies not only in their flavors but in their simplicity and versatility. Whether you're looking for a healthy snack to dip and dive into or seeking to impress with a platter of gourmet bites, this chapter provides the perfect recipe for every occasion. So light up the grill, gather your loved ones, and prepare to indulge in the joy of snacking and sharing — where every bite is a moment to savor and every dish is a memory in the making.

QUICK BITES AND FINGER FOODS

RECIPE 1. GRILLED PROSCIUTTO-WRAPPED ASPARAGUS

PREPARATION TIME: 10 min - **COOKING TIME:** 5 min **MODE OF COOKING:** Grilling - **SERVINGS:** 4
INGREDIENTS: 16 asparagus spears, trimmed; 8 slices prosciutto, halved lengthwise; 1 Tbsp olive oil; Salt and pepper to taste
PROCEDURE: Wrap each asparagus spear with a half slice of prosciutto. Brush lightly with olive oil and season with salt and pepper. Preheat grill to medium-high (375°F/190°C). Grill asparagus, turning occasionally, until prosciutto is crispy and asparagus is tender, about 5 minutes. Serve immediately.
N.V.: Calories: 60, Fat: 3g, Carbs: 3g, Protein: 5g, Sugar: 1g

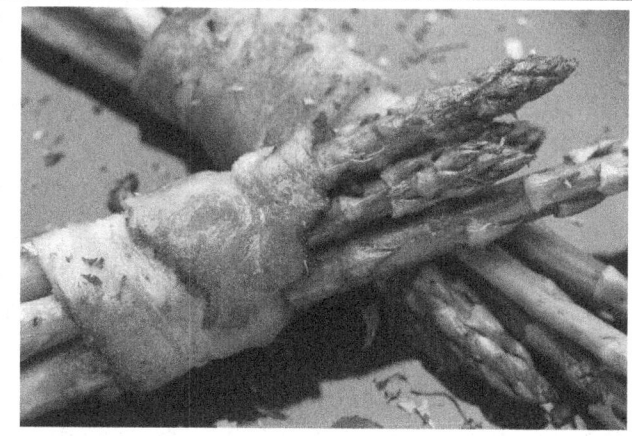

RECIPE 2. MINI GRILLED CHEESE SANDWICHES WITH TOMATO SOUP SHOTS

PREPARATION TIME: 15 min - **COOKING TIME:** 10 min **MODE OF COOKING:** Grilling - **SERVINGS:** 8
INGREDIENTS: 16 mini slices sourdough bread; 8 slices cheddar cheese; 4 Tbsp unsalted butter, softened; 2 cups tomato soup
PROCEDURE: Assemble 8 mini sandwiches with bread and cheese slices. Butter the outside of each sandwich. Preheat grill to medium (350°F/177°C). Grill sandwiches until golden brown and

cheese is melted, about 5 minutes per side. Heat tomato soup and serve in shot glasses alongside grilled cheese sandwiches.
N.V.: Calories: 200, Fat: 12g, Carbs: 15g, Protein: 7g, Sugar: 4g

RECIPE 3. GRILLED SHRIMP AND PINEAPPLE SKEWERS

PREPARATION TIME: 20 min - **COOKING TIME:** 6 min **MODE OF COOKING:** Grilling - **SERVINGS:** 4
INGREDIENTS: 24 large shrimp, peeled and deveined; 24 pineapple chunks; 2 Tbsp soy sauce; 1 Tbsp honey; 1 tsp garlic, minced; 1 tsp ginger, minced
PROCEDURE: Thread shrimp and pineapple chunks alternately onto skewers. Mix soy sauce, honey, garlic, and ginger. Brush mixture over skewers. Preheat grill to high (450°F/232°C). Grill skewers, turning once, until shrimp are pink and opaque, about 3 minutes per side. Serve immediately.
N.V.: Calories: 150, Fat: 1g, Carbs: 18g, Protein: 18g, Sugar: 14g

RECIPE 4. SMOKY GRILLED GUACAMOLE

PREPARATION TIME: 10 min - **COOKING TIME:** 5 min **MODE OF COOKING:** Grilling - **SERVINGS:** 4
INGREDIENTS: 2 ripe avocados, halved and pitted; 1 lime, halved; 1 small onion, quartered; 1 jalapeño, halved and seeded; 1 tomato, halved; Salt and pepper to taste; Cilantro, chopped for garnish
PROCEDURE: Preheat grill to medium-high (375°F/190°C). Grill avocados, lime, onion, jalapeño, and tomato until charred, about 5 minutes. Scoop avocado flesh into a bowl. Squeeze grilled lime juice over avocado. Chop grilled onion, jalapeño, and tomato; add to avocado. Mash together, season with salt and pepper. Garnish with cilantro.
N.V.: Calories: 170, Fat: 15g, Carbs: 12g, Protein: 2g, Sugar: 2g

RECIPE 5. BACON-WRAPPED STUFFED JALAPEÑOS

PREPARATION TIME: 20 min - **COOKING TIME:** 10 min **MODE OF COOKING:** Grilling - **SERVINGS:** 8
INGREDIENTS: 16 jalapeños, halved and seeded; 8 oz cream cheese, softened; 1/4 cup cheddar cheese, grated; 16 slices bacon, halved; Salt and pepper to taste
PROCEDURE: Mix cream cheese, cheddar cheese, salt, and pepper. Fill each jalapeño half with cheese mixture. Wrap each with a half slice of bacon. Secure with a toothpick. Preheat grill to medium (350°F/177°C). Grill jalapeños, turning occasionally, until bacon is crispy, about 10 minutes. Serve immediately.
N.V.: Calories: 200, Fat: 16g, Carbs: 3g, Protein: 10g, Sugar: 2g

RECIPE 6. GRILLED PEACHES WITH BALSAMIC GLAZE

PREPARATION TIME: 5 min - **COOKING TIME:** 6 min **MODE OF COOKING:** Grilling - **SERVINGS:** 4
INGREDIENTS: 4 peaches, halved and pitted; 2 Tbsp balsamic vinegar; 1 Tbsp honey; Mint leaves, for garnish
PROCEDURE: Preheat grill to high (450°F/232°C). Grill peaches, cut side down, until charred, about 3 minutes. Flip, grill for 3 more minutes. In a small saucepan, reduce balsamic vinegar and honey over medium heat until thickened. Drizzle glaze over grilled peaches. Garnish with mint leaves.

N.V.: Calories: 90, Fat: 0.5g, Carbs: 22g, Protein: 1g, Sugar: 20g

RECIPE 7. SPICY GRILLED CORN WITH COTIJA CHEESE

PREPARATION TIME: 10 min - **COOKING TIME:** 10 min **MODE OF COOKING:** Grilling - **SERVINGS:** 4
INGREDIENTS: 4 ears of corn, husks removed; 1/4 cup mayonnaise; 1 tsp chili powder; 1/4 cup cotija cheese, crumbled; 1 lime, cut into wedges; Cilantro, chopped for garnish
PROCEDURE: Preheat grill to medium-high (375°F/190°C). Grill corn, turning occasionally, until charred and tender, about 10 minutes. Mix mayonnaise and chili powder. Brush mixture over grilled corn. Sprinkle with cotija cheese and cilantro. Serve with lime wedges.
N.V.: Calories: 200, Fat: 12g, Carbs: 23g, Protein: 5g, Sugar: 7g

RECIPE 8. GRILLED PARMESAN GARLIC SHRIMP SKEWERS

PREPARATION TIME: 15 min (includes marinating) - **COOKING TIME:** 6 min
MODE OF COOKING: Grilling - **SERVINGS:** 4
INGREDIENTS: 1 lb. large shrimp, peeled and deveined; 1/4 cup olive oil; 3 garlic cloves, minced; 1/4 cup Parmesan, grated; 1 tsp Italian seasoning; Salt and pepper to taste; Wooden skewers, soaked
DIRECTIONS: Whisk together olive oil, garlic, Parmesan, Italian seasoning, salt, and pepper. Marinate shrimp for 10 min. Thread shrimp onto skewers. Preheat grill to high (450°F or 232°C). Grill skewers 2-3 min per side until pink and slightly charred. Serve immediately.
N.V.: Calories: 210, Fat: 10g, Carbs: 2g, Protein: 25g, Sugar: 0g

RECIPE 9. BBQ CHICKEN SLIDERS

PREPARATION TIME: 20 min - **COOKING TIME:** 30 min
MODE OF COOKING: Grilling - **SERVINGS:** 8
INGREDIENTS: 2 lbs. chicken breast; 1 cup BBQ sauce; 1/4 cup apple cider vinegar; 1 Tbsp. brown sugar; 1 tsp garlic powder; 8 slider buns; 1 cup coleslaw; Salt and pepper to taste
DIRECTIONS: Season chicken with salt, pepper, and garlic powder. Preheat grill to medium (350°F or 177°C). Grill chicken 15 min per side, until cooked through. Shred chicken, mix with BBQ sauce, vinegar, and brown sugar. Heap onto slider buns, top with coleslaw.
N.V.: Calories: 300, Fat: 6g, Carbs: 35g, Protein: 25g, Sugar: 10g

RECIPE 10. SPICY GRILLED CORN JALAPEÑO POPS

PREPARATION TIME: 15 min - **COOKING TIME:** 10 min
MODE OF COOKING: Grilling - **SERVINGS:** 6
INGREDIENTS: 6 jalapeños, halved and seeded; 1 cup corn kernels; 1/2 cup cream cheese, softened; 1/4 cup cheddar cheese, shredded; 1/4 cup green onions, chopped; Salt and pepper to taste; 12 bacon strips, halved
DIRECTIONS: Mix corn, cream cheese, cheddar, green onions, salt, and pepper. Stuff jalapeños with mixture, wrap with bacon. Preheat grill to medium (350°F or 177°C). Place jalapeños on grill, cover, cook 10 min, turning once, until bacon is crispy.
N.V.: Calories: 220, Fat: 18g, Carbs: 6g, Protein: 10g, Sugar: 2g

SHARED PLATES FOR SOCIAL GRILLING

RECIPE 1. SMOKY PAPRIKA SHRIMP SKEWERS

PREPARATION TIME: 20 min - **COOKING TIME:** 10 min **MODE OF COOKING:** Grilling - **SERVINGS:** 4

INGREDIENTS: 1 lb. shrimp, peeled and deveined; 1 Tbsp. olive oil; 2 tsp smoked paprika; 1 tsp garlic powder; 1/4 tsp cayenne pepper; Salt and black pepper to taste; 8 wooden skewers, soaked in water

DIRECTIONS: In a bowl, combine olive oil, smoked paprika, garlic powder, cayenne pepper, salt, and black pepper. Add shrimp and toss to coat evenly. Thread shrimp onto skewers. Preheat grill to medium-high heat (about 375°F/190°C). Grill skewers for 4-5 minutes on each side, or until shrimp are opaque and slightly charred.

N.V.: Calories: 120, Fat: 3g, Carbs: 2g, Protein: 20g, Sugar: 0g

RECIPE 2. GRILLED CORN WITH CILANTRO-LIME BUTTER

PREPARATION TIME: 15 min - **COOKING TIME:** 15 min **MODE OF COOKING:** Grilling - **SERVINGS:** 4

INGREDIENTS: 4 ears of corn, husks removed; 4 Tbsp. unsalted butter, softened; 1 lime, zested and juiced; 2 Tbsp. cilantro, finely chopped; Salt and pepper to taste

DIRECTIONS: In a small bowl, mix butter with lime zest, lime juice, cilantro, salt, and pepper. Spread the mixture evenly over each ear of corn. Wrap each ear in foil and grill over medium heat (350°F/177°C) for 15 minutes, turning occasionally. Remove from grill, unwrap, and serve hot.

N.V.: Calories: 200, Fat: 11g, Carbs: 27g, Protein: 4g, Sugar: 6g

RECIPE 3. BALSAMIC GLAZED BRUSSELS SPROUTS

PREPARATION TIME: 10 min - **COOKING TIME:** 20 min **MODE OF COOKING:** Grilling - **SERVINGS:** 4

INGREDIENTS: 1 lb. Brussels sprouts, halved; 2 Tbsp. olive oil; 3 Tbsp. balsamic vinegar; 1 tsp honey; Salt and pepper to taste; 1/4 cup grated Parmesan cheese

DIRECTIONS: Preheat grill to medium (350°F/177°C). Toss Brussels sprouts with olive oil, salt, and pepper. Grill on a vegetable basket over indirect heat for 20 minutes, stirring occasionally. Meanwhile, reduce balsamic vinegar and honey in a saucepan until thickened. Drizzle glaze over grilled Brussels sprouts and sprinkle with Parmesan before serving.

N.V.: Calories: 160, Fat: 8g, Carbs: 18g, Protein: 6g, Sugar: 7g

RECIPE 4. ASIAN-STYLE GRILLED EGGPLANT

PREPARATION TIME: 30 min (includes marinating) - **COOKING TIME:** 15 min **MODE OF COOKING:** Grilling - **SERVINGS:** 4

INGREDIENTS: 2 large eggplants, sliced into 1/2-inch-thick rounds; 1/4 cup soy sauce; 2 Tbsp. sesame oil; 1 Tbsp. honey; 2 cloves garlic, minced; 1 tsp ginger, grated; 1 Tbsp. sesame seeds; 1 green onion, thinly sliced

DIRECTIONS: Whisk together soy sauce, sesame oil, honey, garlic, and ginger in a bowl. Marinate eggplant slices in the mixture for 20 minutes. Preheat grill to medium-high (375°F/190°C). Grill eggplant for 7-8 minutes on each side, or until tender and grill marks appear. Garnish with sesame seeds and green onion before serving.
N.V.: Calories: 180, Fat: 10g, Carbs: 22g, Protein: 4g, Sugar: 12g

RECIPE 5. CHARRED BELL PEPPER DIP

PREPARATION TIME: 10 min - **COOKING TIME:** 15 min **MODE OF COOKING:** Grilling - **SERVINGS:** 4
INGREDIENTS: 3 bell peppers (red, yellow, green), halved and seeded; 1 clove garlic; 1/4 cup olive oil; 1 Tbsp. lemon juice; Salt and pepper to taste; 1/4 cup fresh basil leaves, chopped
DIRECTIONS: Grill bell peppers over high heat (400°F/204°C) until charred on all sides, about 15 minutes. Place in a bowl and cover with plastic wrap for 10 minutes to steam. Peel away the charred skins. Blend peppers, garlic, olive oil, lemon juice, salt, and pepper until smooth. Stir in chopped basil. Serve with grilled bread or vegetables.
N.V.: Calories: 150, Fat: 14g, Carbs: 6g, Protein: 1g, Sugar: 4g

RECIPE 6. ZESTY LIME AND CILANTRO CHICKEN WINGS

PREPARATION TIME: 25 min (includes marinating) - **COOKING TIME:** 20 min **MODE OF COOKING:** Grilling - **SERVINGS:** 4
INGREDIENTS: 2 lb. chicken wings; 1/4 cup olive oil; 1/4 cup lime juice; 1/4 cup cilantro, finely chopped; 2 garlic cloves, minced; 1 tsp chili powder; Salt and pepper to taste
DIRECTIONS: In a large bowl, combine olive oil, lime juice, cilantro, garlic, chili powder, salt, and pepper. Add chicken wings and marinate for at least 20 minutes. Preheat grill to medium-high (375°F/190°C). Grill wings for 10 minutes on each side, or until crispy and fully cooked. Serve with extra lime wedges and cilantro.
N.V.: Calories: 310, Fat: 22g, Carbs: 1g, Protein: 24g, Sugar: 0g

RECIPE 7. SWEET AND SPICY GRILLED PINEAPPLE

PREPARATION TIME: 10 min - **COOKING TIME:** 8 min **MODE OF COOKING:** Grilling - **SERVINGS:** 4
INGREDIENTS: 1 pineapple, peeled, cored, and cut into rings; 1 Tbsp. honey; 1 tsp chili flakes; 1 lime, zested and juiced
DIRECTIONS: In a small bowl, combine honey, chili flakes, lime zest, and lime juice. Brush mixture over pineapple rings. Grill over medium-high heat (375°F/190°C) for 4 minutes on each side, or until grill marks appear and pineapple is heated through. Serve as a dessert or a tangy side dish.
N.V.: Calories: 100, Fat: 0g, Carbs: 25g, Protein: 1g, Sugar: 19g

RECIPE 8. GRILLED PROSCIUTTO-WRAPPED PEACHES

PREPARATION TIME: 10 min - **COOKING TIME:** 8 min
MODE OF COOKING: Grilling - **SERVINGS:** 4
INGREDIENTS: 4 peaches, halved and pitted; 8 slices prosciutto; 1/4 cup balsamic glaze; Arugula for serving; Salt and pepper to taste
DIRECTIONS: Wrap each peach half with a slice of prosciutto. Preheat grill to medium-high (375°F or 190°C). Place peaches on grill, cut side down, grill 4 min until char marks appear. Flip,

grill another 4 min. Serve on a bed of arugula, drizzle with balsamic glaze, season with salt and pepper.
N.V.: Calories: 180, Fat: 7g, Carbs: 24g, Protein: 4g, Sugar: 20g

RECIPE 9. GRILLED VEGETABLE PLATTER WITH ROMESCO SAUCE

PREPARATION TIME: 15 min - **COOKING TIME:** 20 min
MODE OF COOKING: Grilling - **SERVINGS:** 6
INGREDIENTS: 2 bell peppers, sliced; 2 zucchinis, sliced lengthwise; 1 eggplant, sliced lengthwise; 12 asparagus spears; 1/4 cup olive oil; Salt and pepper to taste; **For the Romesco Sauce:** 1 roasted red pepper, 1/2 cup toasted almonds, 2 garlic cloves, 1 tsp smoked paprika, 2 Tbsp. red wine vinegar, 1/2 cup olive oil, Salt to taste
DIRECTIONS: Preheat grill to medium (350°F or 177°C). Toss vegetables with olive oil, salt, and pepper. Grill vegetables until tender and charred, about 5-7 min per side. For the sauce, blend roasted pepper, almonds, garlic, paprika, vinegar, and olive oil until smooth, season with salt. Serve grilled vegetables with romesco sauce.
N.V.: Calories: 250, Fat: 21g, Carbs: 15g, Protein: 4g, Sugar: 6g

RECIPE 10. GRILLED HALLOUMI AND VEGETABLE TACOS

PREPARATION TIME: 15 min - **COOKING TIME:** 10 min
MODE OF COOKING: Grilling - **SERVINGS:** 4
INGREDIENTS: 8 oz. halloumi cheese, sliced; 2 bell peppers, sliced; 1 large onion, sliced; 8 small corn tortillas; 1/4 cup cilantro, chopped; 2 limes, cut into wedges; 1 Tbsp. olive oil; Salt and pepper to taste
DIRECTIONS: Toss bell peppers and onion with olive oil, salt, and pepper. Grill over medium heat (350°F or 177°C) until charred, about 5 min. Grill halloumi until browned, about 3 min per side. Warm tortillas on the grill. Assemble tacos with vegetables, halloumi, top with cilantro. Serve with lime wedges.
N.V.: Calories: 320, Fat: 18g, Carbs: 25g, Protein: 18g, Sugar: 5g

HEALTHY SNACKS AND DIPS

RECIPE 1. AVOCADO HUMMUS

PREPARATION TIME: 10 min - **COOKING TIME:** 0 min **MODE OF COOKING:** Blending - **SERVINGS:** 4
INGREDIENTS: 1 ripe avocado; 1 can (15 oz.) chickpeas, drained and rinsed; 2 Tbsp. tahini; 1 garlic clove; 2 Tbsp. lemon juice; Salt and pepper to taste; 1/4 tsp cumin; 2 Tbsp. olive oil; Water as needed for consistency
DIRECTIONS: Combine avocado, chickpeas, tahini, garlic, lemon juice, salt, pepper, cumin, and olive oil in a food processor. Blend until smooth, adding water as needed to reach desired consistency. Serve chilled with vegetables or whole-grain crackers.
N.V.: Calories: 220, Fat: 14g, Carbs: 20g, Protein: 6g, Sugar: 3g

RECIPE 2. SPICY KALE CHIPS

PREPARATION TIME: 10 min - **COOKING TIME:** 20 min **MODE OF COOKING:** Baking - **SERVINGS:** 4

INGREDIENTS: 1 bunch kale, stems removed, leaves torn; 1 Tbsp. olive oil; 1/2 tsp smoked paprika; 1/4 tsp garlic powder; Salt to taste; 1/4 tsp chili powder

DIRECTIONS: Preheat oven to 300°F (150°C). Toss kale with olive oil, smoked paprika, garlic powder, salt, and chili powder. Spread on a baking sheet in a single layer. Bake for 20 minutes, or until crisp, turning halfway through. Let cool before serving.

N.V.: Calories: 60, Fat: 3.5g, Carbs: 7g, Protein: 2g, Sugar: 0g

Recipe 3. Carrot and Ginger Soup

PREPARATION TIME: 15 min - **COOKING TIME:** 30 min **MODE OF COOKING:** Simmering - **SERVINGS:** 4

INGREDIENTS: 1 Tbsp. olive oil; 1 onion, chopped; 2 cloves garlic, minced; 2 Tbsp. fresh ginger, grated; 1 lb. carrots, chopped; 4 cups vegetable broth; Salt and pepper to taste; 1 can (14 oz.) coconut milk

DIRECTIONS: Heat olive oil in a pot over medium heat. Sauté onion, garlic, and ginger until onion is translucent. Add carrots and vegetable broth; bring to a boil. Reduce heat, cover, and simmer for 30 minutes. Blend until smooth, then stir in coconut milk. Season with salt and pepper to taste. Serve hot.

N.V.: Calories: 250, Fat: 19g, Carbs: 20g, Protein: 3g, Sugar: 6g

Recipe 4. Cucumber Yogurt Dip

PREPARATION TIME: 10 min - **COOKING TIME:** 0 min **MODE OF COOKING:** Mixing - **SERVINGS:** 4

INGREDIENTS: 1 cup Greek yogurt; 1 cucumber, seeded and finely diced; 2 Tbsp. fresh dill, chopped; 1 garlic clove, minced; 1 Tbsp. lemon juice; Salt and pepper to taste

DIRECTIONS: In a bowl, combine Greek yogurt, cucumber, dill, garlic, and lemon juice. Season with salt and pepper to taste. Chill for at least 1 hour before serving. Serve with fresh vegetables or whole-grain pita chips.

N.V.: Calories: 70, Fat: 2g, Carbs: 8g, Protein: 6g, Sugar: 4g

Recipe 5. Roasted Chickpeas

PREPARATION TIME: 5 min - **COOKING TIME:** 40 min **MODE OF COOKING:** Roasting - **SERVINGS:** 4

INGREDIENTS: 1 can (15 oz.) chickpeas, drained, rinsed, and dried; 1 Tbsp. olive oil; 1/2 tsp ground cumin; 1/4 tsp chili powder; Salt to taste

DIRECTIONS: Preheat oven to 400°F (200°C). Toss chickpeas with olive oil, cumin, chili powder, and salt. Spread on a baking sheet and roast for 40 minutes, stirring occasionally, until crisp and golden. Let cool before serving.

N.V.: Calories: 140, Fat: 5g, Carbs: 20g, Protein: 6g, Sugar: 0g

Recipe 6. Quinoa Salad with Lemon Vinaigrette

PREPARATION TIME: 15 min - **COOKING TIME:** 20 min **MODE OF COOKING:** Boiling - **SERVINGS:** 4

INGREDIENTS: 1 cup quinoa, rinsed; 2 cups water; 1/2 cucumber, diced; 1 bell pepper, diced; 1/4 cup red onion, finely chopped; 1/4 cup feta cheese, crumbled; 1/4 cup olive oil; 3 Tbsp. lemon juice; 1 tsp honey; Salt and pepper to taste; 2 Tbsp. fresh parsley, chopped

DIRECTIONS: Bring quinoa and water to a boil in a pot. Reduce heat, cover, and simmer for 15 minutes, or until water is absorbed. Let cool. In a large bowl, combine cooled quinoa, cucumber, bell pepper, red onion, and feta cheese. In a small bowl, whisk together olive oil, lemon juice, honey, salt, and pepper. Pour over salad and toss. Garnish with parsley before serving.
N.V.: Calories: 290, Fat: 15g, Carbs: 33g, Protein: 8g, Sugar: 3g

RECIPE 7. PEANUT BUTTER BANANA BITES

PREPARATION TIME: 15 min - **COOKING TIME:** 0 min **MODE OF COOKING:** Freezing - **SERVINGS:** 4
INGREDIENTS: 2 bananas, sliced; 1/4 cup natural peanut butter; 1/4 cup dark chocolate chips, melted; 1 Tbsp. coconut oil
DIRECTIONS: Spread peanut butter between banana slices to make sandwiches. Freeze for 1 hour. Mix melted chocolate with coconut oil. Dip banana bites in chocolate mixture, then return to freezer until set. Serve cold.
N.V.: Calories: 200, Fat: 11g, Carbs: 24g, Protein: 4g, Sugar: 14g

RECIPE 8. ZESTY LIME AND BLACK BEAN DIP

PREPARATION TIME: 10 min - **COOKING TIME:** 0 min
MODE OF COOKING: Mixing - **SERVINGS:** 6
INGREDIENTS: 2 cups black beans, rinsed and drained; 1 avocado, diced; 1/4 cup red onion, finely chopped; 1/4 cup cilantro, chopped; Juice of 2 limes; 1 tsp cumin; Salt and pepper to taste; Tortilla chips for serving
DIRECTIONS: In a bowl, combine black beans, avocado, red onion, cilantro, lime juice, cumin, salt, and pepper. Mix gently until well combined. Serve immediately with tortilla chips.
N.V.: Calories: 150, Fat: 5g, Carbs: 22g, Protein: 7g, Sugar: 1g

RECIPE 9. CRUNCHY KALE CHIPS WITH SEA SALT

PREPARATION TIME: 5 min - **COOKING TIME:** 15 min
MODE OF COOKING: Baking - **SERVINGS:** 4
INGREDIENTS: 1 bunch kale, stems removed, leaves torn; 2 Tbsp. olive oil; 1 tsp sea salt
DIRECTIONS: Preheat oven to 350°F (175°C). Toss kale leaves with olive oil and sea salt. Spread on a baking sheet in a single layer. Bake for 15 min, until edges are brown but not burnt. Serve immediately.
N.V.: Calories: 80, Fat: 7g, Carbs: 4g, Protein: 2g, Sugar: 0g

RECIPE 10. SWEET POTATO HUMMUS

PREPARATION TIME: 15 min - **COOKING TIME:** 30 min
MODE OF COOKING: Baking/Blending - **SERVINGS:** 6
INGREDIENTS: 1 large sweet potato, peeled, cubed; 1 can (15 oz.) chickpeas, rinsed and drained; 3 Tbsp. tahini; 2 garlic cloves; Juice of 1 lemon; 2 tsp paprika; Salt to taste; Olive oil for drizzling; Vegetable sticks for serving
DIRECTIONS: Preheat oven to 400°F (200°C). Roast sweet potato cubes with a drizzle of olive oil for 30 min. Blend roasted sweet potato, chickpeas, tahini, garlic, lemon juice, paprika, and salt until smooth. Serve with vegetable sticks.
N.V.: Calories: 200, Fat: 8g, Carbs: 28g, Protein: 6g, Sugar: 5g

Recipe 11. Grilled Peach and Mozzarella Skewers

PREPARATION TIME: 10 min - **COOKING TIME:** 6 min
MODE OF COOKING: Grilling - **SERVINGS:** 6
INGREDIENTS: 3 peaches, cut into wedges; 12 mini mozzarella balls; 2 Tbsp. balsamic glaze; 1 Tbsp. olive oil; Fresh basil leaves; Salt and pepper to taste; Skewers
DIRECTIONS: Preheat grill to medium-high (375°F or 190°C). Thread peach wedges, mozzarella balls, and basil leaves alternately on skewers. Brush with olive oil, season with salt and pepper. Grill 3 min per side. Drizzle with balsamic glaze before serving.
N.V.: Calories: 120, Fat: 8g, Carbs: 8g, Protein: 6g, Sugar: 6g

CHAPTER 16: GRILLING AND SMOKING FAQS

As we embark on the smoky path of mastery over our Pit Boss grills, it's inevitable that we'll stumble upon questions that prick our curiosity or challenges that test our resolve. Grilling and smoking, like any great art, is filled with nuances and secrets waiting to be unlocked. Whether it's the whisper of smoke through the vents or the sizzle of a steak hitting the hot grate, every sound and aroma tells a story—a story of tradition, innovation, and culinary exploration.

In this chapter, we delve into the collective wisdom of Pit Boss enthusiasts and experts alike, answering the most frequently asked questions that arise from the glowing embers of our grills. From troubleshooting common issues to uncovering the subtleties of wood pellet flavors, this section is designed to enlighten both the novice and the seasoned grill master.

Grilling and smoking are not just about cooking; they're about creating moments that linger in our memories, flavored with the zest of achievement and the satisfaction of a meal well-made. Here, we address your queries, not only to solve immediate dilemmas but to enrich your understanding and appreciation of this timeless craft.

As you flip through these pages, imagine standing by your grill under a starlit sky, the aroma of smoked delicacies mingling with the cool night air. Each question answered brings you closer to becoming the Pit Boss of your backyard, ready to astonish and delight with every meal you craft. Let's turn the page, stoke the flames, and continue our journey into the heart of grilling and smoking mastery.

OVERCOMING COMMON CHALLENGES

Embarking on the journey of mastering the art of grilling and smoking with your Pit Boss can transform your culinary adventures, offering a pathway to creating delectable dishes that tantalize the taste buds and gather friends and family around the warmth of your backyard. Yet, like any worthwhile endeavor, this journey comes with its set of hurdles. From flare-ups that char your cherished recipes to the intricacies of maintaining the perfect temperature, each challenge invites you to deepen your mastery and understanding of your Pit Boss.

One of the most common challenges grill enthusiasts face is managing flare-ups. These sudden bursts of flame can be daunting, threatening to turn your beautifully marinated creations into charred relics of their former selves. The key to overcoming this lies in preventive measures and quick responses. Always trim excess fat from meats, as fat dripping onto hot coals or burners is a primary cause of flare-ups. Using indirect heat for most of your cooking can also mitigate this risk, positioning your food away from the direct flames and instead, allowing the ambient heat to cook your food evenly.

Temperature control is another crucial aspect of grilling and smoking that can perplex even the most experienced pitmasters. The secret to maintaining a consistent temperature lies in understanding your equipment and the nature of the fuel source. For smoking, the use of a water pan can help stabilize the temperature, adding moisture to the cooking environment and preventing drastic temperature spikes. Remember, the art of low and slow cooking is patience; resist the urge to frequently open the lid, as this can lead to significant heat loss.

Moisture retention in meats, particularly when aiming for that perfect brisket or pork shoulder, is a pursuit that many find challenging. Brining or marinating meats prior to cooking can significantly enhance moisture retention, imbuing your meats with flavors while also helping to keep them juicy. Additionally, allowing your meats to rest after cooking before slicing can help redistribute the juices throughout the meat, ensuring that every bite is as succulent as the last.

Smoke flavoring, a cornerstone of authentic barbecue, can sometimes be elusive, especially when striving for a balance that complements rather than overwhelms your dish. The type of wood used for smoking plays a pivotal role in the flavor profile of your dish. Fruit woods like apple or cherry offer a milder, sweeter smoke, ideal for poultry and fish, while hickory and mesquite impart a stronger, more robust flavor, perfect for beef and pork. Experimentation and personal taste preferences guide this journey, inviting you to explore the vast landscape of wood flavors to find your signature smoke.

Grill cleaning and maintenance, though often overlooked, are essential for ensuring the longevity and performance of your Pit Boss. A clean grill not only operates more efficiently but also reduces the risk of flare-ups and unwanted smoke flavors caused by buildup from previous cookouts. Establish a routine cleaning schedule, paying close attention to the grill grates, the interior surfaces, and the burners or firepit, depending on your model. This not only prolongs the life of your grill but also elevates the quality of your culinary creations.

Beyond the grill itself, the choice of ingredients and their preparation can dramatically influence your grilling experience. The adage "quality over quantity" holds true in the world of barbecue. Investing in high-quality meats and fresh produce can elevate your dishes, providing a robust foundation upon which your grilling skills can shine. Similarly, taking the time to properly prepare these ingredients, from the thickness of your cuts to the composition of your rubs and marinades, can transform a good dish into a great one.

Lastly, the community of Pit Boss enthusiasts, both online and in the real world, offers an invaluable resource for overcoming the challenges of grilling and smoking. From forums and social media groups to local barbecue competitions and events, engaging with fellow grill lovers can provide insights, inspiration, and troubleshooting tips that enhance your grilling journey. Sharing successes and setbacks alike fosters a sense of camaraderie and collective learning, ensuring that no challenge is too great to overcome.

In embracing these challenges as opportunities for growth, you not only refine your skills but also deepen your appreciation for the craft of grilling and smoking. Each obstacle navigated brings with it a sense of achievement and a flavor of success that is uniquely satisfying. So, as you fire up your Pit Boss and lay your ingredients upon the grates, remember that the journey of mastering grilling and smoking is a continuous one, filled with moments of discovery, delight, and, above all, deliciousness.

Pit Boss Tips and Tricks

Navigating the world of grilling and smoking on your Pit Boss Grill is an exhilarating journey, one that transforms the mundane into the extraordinary, turning backyard barbecues into gourmet experiences. Along this savory path, equipped with the right tips and tricks, you can elevate your grilling game, ensuring every dish from your Pit Boss stands out as a masterpiece of flavor and technique. Let's dive into a treasure trove of insider knowledge, designed to turn you into the Pit Boss aficionado you aspire to be.

Understanding the nuances of your Pit Boss Grill is fundamental. Each model, with its unique features and capabilities, is designed to cater to the diverse needs of grill masters. Familiarize yourself with the specifics of your grill, from its temperature controls to its smoking capabilities. Knowing how to manipulate these features can help you achieve precision in cooking, whether you're aiming for a seared steak with a pink center or a slow-smoked brisket that falls apart at the touch.

Temperature control is the cornerstone of successful grilling and smoking. The Pit Boss's ability to maintain consistent temperatures means you can trust it to deliver perfect results. However, mastering temperature control involves understanding the impact of external conditions, such as weather, and adjusting accordingly. On a cold or windy day, your grill might work harder to maintain temperatures, so be mindful of these changes and plan your cooking times accordingly.

The versatility of wood pellets offers a palette of flavors to experiment with. Matching the right wood pellet flavor to your dish can enhance its taste profile significantly. Fruit woods like apple and cherry impart a milder, sweeter smoke, ideal for poultry and seafood, while hickory and mesquite lend a robust flavor to red meats. Experimenting with different wood pellets can uncover delightful flavor combinations and elevate your dishes to new culinary heights.

Achieving the perfect sear on a steak is an art form, one that's easily mastered with your Pit Boss. Preheat your grill to its highest temperature setting to ensure it's scorching hot. A high heat is crucial for creating that flavorful crust on your steak while keeping the inside juicy and tender. Remember, letting your meat rest before and after grilling ensures juices redistribute evenly, resulting in a succulent meal.

Smoke infusion is a technique revered by pitmasters, and your Pit Boss is ingeniously designed to excel at this. To maximize smoke flavor, especially in thicker cuts of meat, consider smoking at a lower temperature for the first hour or two, then increase the heat to finish cooking. This method allows the meat to absorb the delicate smoke flavor gradually, embedding a rich taste that penetrates deep into its fibers.

Cleaning and maintenance might seem mundane but are pivotal in ensuring the longevity and performance of your Pit Boss. Regular cleaning prevents buildup, which can affect the taste of your food and the efficiency of your grill. After each use, allow your grill to cool, then clean the grates and interior surfaces. Periodically, deep clean your grill to maintain its optimal functionality, ensuring it's ready to perform whenever inspiration strikes.

Creativity in grilling is not just about the dishes you cook but also in how you cook them. Don't shy away from experimenting with techniques like reverse searing or using a cast-iron skillet on the grill for dishes you'd typically cook indoors. These methods can introduce new textures and flavors to your meals, expanding your culinary repertoire and impressing your guests with your versatility.

The importance of a meat thermometer cannot be overstated. Investing in a good quality thermometer ensures you cook your meats to the perfect temperature every time, eliminating the guesswork and reducing the risk of under or overcooking. Precision in cooking temperature is key to achieving the desired doneness, whether you're aiming for a rare steak or ensuring poultry is safely cooked through.

Your Pit Boss is more than a grill; it's a gateway to exploring the rich traditions of barbecue and grilling, offering a modern twist on timeless cooking methods. Engaging with the Pit Boss community, both online and in person, can provide a wealth of knowledge, from tried and tested recipes to troubleshooting tips that can save the day. The community is a vibrant space for sharing, learning, and celebrating the joys of grilling and smoking.

Lastly, remember that patience is a virtue in the world of barbecue. The slow and low approach to smoking meats may test your patience, but the results are always worth the wait. Embrace the process, enjoy the aromas wafting from your grill, and anticipate the satisfaction of sharing a meal that's been crafted with care, skill, and a touch of Pit Boss magic.

By embracing these tips and tricks, you're not just cooking; you're embarking on a culinary adventure that brings friends and family together, creating memories that last a lifetime. The path to becoming a Pit Boss master is paved with delicious discoveries, challenges turned triumphs, and the joy of sharing your creations. So, fire up your grill, and let the journey begin.

RECIPE ADJUSTMENTS AND SUBSTITUTIONS

In the grand adventure of grilling and smoking, we often find ourselves at the crossroads of tradition and innovation. As the aromas of charcoal and wood smoke blend with the air, so too does the need to adapt our culinary practices to meet the evolving tastes and dietary needs of our time. The Pit Boss grill, a steadfast companion in our quest for the perfect barbecue, offers a canvas on which to experiment, adapt, and perfect our favorite recipes. In this spirit, we delve into the art of recipe adjustments and substitutions, a crucial skill set for any grill master seeking to cater to a diverse array of dietary preferences and restrictions.

At the heart of any successful recipe adjustment lies the understanding that each ingredient plays a unique role in the dish's final taste, texture, and appearance. However, this doesn't mean that creativity and flexibility can't lead to equally delightful results. Whether you're navigating the world of gluten-free flours, dairy alternatives, or low-sugar sweeteners, the essence of grilling—the smoky flavor, the charred exterior, the juicy interior—remains untouched.

One of the first steps in mastering recipe adjustments is to familiarize oneself with the vast array of alternative ingredients available. Flour, for example, can be replaced with gluten-free blends made from rice, almond, or coconut flour, each bringing its unique flavor and nutritional profile. Similarly, traditional sugars can be substituted with natural sweeteners like stevia or erythritol, allowing for the reduction of added sugars without compromising on sweetness.

Dairy products, so often a staple in marinades, sauces, and toppings, can also be swapped for plant-based alternatives. Coconut milk, almond cream, and cashew cheese offer the creamy texture and rich taste that many dishes require, without the dairy. These substitutions not only open the door to those with lactose intolerance or vegan preferences but also introduce a new dimension of flavors to explore.

The versatility of the Pit Boss grill shines when it comes to accommodating such adjustments. The even heat distribution and precise temperature control make it an ideal tool for cooking with alternative ingredients, which sometimes require more delicate handling. Gluten-free pizza crusts crisp beautifully on its grates, while vegan burgers achieve the perfect char, proving that the grill is not solely the domain of traditional barbecue fare.

Moreover, the smoky essence imparted by wood pellets can enhance the natural flavors of plant-based proteins and vegetables, transforming them into smoky, savory delights that can stand shoulder to shoulder with their meaty counterparts. Experimenting with different types of wood pellets—be it hickory, mesquite, apple, or cherry—allows for a custom smoke profile that complements the substituted ingredients, elevating the dish to new heights.

Beyond the choice of ingredients, technique plays a pivotal role in adapting recipes for the grill. Thinner cuts of meat, for instance, might benefit from a quick sear over high heat, while tougher cuts can be transformed by the low and slow approach. Similarly, vegetables and fruits can be grilled to perfection by adjusting the grill's temperature and the cooking time to suit their varying textures and sugar content.

Embracing the challenge of recipe adjustments and substitutions not only broadens the culinary repertoire but also reflects a commitment to inclusivity and health-consciousness. It's a testament to the belief that the joy of grilling should be accessible to all, regardless of dietary restrictions or lifestyle choices. This journey of exploration and adaptation is not just about substituting ingredients; it's about discovering new flavors, experimenting with uncharted techniques, and, ultimately, about the shared experience of enjoying a meal prepared with care and creativity.

As we continue to navigate the ever-changing landscape of food preferences and dietary needs, the Pit Boss grill stands ready to support our culinary adventures. With a spirit of experimentation and a few adjustments here and there, there's no limit to the delicious, inclusive dishes that can emerge from our backyards. After all, at the heart of grilling lies the simple joy of cooking over an open flame, a pleasure that knows no boundaries and requires no compromises.

Chapter 17: From the Griddle to the Table

As the flames dim and the last sizzle fades away, the journey from the griddle to the table begins—an odyssey that is about much more than merely moving food from one place to another. It is here, in this transition, that we encapsulate the essence of what it means to cook with a Pit Boss. This chapter is a celebration of that journey, an homage to the art of presentation, the craft of pairing, and the joy of sharing that lies at the heart of every meal prepared on the grill.

Grilling is not just a method of cooking; it's a tradition, a communal ritual that brings people together. The path from griddle to table is paved with the anticipation of shared experiences, the crafting of memories around the warmth of a meal. In this chapter, we delve into the nuances of presenting your grilled masterpieces, transforming them from mere dishes to centerpieces that command attention and ignite conversation.

We explore the art of plating, the subtleties of pairing drinks and side dishes, and the theme-based meal planning that turns a simple barbecue into a culinary event. It's about elevating the sensory experience, where the visual appeal on the plate complements the aromas wafting through the air and the flavors bursting on the palate.

Join us as we journey from the griddle to the table, where the grill's heat meets the coolness of the salad, where smoky meets sweet, and where the essence of outdoor cooking enriches not just our meals, but our lives.

Presentation and Plating Techniques

Plating is the final brushstroke on the canvas, a process where each element finds its place to create a harmonious whole. The plate is your canvas, and the food is your medium. The goal is to enhance the visual appeal without compromising the integrity of the dish. This involves a delicate balance of color, texture, and space.

Color:
The allure of a dish often starts with its color. Vibrant, contrasting colors not only catch the eye but also promise a variety of flavors. Consider the deep char of a grilled steak against the bright green of fresh herbs or the rich red of cherry tomatoes. Each color should complement the others, creating a visually appealing palette that entices the senses.

Texture:
Texture plays a crucial role in the presentation. The contrast between the crispy exterior of a grilled fish and the softness of a puree adds depth and interest to the dish. Incorporate a variety of textures to engage the palate and elevate the overall dining experience.

Space:
The concept of space on the plate is akin to whitespace in design—it's not just about what you add, but also about what you leave out. A cluttered plate can overwhelm, whereas thoughtfully placed components with adequate space between them allow each element to stand out. The rule of thirds, often used in photography, can be applied to plating as well, guiding the eye naturally across the dish

Techniques to Elevate Your Presentation
Create a Focal Point:
Choose the main element of your dish and make it the star. This could be a perfectly grilled steak, a beautifully charred vegetable, or an intricately composed burger. Position this element prominently on the plate, using it as an anchor around which the rest of your dish is arranged.

Use Sauces Creatively:
Sauces not only add flavor but also provide an opportunity to introduce color and pattern to your plate. Instead of pouring the sauce over the dish, consider using a spoon or squeeze bottle to drizzle it artfully around the plate or beneath the main components. This adds an element of elegance and invites diners to mix and blend flavors to their preference.

Garnish with Purpose:
Garnishes should do more than just decorate; they should enhance the flavor or texture of the dish. A sprinkle of fresh herbs, a few edible flowers, or a zest of citrus can add a fresh burst of flavor and a pop of color. Remember, every element on the plate should have a purpose.

Experiment with Shapes and Sizes:
Cutting your ingredients into uniform shapes and sizes can create visual harmony, while varying the shapes and sizes can add interest. Consider using cookie cutters for vegetables or layering components to add height and dimension.

Plating Like a Pro
Choose the Right Plate:
The plate itself can dramatically affect the presentation. A plain, white plate offers a neutral background that makes colors pop, while a darker or patterned plate can provide contrast and drama. Consider the size of the plate as well; too small, and the dish can look crowded; too large, and it can appear sparse.

Temperature Matters:
A warm plate keeps hot foods from cooling too quickly, preserving the intended texture and enhancing the flavor. Similarly, chilled plates are perfect for cold dishes, adding a refreshing touch that heightens the experience.

Practice Makes Perfect:
The art of plating takes practice. Experiment with different techniques, arrangements, and styles to discover what works best for you and the dishes you love to create. Remember, the goal is to complement the flavors and textures of your dish, creating a visual feast that matches the culinary delight.

The Joy of Sharing
Ultimately, the journey from the griddle to the table is about sharing—sharing flavors, experiences, and moments. A beautifully plated dish not only showcases your skills and creativity but also conveys your care and passion for the meal you are about to share. It sets the stage for the dining experience, inviting guests to savor not just the taste but the beauty of the food before them.

In embracing the principles and techniques of presentation and plating, you elevate the act of cooking from a mere necessity to an expression of art. It's a celebration of the senses, a tribute to the ingredients, and a testament to the joy of cooking with your Pit Boss grill. So, let your creativity flow, embrace the process, and transform every meal into a masterpiece worthy of the table.

PAIRINGS: DRINKS AND SIDE DISHES

In the symphony of flavors that dance across the grill, the harmony between the main dish, its drink pairings, and side accompaniments plays a pivotal role in elevating the dining experience from the mundane to the sublime. This sub-chapter delves into the art of pairing, a nuanced ballet of flavors, textures, and aromas that, when performed with skill, transforms a simple meal into an unforgettable feast.

The magic of pairing lies not just in matching flavors, but in creating contrasts that highlight each component's unique characteristics. It's about balancing the richness of a smoky brisket with the crisp acidity of a coleslaw or the warmth of a grilled vegetable medley with the cool refreshment of a citrus-infused craft beer. The goal is to enhance the overall dining experience, ensuring that each sip and bite is a journey through a landscape of sensory delight.

Understanding the Basics of Pairing

Pairing is both an art and a science, rooted in understanding the fundamental aspects of taste: sweetness, acidity, bitterness, saltiness, and umami. A well-chosen drink can cleanse the palate, prepare it for the next bite, or contrast with the dish's flavors to highlight its depth and complexity. Similarly, the right-side dish not only complements the main course but also adds its own voice to the culinary choir, creating a richer, more varied performance.

Drinks: A Conduit of Flavor

Wine Pairings

Wine, with its vast spectrum of flavors, can complement or contrast the flavors of your grilled dishes. The tannins in red wine, for example, cut through the richness of fatty meats, while the acidity in white wine can balance the heaviness of a creamy pasta salad.

- **Red Meats and Bold Reds:** A robust steak pairs beautifully with a full-bodied red wine, such as a Cabernet Sauvignon, whose tannins help to cleanse the palate of fats.
- **Poultry and Versatile Whites:** Grilled chicken, with its leaner profile, finds a match in the crisp acidity of a Chardonnay or the fruity notes of a Sauvignon Blanc.
- **Seafood and Light Whites:** Delicate flavors of seafood like grilled shrimp or fish tacos are enhanced by the light, minerally profiles of a Pinot Grigio or a dry Riesling.

Beer and Barbecue

The carbonation in beer makes it an excellent partner to barbecue, cutting through richness and refreshing the palate.

- **Hoppy IPAs and Spicy Dishes:** The bitterness of an IPA can stand up to the heat of spicy foods, balancing the flavors.
- **Amber Ales and Smoked Meats:** The caramel notes of an amber ale complement the deep, smoky flavors of meats like ribs or brisket.
- **Wheat Beers and Vegetarian Options:** The light, sometimes fruity notes of a wheat beer pair well with the char and sweetness of grilled vegetables.

Non-Alcoholic Alternatives

Refreshing, non-alcoholic options like infused sparkling waters, lemonades, and iced teas can be tailored to complement the flavors of your dishes, offering a welcoming option for all guests.

Sides: The Supporting Cast

The role of side dishes is to balance the meal, providing contrast in flavors, textures, and temperatures that enhance the main course.

Cool and Crunchy Salads
A crisp, refreshing salad offers a counterpoint to the rich, smoky flavors of grilled meats. A simple arugula salad with lemon vinaigrette can cleanse the palate, while a tangy coleslaw adds both crunch and a hit of acidity that cuts through fattiness.

Grilled Vegetables
Grilling isn't just for meats. Vegetables like asparagus, bell peppers, and zucchini, when grilled, reveal a smoky sweetness that complements any main dish. A drizzle of balsamic reduction or a sprinkle of coarse sea salt can elevate these simple sides into show-stoppers.

Starches: From Potatoes to Polenta
Hearty sides like garlic mashed potatoes, grilled polenta, or a warm potato salad can anchor a meal, providing a comforting counterbalance to the main dish's complex flavors. These sides offer a canvas for a range of seasonings and additions, from fresh herbs to cheese, allowing for endless customization to match the meal's theme.

Creating Harmony
The art of pairing is ultimately about creating a harmonious meal where each element, from the drink to the side dish, enhances the others. It's about considering the weight of the dish—the richness or lightness of its flavors—and matching it with sides and drinks that offer contrast and complement.

Consider the season, the occasion, and the preferences of your guests when planning your pairings. A summer barbecue might call for lighter fare and refreshing drinks, while a fall grill-out could lean towards heartier sides and warmer, spicier beverages.

Experimentation is key to discovering new and exciting combinations. Don't be afraid to try unconventional pairings; sometimes, the most unexpected matches can result in the most delightful culinary experiences.

From the griddle to the table, the journey of a dish is an opportunity to create moments of joy and connection. Through thoughtful pairings of drinks and side dishes, we can elevate these moments, transforming them into experiences that linger in memory long after the last bite is taken. So, raise a glass and pass the sides; let's celebrate the art of pairing and the joy of shared meals.

THEMED MEAL PLANNING

Themed meal planning is not just a method of organizing a dinner or barbecue; it's a canvas for creativity, an opportunity to take your guests on a culinary journey, and a way to transform a simple gathering into an unforgettable event. Whether you're aiming for a laid-back beach barbecue vibe, a sophisticated wine pairing dinner, or a festive holiday feast, a themed meal creates a narrative that guides your menu choices, presentation, and even your décor, making the dining experience immersive and memorable.

Crafting the Theme
The first step in themed meal planning is selecting a theme that resonates with the occasion, the season, or perhaps a particular cuisine you've been eager to explore. This could range from a "Summer Seafood Fest" to a "Southern Barbecue Night," or even an "Around the World" barbecue showcasing dishes from various cultures. The key is to choose a theme that excites you, as this enthusiasm becomes contagious and will be felt by your guests.

Menu Selection: The Heart of the Theme

Once your theme is set, crafting a menu that reflects and enhances this concept is next. Every dish, from the appetizers to the desserts, should echo the theme, providing a coherent dining experience. For instance, a "Tex-Mex Fiesta" might feature grilled fajitas, corn on the cob with lime butter, a vibrant salsa, and a tequila-infused watermelon for dessert.

Appetizers and Starters

Begin with appetizers that introduce the theme without overwhelming the palate, setting the stage for the main course. For a "Mediterranean Soiree," consider offering a selection of grilled vegetable skewers with a yogurt-tzatziki dip or a platter of olive oil-drizzled bruschetta topped with fresh tomatoes and basil.

Main Course: The Centerpiece

The main course is where your theme shines brightest. Choose a centerpiece dish that is both a crowd-pleaser and a testament to the theme's essence. In a "Hawaiian Luau," this might be a beautifully grilled pineapple and ham, while a "Rustic Italian Gathering" could be anchored by a hearty grilled Tuscan steak, seasoned with rosemary and garlic.

Sides: Complementing the Narrative

Side dishes should complement the main course and reinforce the theme. They offer an opportunity to incorporate a variety of textures and flavors that balance the meal. A "Caribbean Carnival" might feature coconut rice and beans and a mango salad, adding sweet and spicy notes that dance with the main course's flavors.

Desserts: The Sweet Conclusion

Desserts are your final act, the sweet conclusion to your themed meal. They should continue the theme's narrative while offering a refreshing contrast to the preceding courses. For a "French Countryside Picnic," lavender-infused grilled peaches served with a dollop of crème fraiche could provide a fitting finale.

Beverage Pairings: Enhancing Each Bite

Beverages, both alcoholic and non-alcoholic, play a crucial role in themed meal planning. They should complement the food's flavors and enhance the overall dining experience. For a "Spicy Latin Fiesta," margaritas or sangrias alongside refreshing ague fresca can provide balance to the meal's spicy elements.

Presentation and Ambiance: Setting the Scene

The presentation of each dish should reflect the theme, using appropriate serving ware and garnishes that accentuate the theme's aesthetics. Table settings, decorations, and even background music can help to immerse your guests fully in the theme. For an "Asian Street Food Night," serving dishes on bamboo platters with chopsticks and decorating the table with lanterns can transport your guests to the bustling streets of Southeast Asia.

Engagement: Inviting Participation

Consider ways to involve your guests in the themed experience. This could be through dress codes, themed games, or even inviting guests to contribute a dish that fits the theme. Engagement adds a layer of personalization and fun, making the meal memorable and interactive.

Flexibility: Adapting to Preferences and Dietary Needs

While staying true to your theme, remain flexible to accommodate dietary preferences and restrictions. Offering vegetarian, vegan, or gluten-free options ensures that all guests can enjoy the meal. For example, in a "Classic American Barbecue," offering a selection of grilled portobello mushrooms alongside the traditional meats ensures that everyone's dietary needs are respected.

CHAPTER 18: THE JOURNEY AHEAD

As the embers of our culinary adventure begin to glow with the warmth of acquired knowledge and shared experiences, we stand at the threshold of a new dawn in our journey with the Pit Boss. This chapter, "The Journey Ahead," is not merely a conclusion but a beacon guiding us toward the limitless horizons that await. It's here we recognize that mastering the art of grilling and smoking is a lifelong pursuit, one that continually evolves as we explore new flavors, techniques, and traditions.

The path forward is paved with the promise of meals yet to be shared, dishes yet to be created, and techniques yet to be mastered. It's a journey that invites us to remain curious, to embrace the unexpected, and to celebrate the joy of discovery that lies at the heart of cooking. Whether you're a seasoned pitmaster or a novice just beginning to explore the wonders of wood pellet grilling, the road ahead is filled with opportunities to deepen your connection with food, with nature, and with those you hold dear.

In this chapter, we'll explore how to continue your education in the culinary arts, connect with a community of like-minded enthusiasts, and take your grilling game to new heights. The end of this book marks the beginning of your own unique story with the Pit Boss, a story that you write with every meal you grill and every memory you create. So, let's turn the page together and step into the journey ahead, ready to embrace the adventures that await with open hearts and hungry appetites.

CONTINUING YOUR GRILLING EDUCATION

Embarking on the path of grilling and smoking is much like setting out on an unending voyage of culinary discovery. This journey, with its highs and lows, successes and learning opportunities, is what molds us into adept pitmasters and seasoned grill enthusiasts. "Continuing Your Grilling Education" is a commitment to lifelong learning, a pursuit that enriches not just our plates but our lives.

The Ever-Evolving World of Grilling

The beauty of grilling and smoking lies in its dynamic nature. Just when you think you've mastered a technique, a new trend, ingredient, or piece of equipment emerges, beckoning you to explore unfamiliar territories. Staying abreast of these developments is crucial. It invigorates your passion and ensures your skills remain sharp and your meals exciting.

Dive Into Books and Blogs

A wealth of knowledge awaits in the pages of books and the posts of blogs dedicated to grilling and smoking. Authors and bloggers often share not just recipes but also their personal journeys, offering insights into the challenges they've faced and how they've overcome them. These narratives can be a source of inspiration and practical advice.

Online Courses and Videos

The digital age has brought the classroom into our homes. Online platforms offer courses ranging from the basics of grilling to advanced smoking techniques. Accompanied by videos, these courses allow you to see the subtleties of the craft in action, providing a visual and interactive element to your learning.

Attend Workshops and Classes
There's something irreplaceable about the hands-on experience gained in workshops and classes. These sessions often provide the opportunity to ask questions in real-time, receive immediate feedback, and learn alongside fellow enthusiasts. Many communities and culinary schools offer such classes, making them accessible to grillers at all levels.

Building on Experience
Experiment with Recipes
The true test of learning is in the doing. Experimenting with new recipes challenges you to apply your knowledge and skills, pushing you out of your comfort zone. Each recipe is a lesson in flavors, techniques, and adaptations, offering a chance to reflect on what worked, what didn't, and how you can improve.

Master New Techniques
Grilling and smoking are arts founded on techniques that can take years to master. Whether it's perfecting the reverse sear method, experimenting with different smoking woods, or exploring the nuances of indirect grilling, there's always a new technique to learn and master.

Explore New Cuisines
The grill knows no borders. It's a tool that can bring the world to your backyard. Exploring new cuisines opens your palate to a range of flavors and ingredients, broadening your culinary repertoire and introducing you to grilling and smoking traditions from around the globe.

Engaging with the Community
Join Forums and Social Media Groups
The grilling community is vast and vibrant, with forums and social media groups bringing together enthusiasts from all corners of the world. These platforms are invaluable for sharing experiences, seeking advice, and staying updated on the latest in the grilling world.

Participate in Competitions
For those who thrive on challenge and competition, participating in grilling and smoking contests can be a thrilling way to test your skills. Competitions offer a unique learning experience, allowing you to see how your techniques and flavors stand up under the scrutiny of judges and against the talents of other grillers.

Share Your Knowledge
As you continue your grilling education, sharing your knowledge with others can be immensely rewarding. Teaching a friend, writing a blog, or hosting a grilling workshop not only helps others on their journey but also deepens your understanding and appreciation for the craft.

Embracing Technology
Stay Updated with the Latest Gadgets
The world of grilling gadgets and accessories is ever-expanding. From Bluetooth thermometers to advanced grilling systems, new technologies can enhance your grilling experience, making it more precise, convenient, and enjoyable. Keeping an eye on these developments ensures your grilling setup evolves with the times.

Utilize Apps
Numerous apps are designed to assist grillers, offering features from recipe databases and temperature guides to timer functions and weather advisories. Leveraging these tools can streamline your grilling process, allowing you to focus more on the art and less on the logistics.

Reflecting and Growing
Keep a Grilling Journal
A grilling journal is more than a collection of recipes; it's a record of your journey. Documenting your experiences, from the triumphs to the mishaps, provides valuable insights into your growth as a griller. It serves as a reminder of how far you've come and where you wish to go.
The Path Ahead
The journey ahead in your grilling education is boundless, filled with opportunities to learn, grow, and connect. It's a path paved with the anticipation of the next great meal, the next challenge to overcome, and the next lesson to learn. Embracing the continuous nature of this education not only makes you a better griller but also enriches the experiences you share around the fire. So, stoke the flames of curiosity, wield your tongs with confidence, and step forward into the journey ahead, ready to explore the vast, smoky horizons of the grilling world.

JOINING THE PIT BOSS COMMUNITY

The journey of a Pit Boss enthusiast is not a solitary one. It's a path shared with a vibrant, passionate community that stretches across backyards, across cities, and even across countries. Joining the Pit Boss Community is more than becoming part of a group; it's about connecting with a family of like-minded individuals who share your passion for grilling, smoking, and exploring the limitless possibilities that open up when you fire up your grill.
The Essence of Community
At its core, the Pit Boss Community is built on a foundation of shared experiences, knowledge, and a genuine love for the art of grilling and smoking. It's a place where novices and seasoned pitmasters alike can come together to learn, inspire, and support one another. In this community, every question is welcomed as an opportunity for collective learning, and every success is celebrated as a communal triumph.
Engaging with the Community
Online Forums and Social Media
The digital age has made it easier than ever to connect with fellow grilling enthusiasts. Online forums and social media platforms dedicated to Pit Boss users serve as bustling hubs of activity where members exchange tips, share recipes, and offer troubleshooting advice. Here, you can dive deep into discussions about the nuances of smoking woods, the best techniques for achieving the perfect sear, and the latest accessories that can take your grilling to the next level.
Pit Boss Events and Competitions
Throughout the year, Pit Boss and its community members organize events and competitions that bring people together to celebrate their love for grilling. Participating in these events not only allows you to showcase your skills but also to learn from others, witness new techniques firsthand, and experience the camaraderie that comes from cooking and competing side by side with your peers.
Community Cookouts and Meetups
Imagine the aroma of smoking wood mingling with the sizzle of meats on the grill, surrounded by a group of people who share your enthusiasm for all things barbecue. Community cookouts and local meetups offer a chance to turn online connections into real-world friendships, providing a space to share stories, swap recipes, and enjoy the fruits of your collective labor.

Contributing to the Community
Sharing Your Journey
Every griller has a story to tell, and the community thrives on these personal narratives. Whether it's posting about your first successful brisket smoke, a family recipe that's been perfected on the grill, or a creative workaround to a common grilling challenge, your experiences add value and depth to the community's collective knowledge.
Offering Support and Encouragement
Remember the challenges you faced when you first started? By offering support and encouragement to newcomers, you help foster an environment of growth and learning. Answering questions, providing constructive feedback, and cheering on the successes of others not only helps them on their journey but also strengthens the bonds within the community.
Collaborating on Projects
The community is a melting pot of creativity, and collaboration is the key to unlocking its full potential. Working together on projects—be it a charity cookout, a community cookbook, or a grilling accessory invention—can lead to amazing outcomes that benefit not just the community members but also the wider world.
The Benefits of Belonging
A Sense of Belonging
In the Pit Boss Community, you're never just another griller. Your part of a family that understands your passion, shares your challenges, and celebrates your achievements. This sense of belonging is what makes the community not just a valuable resource, but a source of inspiration and motivation.
Continuous Learning
The collective wisdom of the community is a treasure trove of grilling and smoking knowledge. Being part of this community means you have access to a wealth of information and experiences that can help you grow and refine your skills, no matter where you are on your grilling journey.
Inspiration and Innovation
The community is a hotbed of innovation, where creative ideas and novel techniques are shared freely. Here, you're exposed to a wide array of culinary styles and practices that can inspire you to push the boundaries of what you thought was possible with your Pit Boss grill.
Looking Ahead
Joining the Pit Boss Community is a step into a world where every meal is an adventure, every challenge is an opportunity for growth, and every member is a friend waiting to be made. As you move forward on your grilling journey, remember that the community is here to walk with you, offering support, knowledge, and companionship every step of the way.

So, fire up your grill, share your stories, and embrace the endless possibilities that await in the company of fellow Pit Boss enthusiasts. Together, let's continue to explore, learn, and celebrate the art of grilling and smoking, forging ahead on a journey that's enriched by the community we build around us.

ELEVATING YOUR GRILLING GAME

As the flames of our grills burn brightly into the night, casting a warm glow on the faces of those gathered around, we're reminded of the journey we've embarked upon with our Pit Boss grills. It's a journey not just of flavors and techniques but of constant growth and discovery. "Elevating Your Grilling Game" is about pushing beyond the boundaries of what we know, embracing the vast, smoky horizons of what we have yet to learn.

The essence of elevating your grilling game lies in the pursuit of perfection—a perfection that's not defined by flawless execution but by the joy of experimentation, the willingness to embrace failure, and the relentless quest for improvement. It's about transforming the ordinary into the extraordinary, one meal at a time.

Mastery Through Experimentation

Experimentation is the heartbeat of culinary innovation. It's what turns a simple steak into a masterpiece of flavors and what transforms a backyard barbecue into a gourmet experience. Dare to combine unconventional flavors, try new smoking woods, or adopt techniques from other culinary traditions. Each experiment, whether successful or not, is a step forward in your grilling journey.

The Art of Flavor Layering

Understanding and mastering the art of flavor layering can significantly elevate your grilling game. This involves more than just seasoning your meats; it's about building a profile of flavors that complement and enhance each other. From the choice of marinade to the selection of smoking wood, every element should contribute to the final taste, creating a multi-dimensional culinary experience.

Precision and Control

Precision in cooking times and temperatures is crucial for achieving the perfect cook. Investing in a quality thermometer and learning to manage your grill's heat zones can make a significant difference in the outcome of your dishes. Mastering the control of your grill allows you to tackle more challenging recipes with confidence, knowing that you can deliver consistent results every time.

Presentation: The Final Touch

Never underestimate the power of presentation. The visual appeal of a dish can set the tone for the dining experience, adding an extra layer of enjoyment. Simple touches like thoughtful plating, garnishing with fresh herbs, or adding a splash of color with side dishes can turn a meal into a feast for the eyes as well as the palate.

Continuous Learning

The landscape of grilling and smoking is ever-evolving, with new techniques, tools, and flavors emerging all the time. Engage with the community, attend workshops, and seek out new sources of inspiration. The more you learn, the more you'll find your grilling style evolving, reflecting your unique blend of experiences and influences.

Teaching and Sharing

One of the most rewarding ways to elevate your grilling game is to teach and share your knowledge with others. Whether it's hosting a grilling class, sharing tips online, or simply cooking for friends and family, teaching allows you to refine your understanding and deepen your appreciation for the art of grilling.

Sustainability and Ethics

Elevating your grilling game also means being mindful of sustainability and ethical choices. From choosing responsibly sourced meats and produce to minimizing waste and conserving energy, responsible grilling practices ensure that our passion for barbecue also respects the planet and its resources.

Embracing Technology

In the digital age, technology offers tools that can revolutionize the way we grill. Smart grills, Bluetooth thermometers, and grilling apps can provide precision and convenience, allowing us to focus on the creative aspects of cooking. Stay open to these innovations, as they can be powerful allies in your quest to elevate your grilling game.

The Road Ahead

As we stand before our grills, the road ahead is filled with endless possibilities. The journey of a griller is one of perpetual growth, fueled by passion, curiosity, and the relentless pursuit of excellence. Elevating your grilling game is a commitment to this journey, a promise to never settle for the ordinary, and to always seek out the extraordinary.

So, let us embrace the challenges, savor the successes, and learn from the failures. Let us share our discoveries, celebrate our achievements, and, above all, continue to explore the boundless potential that lies within us and our grills. The journey ahead is not just about perfecting our craft; it's about the stories we'll tell, the memories we'll create, and the community we'll build around the warm glow of our grills. Here's to the adventures that await, to the meals that will bring us together, and to the endless quest to elevate our grilling game.

CONCLUSION

As we draw the curtains on this guide, standing at the cusp of the journey ahead with our Pit Boss grills by our side, it's imperative to pause and reflect on the essence of what we've traversed together. This odyssey through the realms of grilling and smoking wasn't just about mastering techniques or perfecting recipes; it was about igniting a passion that transforms mere meals into experiences, kindling connections that bridge hearts, and fostering a community that thrives on shared wisdom and joy.

The Heart of Our Journey

At the heart of our journey lies the unwavering belief that grilling goes beyond cooking—it's an art, a form of expression that allows us to convey our love, creativity, and passion through the medium of food. It's a ritual that brings us closer to nature, to the primal elements of fire and smoke, grounding us in the moment and reminding us of the simple joys that life offers.

The Evolution of a Pitmaster

Through the chapters, we've evolved—not just as grillers but as individuals who appreciate the nuances of flavors, the value of patience, and the importance of persistence. We've learned that every mistake is a lesson in disguise, every challenge an opportunity to grow, and every meal a chance to make memories that linger long after the last bite is savored.

The Tapestry of Community

This guide also wove us into the vibrant tapestry of the Pit Boss community, a mosaic of individuals united by a common passion. It's in this community that we find our tribe, a supportive and inspiring collective that encourages us to reach new heights, to push boundaries, and to keep the flames of our curiosity burning bright.

The Art of Sharing

One of the most profound lessons learned is the art of sharing—not just sharing our culinary creations but sharing our knowledge, our experiences, and our time. In sharing, we multiply the joy, enriching not just our lives but the lives of those around us, forging bonds that transcend the ordinary.

The Path Ahead

As we stand at the threshold of what lies ahead, it's clear that this journey doesn't end here. It stretches into the horizon, an endless road of discovery, innovation, and growth. The future beckons with promises of meals yet to be grilled, techniques yet to be mastered, and stories yet to be told.

The Legacy We Build

What we carry forward from here is more than just recipes or skills; it's a legacy built on the flames of our grills—a legacy of warmth, of generosity, and of a life well-lived. It's about leaving a mark, not just on the plates we serve but on the hearts of those we serve them to.

The Invitation to Continue

So, as we close this chapter, let it not be a farewell but an invitation—an invitation to continue exploring, learning, and growing. Let's keep the fires of our grills and our passions burning, always ready to embrace the adventures that await, the challenges that inspire, and the moments that bring us together.

The Gratitude We Share

In parting, let's extend our heartfelt gratitude to the flames that have fueled our journey, to the foods that have graced our tables, and to the community that has walked this path with us. Thank you for the lessons learned, the laughter shared, and the love that has seasoned every meal.

The Promise of Tomorrow

As we step into tomorrow, let's carry with us the promise to remain students of this craft, ever eager to learn, to experiment, and to share. Let's vow to keep the spirit of the Pit Boss alive in our hearts, in our kitchens, and in our lives, forever pushing the boundaries of what's possible with a grill and a handful of ingredients.

This isn't the end; it's merely the beginning of a new chapter in our grilling saga, a chapter that each of us will write with our adventures, our discoveries, and our dreams. So, here's to the journey ahead, to the roads less traveled, and to the endless possibilities that lie within each of us. Keep grilling, keep exploring, and most importantly, keep sharing the warmth and joy that comes from cooking over an open flame.

In the words of a fellow Pit Boss enthusiast, "The grill is not just a tool; it's a portal to a world of infinite flavors, a bridge to bring us together, and a reminder that, in the end, it's the simple pleasures that make life truly rich." Let's cherish this journey, for it's one that enriches not just our palates but our souls. Here's to the journey ahead, may it be as flavorful and fulfilling as the meals we've shared and the memories we've created.

INDEX

The complete index for "Pit Boss Wood Pellet Grill & Smoker Cookbook for Beginners" spans across multiple culinary adventures, starting from the very basics of understanding and operating your Pit Boss Grill to mastering the art of grilling, smoking, and beyond. Here's a structured look at what this guide offers:

1. **Introduction**
   - Embark on a culinary adventure, unlocking a universe of flavors, techniques, and experiences with the Pit Boss Wood Pellet Grill & Smoker.
2. **Chapter 1: Discovering the Pit Boss Wood Pellet Grill & Smoker**
   - Dive into the world of Pit Boss, exploring its versatile capabilities from smoking, grilling, baking, to roasting. This chapter sets a strong foundation for your grilling journey.
3. **Chapter 2: Honing Your Pit Boss Skills**
   - This chapter is all about refining your grilling techniques, from perfect grill marks to mastering heat zones, aiming to transition you from a novice to a seasoned pitmaster.
4. **Chapter 3: Maintenance and Care for Your Pit Boss**
   - Focuses on the essential practices of maintenance and care to enhance your grill's performance and longevity. It turns routine upkeep into an act of respect for the art of grilling itself.
5. **Chapter 4: The Pit Boss Toolkit**
   - A guide through essential grilling equipment and enhancements that elevate your grilling sessions. From basic tools like tongs and thermometers to advanced gadgets like Bluetooth thermometers and custom grill grates.
6. **Chapter 5: Expanding Your Culinary Horizons**
   - Invites you to push beyond traditional grilling. Explore vegetables, grilled desserts, and global flavors that span continents, transforming simple meals into gourmet experiences.
7. **Chapter 6: Seasonings and Marinades Mastery**
   - Delve into the alchemy of flavors with a focus on crafting marinades and rubs that enhance flavor, tenderize, and transform the texture of your dishes. It also explores the art of balancing and blending spices and herbs.
8. **Chapter 7: Smoke Crafting Techniques**
   - Dedicated to the mastery of smoke, this chapter guides you through selecting woods, managing smoke density, and controlling temperature to achieve the perfect smoke flavor in your dishes.

The book is designed not just as a collection of recipes but as a comprehensive guide to mastering the Pit Boss Grill, emphasizing the joy of grilling, the creativity involved in seasoning and marinade preparation, and the artistry in smoke crafting. Each chapter builds on the previous, ensuring you're well-equipped to tackle any culinary challenge with your Pit Boss Grill, making every meal a memorable experience.

Measurement Conversion Table

Volume Equivalents (Liquid)

US Standard	US Standard (ounces)	Metric (approximate)
2 tablespoons	1 fl. oz.	30 mL
¼ cup	2 fl. oz.	60 mL
half cup	4 fl. oz.	120 mL
1 cup	8 fl. oz.	240 mL
1 half cups	12 fl. oz.	355 mL
2 cups or 1 pint	16 fl. oz.	457 mL
4 cups or 1 quart	32 fl. oz.	1 L
1 gallon	128 fl. oz.	4 L

Volume Equivalents (Dry)

US Standard	Metric (approximate)
1/8 teaspoon	0.5 mL
¼ teaspoon	1 mL
half teaspoon	2 mL
¾ teaspoon	4 mL
1 teaspoon	5 mL
1 tablespoon	15 mL
¼ cup	59 mL
1/3 cup	79 mL
half cup	118 mL
2/3 cup	156 mL
¾ cup	177 mL
1 cup	235 mL
2 cups or 1 pint	475 mL
3 cups	700 mL
4 cups or 1 quart	1 L

Oven Temperatures

Fahrenheit (F)	Celsius (C) (approximate)
250°F	120°C
300°F	150°C
325°F	165°C
350°F	180°C
375°F	190°C
400°F	200°C
425°F	220°C
450°F	230°C

Weight Equivalents

US Standard	Metric (approximate)
1 tablespoon	15 g
half ounce	15 g
1 ounce	30 g
2 ounces	60 g
4 ounces	115 g
8 ounces	225 g
12 ounces	340 g
16 ounces or 1 pound or 1 lb	455 g